D0772730

DAVID O. McKAY LIBRARY
RICKS COLLEGE
REXBURG, IDAHO 83460-0405

WITHDRAWN

JAN 1 2 2023

DAVID O. McKAY LIBRARY
BYU-IDAHO

THE JUDGMENT
of
EXPERTS

Thou wilt bring to distruction
the speakers of lying-falsehood,
the lord will make to be abhor'd
the man deceitfull, and of blood.

Psalm V
The Whole Booke of Psalmes
(Cambridge, Mass., 1640)

The Judgment of Experts

Essays and Documents about the Investigation
of the Forging of the *Oath of a Freeman*

Edited by James Gilreath

WORCESTER

AMERICAN ANTIQUARIAN SOCIETY

1991

Library of Congress Cataloging-in-Publication Data

The Judgment of experts: essays and documents about the investigation of the forging of the oath of a freeman / edited by James Gilreath.

271 pp. 26 cm.
ISBN 0-944026-14-1
1. Oath of a free-man. 2. Oath of a free-man—Bibliography. 3. Broadsides—United
States—Forgeries—History—20th century. 4. Oaths—Massachusetts—Bibliography.
5. Hofmann, Mark.
I. Gilreath, James, 1947-
F67.J83   1991   89-14947
364.1'63—dc20   CIP

Copyright © 1991 by American Antiquarian Society
No part of this book may be reproduced in any form or by any electronic or
mechanical means including information storage and retrieval systems without
permission in writing from the publisher.
Printed in the United States of America

Table of Contents

Chronology of Events

MARCH 13, 1985

Mark Hofmann purchases for twenty-five dollars a nineteenth-century broadside hymn on which he had printed the title *Oath of a Freeman,* which he had planted in Argosy Bookstore in New York. See Appendix F.

MARCH 14, 1985

Hofmann telephones Justin Schiller to tell him about finding the *Oath of a Freeman.*

MARCH 25, 1985

Hofmann purchases a printing plate from DeBouzek Engraving Company in Salt Lake City, which he will use to fabricate the *Oath* that he will offer to the Library of Congress and the American Antiquarian Society through Justin Schiller. During the evening of March 25 and the following morning, according to his later testimony, Hofmann produces the forgery in his basement workroom.

MARCH 28, 1985

Justin Schiller telephones James Gilreath at the Library of Congress and Marcus McCorison at the American Antiquarian Society to inform them of the existence of the *Oath of a Freeman.*

APRIL 5, 1985

Gilreath travels to New York City to see the *Oath* firsthand.

APRIL 8, 1985

Raymond Wapner brings the *Oath* to the Library of Congress.

APRIL 29, 1985

The Library's Conservation Office completes its scientific analysis of the *Oath.*

MAY 22, 1985

After the completion of all scientific and historical analyses, Library officials meet to determine a course of action.

JUNE 5, 1985

The Library of Congress notifies Justin Schiller that it has decided not to purchase the *Oath* because of questions about its price, provenance, and title.

JUNE 14, 1985

Raymond Wapner arrives in Washington to pick up the *Oath* and return it to New York City.

JUNE 27 OR 28, 1985

Raymond Wapner delivers the *Oath* to the American Antiquarian Society in Worcester, Massachusetts.

JUNE 28, 1985

Hofmann receives a $185,000 loan from First Interstate Bank in Salt Lake City, citing the alleged purchase of the *Oath* by the Library of Congress for $1.5 million as the means of repayment.

AUGUST 16, 1985	Robert Mathiesen of Brown University writes a report about the *Oath* after his examination of it at the request of the American Antiquarian Society.
SEPTEMBER 4, 1985	If certain conditions are met, the American Antiquarian Society offers to purchase the *Oath* for $250,000. The offer is declined by Schiller-Wapner Galleries.
SEPTEMBER 11, 1985	Georgia Barnhill of the American Antiquarian Society returns the *Oath* to New York City.
MID-SEPTEMBER 1985	Hofmann manufactures a second *Oath* and sells an interest in it to Thomas Wilding, a Salt Lake City businessman, and Sid Jensen, Hofmann's brother-in-law.
OCTOBER 15, 1985	Kathleen Sheets and Steve Christensen are killed in Utah by pipe bombs manufactured by Hofmann, who hopes to divert his creditors' attention away from his debts.
OCTOBER 16, 1985	Mark Hofmann is critically injured while transporting a pipe bomb of his own making. Salt Lake City police immediately make Hofmann the prime suspect in all three bombings.
FEBRUARY 4, 1986	Charges are filed against Mark Hofmann for the murders of Kathleen Sheets and Steve Christensen and for crimes relating to the forgery of historic documents.
APRIL 3, 1986	Keith Arbour of the American Antiquarian Society writes a report for Detective Ken Farnsworth of the Salt Lake City Police to inform Farnsworth about his findings concerning the text of the *Oath*.
APRIL 14, 1986	Preliminary hearing for Hofmann begins. He ultimately is bound over for trial.
APRIL 17, 1986	The Schiller-Wapner *Oath* and the Rosenbach Museum & Library's *The Whole Booke of Psalmes* are sent to the Crocker Nuclear Laboratory at the University of California at Davis for comparative testing by the cyclotron.
JUNE 25, 1986	Marvin Rennert, a forensic document examiner for the Bureau of Alcohol, Tobacco and Firearms, and George Throckmorton, a forensic specialist working for the Salt Lake City Police Department, examine the Schiller-Wapner copy of the *Oath* in New York City. They report their findings confidentially to the Salt Lake City authorities.

JANUARY 7, 1987	Hofmann secretly signs a plea agreement, which is entered on January 22, 1987. He agrees to plead guilty to two counts of murder and two counts of theft by deception in return for answering questions about certain criminal charges and "the surrounding circumstances of those offenses and any other related activities."
JANUARY 19, 1987	Walter C. McCrone of the McCrone Institute in Chicago examines the *Oath* using optical microscopy.
JANUARY 24, 1987	Hofmann enters the Utah State Prison at Draper, Utah.
FEBRUARY 11 - MAY 27, 1987	Hofmann is interviewed about his crimes by members of the Salt Lake County Attorney's Office. The Hofmann interviews will not be published until July 1987.
MARCH-MAY, 1987	Roderick McNeil tests the Schiller-Wapner *Oath* using the Scanning Auger Microscopy technique.

Glossary

THE WHOLE BOOKE OF PSALMES

Originally printed in England for the religious use of the Puritans, it was the first book printed in the United States after the sect left Great Britain for its new home in Massachusetts. Printed in Cambridge, Massachusetts, by Stephen Daye in 1640, it is also sometimes called the Bay Psalm Book. The volume contained psalms that were meant to be sung during religious ceremonies.

BROADSIDE

This is a single sheet of paper printed on one side only. Legal forms and public notices were often printed in this format. Hofmann's forgery of the *Oath of a Freeman* was printed as a broadside.

CHAIN LINES

When handmade paper is held up to the light, thin parallel lines, usually spaced one or two inches apart, become visible, because they transmit more light than the rest of the sheet of paper. These chain lines are produced on handmade paper by wires used to make the bottom of the mold in which the paper is produced. Papermaking molds vary from one establishment to another and so the chain lines on a piece of paper can sometimes be helpful in determining at which shop a particular sheet of paper was made and when it was produced.

RECTO

When a book is open, the right-hand page is called the recto. Also, the front of a broadside is called the recto.

VERSO

This is the opposite of recto: the left-hand page of an open book or the back of a broadside.

WATERMARK

Each hand papermaker usually has his own unique mark or symbol. A representation of this mark is sewn onto his mold. When a sheet of paper is made in one of these molds, this unique mark can be seen on the paper when it is held up to light, in the same fashion that the chain lines are visible.

Introduction

James Gilreath

Many readers of this volume will undoubtedly be familiar with the general outline of the story of Mark Hofmann's forgeries of Mormon and other rare American manuscripts, books, and broadsides, including the *Oath of a Freeman*. Some may be thoroughly versed in the sequence of tragic events that threatened to undermine the religious foundations of the Mormon Church, bilked numerous investors out of hundreds of thousands of dollars, cost two people their lives, and almost deceived the American people into thinking that one of their society's long-lost and most important documents had been discovered. To date, four books about Mark Hofmann's murderous and duplicitous career have been published: Jerald and Sandra Tanner's *Tracking the White Salamander;* Steven Naifeh and Gregory White Smith's *The Mormon Murders: A True Story of Greed, Forgery, Deceit, and Death;* Linda Sillitoe and Allen D. Roberts's *Salamander: The Story of the Mormon Forgery Murders;* and Robert Lindsey's *A Gathering of Saints: A True Story of Money, Murders, and Deceit.* Each book has its own strengths and weaknesses, and all contribute something to our understanding of the situation.

However, for reasons that will be given later, none of these works comes close to presenting an accurate picture of the story of the *Oath of a Freeman,* allegedly the first document printed in America (1638/39) and necessary for every freeman of the Massachusetts community to swear to before he could attain the full privileges of citizenship. This book is a compilation of the first-hand accounts of those who were actually involved in trying to solve the mystery of the *Oath.* Few of the writers were ever interviewed by any of the chroniclers of what have come to be called the Mormon murders.

For those to whom the story is new, a brief recapitulation is in order. Mark Hofmann began a career of forging manuscripts and printed documents relating to Mormon history in the late 1970s. He successfully fooled numerous collectors, experts, research institutions, and the Church of Jesus Christ of Latter-day Saints, which had purchased these forgeries for thousands of dollars, into thinking that his productions were authentic. He began modestly, but as his reputation grew so did his need for more cash, which fueled his ambitions as a forger. In 1983, Hofmann produced his most significant forgery up to that time: a letter from Martin Harris, a friend of the founder of the Mormon church, Joseph Smith. The letter was popularly dubbed "the Salamander Letter" because its contents stated that when Smith discovered the golden plates given by the angel Moroni he also saw a white salamander, an animal that figures prominently in early nineteenth-century magic accounts. The contents of the letter suggested that Smith was a spiritual charlatan rather than a prophet of faith. After some negotiation, Utah collector Steve Christensen purchased the Salamander Letter from Hofmann for $40,000 on January 6, 1984.

Soon, Hofmann's forging picked up in pace and dramatically increased the amounts of money with which he dealt. He devised a kind of pyramid scheme: he would talk investor A into putting up a sizable amount of money to purchase a rare item or collection in order to sell it for a profit. He next approached collector B to stake an even larger amount than did investor A, paying back investor A with a profit using B's money—only to try to get A to make an even larger amount of money available.

In the midst of these activities Hofmann produced his most spectacular forgery, the *Oath of a Freeman*, and used two New York City booksellers, Justin Schiller and Raymond Wapner, to try to sell it first to the Library of Congress and then to the American Antiquarian Society for $1.5 million. Confident of completing the sale, Hofmann went on a buying and borrowing spree that included a $600,000 house and more than $400,000 in loans from private investors and a bank. When the Library of Congress turned down the offer to acquire the *Oath* and the American Antiquarian Society contemplated a much lower figure, Hofmann found himself hounded by his various angered creditors. His back to the wall, he killed two people to relieve the pressure and to divert suspicion from himself. Subsequently, the saga of the attempts to prove the *Oath* a forgery became an important part in the fraud and murder charges against Hofmann in what was to become the largest criminal investigation in the history of the state of Utah.

Hofmann's deception of the collecting community, his creation of the manuscript forgeries (many remain in circulation), and his commission of the two murders have been documented by the four volumes mentioned in the first paragraph of this introduction and by the avalanche of news media reports. However, extracting the true story of the *Oath of a Freeman*—which is of special concern to those in the rare book world—from this complex narrative is especially difficult for several reasons. First, Hofmann plea-bargained with Utah authorities, and he never went to trial, leaving unreported much of the case developed against the *Oath* by government forensic specialists and others. Second, the results of the analyses of the *Oath* made by private individuals were not made public, because the analyses had been commissioned by Justin Schiller and Raymond Wapner for their own use. Last, the Library of Congress and the American Antiquarian Society, the two institutions to which the *Oath* was offered for sale, considered the broadside in secret, as is normally the case when a very important item is offered to a research institution or a private collector by private treaty. This secrecy is usually imposed by the seller.

The necessary restriction of information related to the investigation of the *Oath* allowed rumor, error, and innuendo to monopolize the public's knowledge of the document. To give only one example, the *Wall Street Journal* carried an article about Hofmann's forgeries on September 9, 1987,

2

that alleged: (1) federal historians had appraised the *Oath* at $1.5 million; (2) the Library of Congress had authenticated the broadside as being printed in 1638; (3) the Library of Congress considered displaying Hofmann's forgery next to the *Declaration of Independence* (the engrossed copy of the *Declaration of Independence* is actually on display at the National Archives and Records Administration); (4) the Library of Congress had arranged for a private group of investors to purchase the *Oath* and donate it to the Library, and (5) the Library of Congress had lost its ardor to acquire the *Oath* only after Hofmann had been arrested for murder. Each of these assertions makes for part of a good story, but in fact none is true. The *Wall Street Journal* article simply picked up errors from a variety of other newspaper and media accounts and cumulated them into a single story that bore little resemblance to actual events.

This volume attempts to lift the veil of secrecy and provide an accurate account of the affair. Justin Schiller relates his and Raymond Wapner's dealings with Mark Hofmann and how the *Oath* was brought to their attention. The results of the tests arranged by Schiller and Wapner are for the first time publicly revealed, including those from the cyclotron conducted by Dr. Thomas Cahill and his associates; microscopy examination by Dr. Walter C. McCrone; and scanning auger microscopy by Roderick McNeil. Keith Arbour's conclusions based on research about the text are presented as an appendix. I discuss the Library of Congress's preliminary inspection and its negotiations with Schiller and Wapner over the sale. The Library's scientific test is made public for the first time. Marcus McCorison, director of the American Antiquarian Society and Dr. Robert Mathiesen of Brown University, who was invited to the Society to inspect the *Oath*, give their accounts. Marvin Rennert of the Bureau of Alcohol, Tobacco, and Firearms, who would have been a crucial prosecution witness against the *Oath* had Hofmann gone to trial, reflects on his role in the investigation, something rarely done by the Bureau's agents in the field. Detective Kenneth Farnsworth of the Salt Lake City Police Department, upon whose shoulders fell the awesome burden of piecing together the myriad pieces of evidence about the forgeries into a coherent case, tells his story for the first time in print. Finally, I have excerpted and included those sections dealing with the *Oath* from Mark Hofmann's interviews with the Salt Lake Attorney's office, which he gave as part of the plea-bargaining settlement.

The question of the text of the *Oath* requires special comment. Keith Arbour's analysis of the *Oath*, arguing that its text demonstrated that the document was a forgery, is published as an appendix to Ken Farnsworth's article. Arbour's argument was not formally developed until after the bombings. Earlier, Paul Sternberg of New Mexico provided Justin Schiller with a report, which Sternberg would not allow to be published in its original form in this volume, that contended that the *Oath*'s text contained nothing that would eliminate it from being considered genuine, though emphasizing that the text did not prove it was authentic. Indeed, the unofficial word that I received from the American Antiquarian Society throughout the summer and early fall of 1985 supported the position that there was no detectable flaw in the textual evidence present in the *Oath*. Nonetheless, the two strongly held, opposing arguments made, in my mind, textual analysis a confusing methodology in this instance, one I thought would certainly face stiff challenges in a courtroom and probably in the scholarly community as well.

Some of the articles in this volume are presented in facsimile and contain all the usual marks of works in progress undertaken under intense pressure, including typos, misspellings, and other infelicities. These documents were not originally intended for publication, and the generosity of the authors in allowing them to be reproduced here allows us to understand the story as it was unfolding.

However, I hope that this volume serves a purpose larger than simply to present an accurate account of the *Oath* and its examination, as important as that may be. No printed document with which I am acquainted has ever been subjected to such a wide array of scientific, forensic, historical, and verbal tests as has the Hofmann forgery of the *Oath of a Freeman*. Each essay in this book tries to acquaint the reader in layman's language with one kind of methodology for detecting forgery, in effect making this book a partial inventory of the various means investigators have available to test a printed document's authenticity. In this vein, I hope that the story presented here will serve as a lesson that will be useful at some later time when the next sophisticated forgery comes onto the market. Significant forgeries seem to appear with cyclical regularity. The Thomas J. Wise fabrications of Victorian and Romantic poetic works surfaced in the 1920s and 1930s. Approximately thirty years later, the Vinland Map, acquired by Yale University, was declared a hoax, though the matter is still subject to debate. Roughly thirty years after the Vinland Map, Hofmann's forged *Oath of a Freeman* arrived on the scene. Can anyone doubt that during the next thirty years another well-crafted forgery will appear?

Recently, many forged nineteenth-century broadsides dealing with Texas history were discovered in Texas by Austin rare book seller Tom Taylor. Forgeries like these can be detected by a careful examination of the paper and print of the disputed document when such examination is grounded in a thorough understanding of the history of paper, printing, and other historical matters. Such connoisseurship, to borrow a word more frequently used in the art world, unmasks many forgeries every year. However, connoisseurship failed in the case of the *Oath of a Freeman*, at best producing contradictory and inconclusive results. At such times, it is natural to turn to science to provide the final judgment. Science has been a part of past investigations of printed frauds such as the Thomas J. Wise forgeries. But the increasingly more powerful and precise scientific tests and tools recently available so far exceed anything known in the past that they would naturally lead one to think that we are in a new age of scientific detection. How could a forger produce something that would deceive science's minutely focused eye? Yet, when put to the test in the Hofmann case, almost all of the scientific tests showed that their results could be as ambiguous as the more subjective view of the connoisseur. It was only due to the fact that the Salt Lake City police were able to uncover the original negative used to produce the forger's printing plate that forensic examiners like Marvin Rennert were able to uncover the deception. But how often can we have the luxury of possessing the forger's own negative? Roderick McNeil's newly developed technique was allegedly able to determine how long the ink had been on the paper without recourse to the negative. But who can doubt that an enterprising and knowledgeable (or even lucky) forger might beat the McNeil test at some time in the future?

When the *Oath of a Freeman* was at the Library of Congress, I did a great deal of reading about past forgeries that had been exposed. Whether or not these forgeries were discovered by connoisseurship or by scientific tests, one thing remained constant in every instance: those who were willing to accept the forgeries as authentic were willing to ignore provenance as an important proof of authenticity. Provenance is the one unfailing guide when used in conjunction with a critically intelligent examination of the physical properties and text of any document. I do not refer to the type of flimsy provenance that Hofmann tried to create (which will be detailed in Ken Farnsworth's essay), but one that is credible and extends back for many years. Preferably, the document's provenance should reach back through two unrelated owners or transactions, thus decreasing the chance for collusion. Such a provenance will not guarantee authenticity; but, when considered along with other methods of checking a document, it will certainly improve the reliability of any conclusion.

For a variety of reasons, rare book dealers often do not reveal their source when offering a rare item for sale. Any institution or collector purchasing a very important or very valuable piece (especially a manuscript, broadside, or short pamphlet, which are more easily forged than a book) without fully verifying the item's provenance is playing a dangerous game that may entail years of embarrassment and controversy. It is the mark of a forger to not want to disclose his identity or his document's provenance, both of which are obviously suspect.

During the years when the authenticity of the *Oath* was in doubt, many who discussed the broadside confused two very different ideas. It is one thing to theorize about the means by which such a document *could* have been produced, but something quite different to cite categorically a *particular* means of production based upon certain specific and clearly identifiable traits—because such proof must be irrefutable in a court of law. For instance, there was never any doubt that the *Oath* could have been printed by rearranging letters cut out from a Bay Psalm Book to form the text of the *Oath*, and then procuring a printing plate made from this artwork. A forger could file down certain letters to create the illusion that any impression made from the plate had come from movable type. He could then find a blank piece of paper from a seventeenth-century book, create a carbon-based ink, and then print the text of the *Oath* on this blank piece of paper

5

from the plate. But to prove from the physical evidence of the broadside itself that this particular document was produced in this manner is much more difficult than making theoretical speculations. It is not enough to say that the broadside looked or "smelled" wrong. A witness for the defense could have easily refuted such an argument by saying that it "smelled" just fine to him.

After the bombings, many theories were offered that allegedly proved that the *Oath* was suspect by using arguments such as the flow or density of the type being incorrect, or that the ornaments didn't move on the page in the right way, or even wilder logic. When I discussed these so-called proofs with Marvin Rennert, Ken Farnsworth, and their colleagues, I argued against their relying on them, which probably discouraged the investigators. I did so not because I was confident that the *Oath* was genuine, but rather because I was certain that these theories could be easily discredited. At the same time, I encouraged Justin Schiller and Raymond Wapner to send the *Oath* to Walter McCrone of the McCrone Institute in Chicago, to supply it to Tom Cahill of the Crocker Nuclear Laboratory in Davis, California, and to make it available to Marvin Rennert of the Bureau of Alcohol, Tobacco, and Firearms. Schiller and Wapner were under great emotional and financial stress during this period and should be given more credit than they have received for going through the sometimes great difficulties in seeking these experts' advice. Later, a conversation with Antonio Cantu of the United States Secret Service led me to convince Schiller and Wapner to send the *Oath* to Roderick McNeil's laboratory in Polson, Montana, because of a test McNeil had developed for discovering the age of ink on a piece of paper without having to compare it to any control document. McNeil's description of his test in this volume will be of great interest to forensic scientists who may at some time be faced with a situation similar to the one described in this book.

The two camps that formed are joined together in this volume, though during the investigation they were often at tense odds with each other. I anticipate that there will be a number of surprises in these articles for readers, even for those who have closely followed the case. But even more interesting is the fact that I know there will be some surprises for the authors of these essays when they read essays other than their own. But no matter whether an investigator's method produced an answer that was correct, inconclusive, or even wrong, all of them deserve our respect for having had the courage to offer a definite opinion under a great deal of pressure—when large amounts of money, personal or institutional reputation, and even human life hung in the balance. How much more difficult was their job than that of others who have had the luxury of composing elaborate theories based on hindsight? We owe our profound thanks to all of them.

I asked each of the authors to compose as much of his essay as possible in the first person in order to make the style of writing as engaging as possible for the reader, as well as to ease somewhat the strain of writing for

6

those not used to producing finished texts. As a matter of editorial principle, I did not try to impose a uniform style on all the essays but rather tried to maintain each author's distinctive voice. For this reason, some articles are composed primarily in short sentences, while others have a more elaborate sentence structure. Because of the overlap between stories told in the essays, some details may seem repetitive. I have let these repetitions stand because various narrators will approach the same fact from different angles, giving it varying degrees of importance.

Also, I have allowed to appear unedited, or with only the minor changes that are noted at the beginning of the document, any contribution to this book that was written during the original investigation of the *Oath*. Such contributions include: the Library of Congress's "Preliminary Report"; Robert Mathiesen's "Preliminary Report"; a portion of Thomas Cahill's "Compositional Comparison of the Mark Hofmann *Oath of a Freeman* and the *Whole Booke of Psalmes*"; Walter McCrone's January 19, 1987, letter to Justin Schiller; almost all of the appendices to Ken Farnsworth's "The Investigation of the 1985 Mark Hofmann Forgery of the *Oath of a Freeman*"; and excerpts from the *Mark Hofmann Interviews*.

I want to thank John Hench of the American Antiquarian Society for his staunch work in helping to overcome the enormous difficulties posed by this book; Sheila McAvey of the American Antiquarian Society for her diligent editorial assistance; and Libby Kaiser, acting special assistant to the chief of the Rare Book and Special Collections Division, who made numerous valuable contributions. Leonard Beck, former subject collections specialist in the Rare Book and Special Collections Division at the Library of Congress, and Richard E. Turley, Jr., managing director of the Historical Department of the Church of Jesus Christ of Latter-day Saints, both carefully read the proofs and saved me from errors of fact. Jennifer Larson, chair of the Questioned Imprints Committee of the Antiquarian Booksellers Association of America, made many useful suggestions and spotted errors in the manuscript that all others missed. I take sole responsibility for all editorial decisions, including the arrangement of the contents and the selection of the contributors.

Note:

Most of the facsimiles in this book have been printed from photocopies, as supplied by the contributors.

'In the Beginning . . .'
A Chronology of the 'Oath of a Freeman' Document as Offered by Schiller-Wapner

Justin G. Schiller

I first met Mark and Doralee Hofmann at the Spring 1984 Book Fair sponsored by the Antiquarian Booksellers Association of America at the 67th Street/Park Avenue Armory in New York. They were a young couple who expressed interest in beginning a rare book collection, asked lots of questions about children's literature, and then purchased from Schiller-Wapner Galleries a presentation copy of Eugene Field's poetry with an accompanying holograph letter. A few telephone conversations followed during the next months, and by late summer the Hofmanns were back in New York declaring their intent to build a first-class collection of rare and unique children's books. During the next year they mostly used us as their agents to purchase things either at auction or by private treaty from other collectors. We did occasionally sell them important books from our own inventory; but they were searching for big-ticket items, first editions of *Pinocchio* in the original Italian, and the two-volume *Heidi* in German. We made one purchase from them, a Louisa May Alcott letter, circa 1880, regarding the death of her sister in Paris and the subsequent arrival of her niece Lulu, a modest letter that the Hofmanns had acquired during a brief bout with collecting autographs and that we have subsequently authenticated as genuine. We had a comfortable rapport and mutual regard with our new customers, and in this context the events of March 1985 began to unfold.

To promote a sale of printed and manuscript Americana from the Sang Collection on March 27, Sotheby's (New York) announced one of its star items: a first edition *Uncle Tom's Cabin*, inscribed by Harriet Beecher Stowe to Mrs. Luther Dana, a close family friend, dated by its author just eleven days after publication. Mark Hofmann was in New York during the second week of March, and at this time we both previewed the Stowe book. He was in and out of our shop on several occasions during that week, and on the last day of his visit (Thursday, March 14) we received the Sotheby's catalogue and handed him a copy as he was departing for his hotel before going off to the airport. We decided to discuss final details over the telephone. He thought he would be able to return to New York for the auction, though Schiller Ltd. would still be bidding at the sale on his behalf.

That same evening at home, I received a telephone call from Mark Hofmann, rather late at night by Eastern time, but then he had just arrived back in Salt Lake City. He told me that he had been reading the Sotheby's catalogue on the plane and that an annotation for lot #32 especially caught his notice. Had I ever heard of a book by John Child called *New-Englands Jonas Cast Up at London* published in 1647? The auction description noted, "This book also provides the earliest reprint of 'The Freeman's Oath,' the first issue of Stephen Daye's Cambridge press, of which no copy of the original printing survives." He explained that he had purchased a few miscellaneous papers from Argosy Book Store when he was in New York. At the time, he considered them just wall decorations and not having any serious value. But one of them was a little broadside entitled the *Oath of a Freeman*. Did I think this might be "The Freeman's Oath" referred to in the Sotheby's catalogue? I confessed not knowing anything about such matters, aside from having seen the Bay Psalm Book a few times, but if he wanted to send me a photocopy of this document I would send it to the American Antiquarian Society on his behalf for their opinion. Instead, he said he would just send us the original in the mail. I cautioned him about doing so, in case it was of exceptional value. There the matter rested.

Several days later Hofmann again called to say that he had confirmed that his Oath of a Freeman text was essentially the same as the one reprinted in the 1647 *New-Englands Jonas,* which he had tracked down on microfiche at Brigham Young University Library. He also looked at the 1640 Bay Psalm Book on microfiche at Brigham Young and found a similar use of ornaments and typeface as that appearing in his broadside. It sounded potentially very exciting, but I cautioned that I would have to look at the sheet of paper with him before I could offer any professional opinion. He confirmed his plans to return to New York with the broadside in hand, because he planned to attend the Sotheby's auction on the twenty-seventh. It was not until the day before the auction, Tuesday the twenty-sixth, that he arrived at our shop during mid-afternoon. He showed me the document and a facsimile of the Bay Psalm Book, which he had recently borrowed from Brigham Young. The similarities between the two were certainly obvious. Moreover, the endorsement on the verso of the printed sheet appeared to be in a seventeenth-century handwriting. The situation now required the eye of a specialist, one who knew early American printing as well as I knew children's books; so with Hofmann's permission I telephoned my good friend and erstwhile colleague Michael Zinman to seek his counsel.

After convincing Michael that I was not prematurely calling him up for an April first prank, he agreed to leave work early, stop off at home to pick up his reference books on Massachusetts Bay printing, and be at our bookshop within the hour. When he arrived and looked at the document, he thought it simply looked too good to be right. But checking it against everything that he cross-referenced, he could not find any evidence that it was a forgery or counterfeit. Perhaps the *Oath* really had resurfaced after nearly 350 years. Hofmann, Zinman, and I went out to dinner that evening to discuss the next steps. We talked about relative values, assuming that the *Oath* could be authenticated; and, much to Hofmann's surprise, both Michael and I felt that if genuine it should be worth the same as a complete copy of the 1640 Bay Psalm Book. Hofmann at first suggested a value up to $50,000 and looked as if he would have been pleased had we suggested doubling that figure. But if it was worth the same as a Bay Psalm Book—the last having fetched $151,000 in 1947 at public auction—then it was far more valuable than he had ever dreamed. As to the precise dollar amount, that needed more thought. Clearly, we were now speaking of at least $1 million and quite probably somewhat more.

Authentication was absolutely essential, so we thought that a direct comparison with a real Bay Psalm Book would be a reasonable beginning. Only one copy is in the New York area, and it was currently on exhibition at the "Treasures" show of the New York Public Library. The next day, I telephoned Francis Mattson, NYPL curator of rare books, and he made arrangements with the registrar's office to have the exhibition case opened early morning on Thursday the twenty-eighth before the general public was admitted to the library and exhibition rooms. Comparing the book and the broadside, we found that the type and ornaments looked very similar, but it was not until I found a gathering of pages near the end of the book with virtually the same chain-line measurements as the paper on which the *Oath of a Freeman* was printed that I became personally excited. Afterwards, Mr. Mattson took me up to the rare books room, and we examined other examples of early 1640s printing from the Stephen Daye press, noting the unusual occurrence of contraction marks, irregular line-endings, and poor imposition of type—all of which were characteristic of Hofmann's document. All told, these were persuasive pieces of evidence to me as a nonspecialist that we had a genuine document, especially since there was no other specimen with which to compare the broadside. And we felt compelled to pursue further investigations.

After my return to the office that morning, I brought my partner Raymond Wapner up to date on what was happening and explained as best I could the importance of the 1638/39 "Oath of a Freeman." Then together, we had a meeting with Hofmann to discuss our continued role in these proceedings. Although early American documents are somewhat out of the range of our usual dealings, we once had handled an original 1692 holograph indictment for one of the Salem witchcraft prosecutions. Hofmann seemed exceedingly pleased about what had been accomplished in so brief a time and also about our estimate of the document's commercial value. We were hoping he would offer us a minimal percentage of the eventual selling price to continue as his representative, but to our amazement he instead offered to give us a large commission that later was converted to a part ownership in the document, in exchange for our efforts to sell the *Oath* for the most advantageous price. We had him repeat his offer several times. I can remember not believing it. *That* is a way to get someone committed to a project!

I did not know what the next step should be, but I realized it would probably include scientific testing of both paper and ink. To know how to proceed, I telephoned James Gilreath at the Library of Congress on March 28. Initially, he asked for a photocopy of the document; and after its receipt, he suggested coming up to New York (April 5) to examine personally the document under magnification and ultraviolet and natural light. We saw him as scheduled; and after his inspection of the "Oath," he recommended that it be brought to the Library of Congress for more in-depth analyses using sophisticated laboratory equipment in consultation with various specialists. By this time Hofmann had returned to Salt Lake City, but with his permission we made arrangements with William Matheson, chief of the Rare Book and Special Collections Division at LC, to have the *Oath* delivered to Washington by Ray Wapner (on April 8). Another telephone conversation that week with Mr. Matheson indicated that LC desired to establish a selling price on the *Oath*, assuming that it would be for sale if the tests showed the document to be authentic. I explained that we had not yet firmed up the specific amount to be asked, but I used the equation of its value being comparable to a complete Bay Psalm Book. As for actually quoting a dollar figure, I declined, except to say that we had not yet determined what a Bay Psalm Book would be worth in today's marketplace. He asked me to define the price area we were considering—$100,000, $500,000, $1 million, $5 million—and I said somewhere above one million, which afterwards was mistaken as our having fixed a price and then having tried to raise it 50 percent when the document was formally offered at $1.5 million. Ultimately, we realized that a complete Bay Psalm Book would certainly bring in excess of $1 million today, and so we decided to take the 1947 auction price and multiply it by a factor of ten. Actually, if the *Oath* were genuine, one could probably double even this figure without too much imagination, taking 1990 values into account.

I should also emphasize that at first Hofmann did not want either himself or his source for the *Oath* identified, even though he had shown us a dated receipt from Argosy Bookstore on which the document was separately itemized for $25. We explained to Hofmann that provenance is very important in matters such as this. He said he would inquire directly with the staff at Argosy to see if one of them might remember where they acquired the broadside. Meanwhile, he gave us permission to identify both him as the owner and Argosy as the place of purchase but only to the eventual purchaser. Also, he claimed that his copy of the *Oath* had been pasted down on its corners to a piece of old cardboard, the type used by laundries when returning shirts fifty years or so ago. Since he could see the written endorsement on the reverse side of the document, he wanted to lift the piece of paper off the cardboard in order to read the inscription, and so he immersed the entire board with affixed paper in a shallow pan of Salt Lake City tap water. After the board had been submersed for a while, the paper loosened on all corners and a tremendous amount of dirt and soiling had also come off the document. It has been conjectured that the board

11

might have contained a high starch content; and being soaked in water, the starch formed a solution that bleached the document clean. It all sounded quite convincing and would explain the presence of salt, if any turned up in a chemical analysis.

We sent photocopies of the *Oath* broadside to Katharine F. Pantzer of the Houghton Library at Harvard, and to Jean Archibald at the Department of Printed Books of the British Library, to learn what they thought about the typographical makeup of the document. And shortly afterwards (as word quietly infiltrated the scholarly community), the original document was shown to such visiting luminaries as Arthur Freeman of Bernard Quaritch, in London, and Nicolas Barker of the British Library. Both independently expressed caution because of the importance of the discovery but agreed that the document looked good enough to warrant further scientific testing. More recently, autograph dealer Kenneth Rendell and Dr. Paul Needham of the Pierpont Morgan Library generously spent time looking at the original broadside with considerable enthusiasm.

When the suggestion of forgery was first raised, I contacted Sotheby's to verify who consigned the *New-Englands Jonas* and learned it was Mrs. Sang, a collector from Chicago. Though Child's book is extremely rare in the marketplace, it is not valuable enough for there to have been any prior notice of its forthcoming appearance in the salesroom, nor is it likely that it could have been casually noticed when Hofmann and I previewed the *Uncle Tom's Cabin* earlier that month (allegedly the same week Hofmann purchased the broadside from Argosy). Consequently, Hofmann's use of the auction catalogue annotation to introduce the *Oath* could not have been planned long in advance. Likewise, it was always our intention that upon reaching an agreement of sale for the *Oath*, a period of one year would be granted for the purchaser to do continued testing. During that time, the funds would be held in escrow; and the sale would be negated if the broadside could be discredited. In fact, we did have an investor ready to buy Hofmann's remaining interest in the *Oath* in early October 1985 at a negotiated discount (see Sillitoe and Roberts, *Salamander*, 1988, p. 348) but the agreement required Hofmann to sign a contract. Once the bombs started going off, the purchase was understandably canceled.

So ends this preamble. What follows will be reports on the study of our *Oath* once it was turned over first to the Library of Congress and next to the American Antiquarian Society. A textual study was made by Paul Sternberg, and we commissioned cyclotron comparisons at the University of California (Davis) with Messrs. Cahill and Schwab. Through the courtesy of Ellen Dunlap and the trustees of the Rosenbach Museum & Library, the University of California team was able to use the Rosenbach Bay Psalm Book as a control when examining the *Oath*. And we asked Walter McCrone of Chicago to test the ink, with the document being couriered back and forth under the protection of the district attorney's squad of the New York City Police Department. One obstacle that confronted us for many months was contacting Roderick McNeil of Polson, Montana, who eventually agreed to examine the Hofmann *Oath* entrusted to our care. It was in his possession for nearly six weeks, from March to May 1987. In a brief telephone conversation shortly before the document was returned to us, he stated that the document was similar to other Hofmann papers he had tested for the prosecutor's office in Utah, which he believed were not authentic. This was the only examination we commissioned that suggested the document was a fake. Despite our requests to receive a copy of Mr. McNeil's report, one was never provided. Consequently, our inability to secure his evaluation during these past thirty-six months, precluded us from analyzing his conclusions.

The 'Oath of a Freeman' and
the Library of Congress:
An Ambiguous First Impression
and an Elusive Finish

James Gilreath

March sometimes plays cruel tricks in Washington. Everyone expects the balmy weather that quickly streaks the city's broad avenues with bright azaleas, cherry blossoms, and blooming apple trees. If the warm breezes do not arrive, people feel deceived and strangely suspicious, as if some unspoken promise had been broken. But March 28, 1985, satisfied all expectations, as the temperature climbed into the seventies, and it was certain that winter's unpredictability was safely behind.

But not even the sanguine prospects of the season could encourage much hope that what Justin Schiller told me during a telephone conversation that day could possibly be true. I had occasionally bought rare early children's books from Schiller for the Library of Congress's collections for a number of years. He is a well-known dealer in rare juvenile literature, and I knew that he had helped form some of the best private libraries throughout the country. But nothing that he had uncovered in the past could match what he described that day. In a tone that expressed simultaneously both his incredulity and his excitement that such astonishing good fortune might possibly visit his doorstep, he said that a client had just brought to his store a broadside that might be the long-lost copy of the *Oath of a Freeman*, the first printed document in English North America. Issued in Cambridge, Massachusetts, the *Oath* was the promise that freemen of the colony made when they assumed the full responsibilities of citizenship in the settlement.

If genuine, its discovery would have been an extraordinary event. Such remarkable finds are occasionally made in the field of rare Americana. In 1906, a unique copy of the 1648 *The Book of the General Laws and Libertyes Concerning the Inhabitants of the Massachusetts*, the first compilation of the Massachusetts Bay Colony's code of laws, was uncovered in a small private English library. However, the appearance of the first piece of printing in what is now the United States would certainly lead the list of notable discoveries. The reserved bibliographer Charles Evans once thought that he had chanced upon a record indicating that an *Oath* existed in the British Museum. After sailing across the Atlantic, he submitted his call slip in the

14

reading room and waited for the broadside to be retrieved. In an article in the *Proceedings of the American Antiquarian Society* published in 1921, he described himself at that moment as feeling as if he had entered "into the holy of holies of delight, when the whole body thrills with suppressed emotions, the eyes moisten." Unfortunately, the document was not in its place on the shelves and is presumed lost.

Though I was cynical about the *Oath*'s genuineness, Schiller is a knowledgeable bookseller of rare material, and so the broadside could not be dismissed out of hand. He understood my doubts, but he insisted that he could find nothing wrong with it, at the same time knowing that it would require much more scrutiny. We closed the conversation by agreeing that going to the New York Public Library would be a good first step. Comparing two pieces of printing that allegedly were made at the same place, from the same press, by the same man, at about the same time, potentially could offer clues about whether or not the real *Oath of a Freeman* was in Schiller's hands. I asked him to keep me informed and to send a photocopy of what he had.

After returning from a weekend trip, I received on the inauspicious date of April 1 a photocopy of the *Oath of a Freeman* broadside and Schiller's report on his visit to the New York Public Library. He thought that the chain lines of the broadside's paper matched those on several pages in a section of the Bay Psalm Book, that the typefaces in both documents measured the same size, and that the ornaments surrounding the text of the *Oath* were very similar to those used in the Bay Psalm Book. Furthermore, he was certain that the writing on the back of the broadside was in a seventeenth-century style of handwriting. If this copy of the *Oath* were forged, then someone had clearly taken the time to do detailed homework. Schiller's letter also mentioned that he had sent photocopies of the *Oath* to Katherine Pantzer at Harvard's Houghton Library (editor of the *Short-Title Catalogue*, a bibliography of English books printed between 1641 and 1700) and Jean Archibald (assistant keeper of English printed books) at the British Library in London.

Photocopies seldom offer conclusive information about the authenticity of a suspicious document. Many mistakes a forger might make, such as using paper that was not consistent with the purported date of printing, would be apparent only when looking at the original and not at a reproduction. Additionally, the image reproduced on a photocopy is always slightly different from the one found on the original; often, fine lines are not copied and sometimes disappear altogether. Such tiny pieces of evidence are of paramount importance in many instances. However, a reproduction does give the investigator the opportunity to check the text of the document. In this case, the spelling of a word or the use of a phrase might be inappropriate to the early seventeenth century and show the item to be a fake. The text of the *Oath* exists in several extant manuscripts done in the 1630s and was reprinted in several other contemporary sources. Each varies in slight ways from the others, and this new broadside needed to fit in a consistent way with these other known, valid versions. Though time did not permit me the opportunity to do as thorough a textual analysis as possible, I felt, after comparing all the versions of the text that nothing was egregiously wrong with the text of the *Oath* that Schiller had sent.

Though much remained to be learned about the broadside, there now seemed reason enough to visit New York to inspect the *Oath* personally. I made arrangements to visit Justin Schiller on Thursday, April 5. Anything as important as the *Oath of a Freeman* should not be allowed to float in a limbo of uncertainty. We should know if it is real or fake beyond any reasonable doubt. In the few days before my departure, I consulted with Karen Garlick, the Library's paper conservator, and Don Sebera, a research scientist in the Library's Preservation Office. I wanted to glean from Garlick as much as possible about ink and paper from her extensive experience with them, and to learn from Sebera which scientific tests the Library might be able to conduct in order to determine whether the *Oath* was genuine. I also spent as much time as possible looking over the Library's copy of the Bay Psalm Book and reading as many books as I could about early Massachusetts printing.

George Parker Winship's *The Cambridge Press, 1638-1692* and Zoltan Haraszti's *The Enigma of the Bay Psalm Book* proved two of the most helpful works. The printing press that produced the Bay Psalm Book and the *Oath of a Freeman* traveled to Massachusetts in the hold of the ship *John of London* in 1638. Rev. Josse Glover, who intended to immigrate to America with his wife and children but died during the hard passage, arranged for the press to be brought on the trip. A fellow immigrant, Stephen Daye, a locksmith, set up the press in America and became the country's first printer. Since Daye was not a printer by trade, his first pieces of work were not skillfully accomplished, and wildly eccentric presswork and composition are the hallmarks of these early imprints. Very little printing was done during the seventeenth century in Massachusetts. In the first fifty years after the press arrived in America, fewer than five hundred books and broadsides were printed in all the colonies. However, the few products from Daye's press were all essential for the Puritan community and culture. The *Oath of a Freeman* symbolized a colonist's transition to full participation in citizenship in the Massachusetts Colony and was clearly an important civil document. The Bay Psalm Book contained the hymns that the Puritans sang during their ceremonies and so was a centerpiece of their spiritual life.

On April 5, I flew to New York and took a cab to the Schiller and Wapner bookstore. During the trip, I was troubled by the fact that they would not normally handle an important early American item like the *Oath* that was not related to children's books. Arriving at their store at the corner of East 61st Street and Fifth Avenue, across from the Hotel Pierre, I remembered that they were located within view of some of the legendary sights in mid-Manhattan, made famous by numerous movies and television shows: the Plaza Hotel, the cluster of horse-drawn carriages that congregate on 59th Street to take tourists on trips through Central Park, and the statue of

General Sherman at the intersection of 59th Street and Fifth Avenue. The place evoked the aura of wealth of the country's foremost consumer capital. I took a guess that whoever consigned the *Oath* to Schiller and Wapner might be from out of town, and that the store's prominent location might have made him feel comfortable.

I carried an ultraviolet lamp in order to detect any irregularities in the paper not visible to the human eye such as erasures, and also a small magnifying instrument in order to get a closer look at the typeface and ornaments. These were elementary tests but essential first ones. As I walked through the door, both Schiller and Wapner greeted me warmly. Inside, they presided over a veritable fantasyland, a dream world of original Sendak illustrations, nineteenth-century toybooks that twirled or popped up, and the images of characters that have danced for years through childhood imaginations: Mickey Mouse, the Three Bears, the Little Prince, Alice in Wonderland, and many more.

Putting the *Oath* on a desk in their office, they told me that they had retrieved it that morning from a bank vault. Then they left the room, leaving me to examine it alone. Its appearance immediately surprised me. The paper was much whiter than the paper in the Library of Congress's Bay Psalm Book. However troubling the paper's color might be, it did not immediately disqualify the broadside as being authentic. The copy of the Bay Psalm Book in the Rare Book and Special Collections Division had been exposed at an earlier time to poor environmental conditions that would have naturally browned its pages. This copy of the *Oath* might have been inserted in a book for most of its life, protecting it from the atmosphere and explaining its comparatively clean condition.

The way the type looked was also disquieting. The printing in the Bay Psalm Book was dark and many of the individual letters looked uneven and battered. However, the letters in this *Oath* seemed perfectly formed and the color of the ink was much lighter than that in the later book. But balancing out this problem was the design of the typeface itself. At the time that the *Oath* was printed, each individual letter was made from a piece of lead that had been cast into its particular shape in an iron mold. There were many different designs of type made by the many commercial typefoundries, each of which had its own unique characteristics. When studying the Bay Psalm Book, I discovered several idiosyncrasies in the design of its type that were not characteristic of typefaces used at this time. For instance, the letter "o" had thicknesses at certain places in the circle that were unusual. I was quickly able to spot several of these idiosyncrasies in the *Oath*, suggesting that the two documents were composed from the same or related typefaces. Of course, the possibility that the *Oath* was in some way photographically reproduced from letters cut from one of the easily available facsimile editions of the Bay Psalm Book immediately occurred to me. A forger would rearrange these cut-out letters into new words to form the text of the *Oath*, which would then be photographed to be transferred in some way to a blank piece of old paper. However, the back of the *Oath* showed

17

the clear impressions made by metal biting into the paper, thus eliminating the possibility that it had been reproduced by some planographic process such as lithography. Furthermore, the depth of the impression of the letters into the page varied from place to place. Because the letters used to print a document from movable type could never be perfectly adjusted to the same height before the paper was pressed against them for printing, a slightly varying bite from letter to letter is expected. If the impression into the paper had been even over the entire printed surface, it would have been a sure sign that the broadside was produced from a plate and was not almost 350 years old.

At this point, I took the *Oath* to a dark room and inspected it under ultraviolet light. The broadside did not reflect any unusual or suspicious colors during this examination. I returned the broadside to Schiller and Wapner and told them that I was finished with it for the time being. Walking to lunch with them at the Society of Illustrators Club, I said that in my opinion the odds were against their broadside being genuine because of the paper and the coloring of the type, but I admitted that I had a divided mind. The similarities of the typefaces between the two documents gave me pause. It would have been impossible to cast type to produce the *Oath* that would match the small details of design that I had identified in the Bay Psalm Book. As long as I could not prove that the *Oath* was produced from a plate, the broadside could not be ruled out. On the chance that this might be the lost *Oath of a Freeman,* a great national treasure, I suggested that it be sent to Washington for sophisticated scientific tests and closer historical analysis. Over lunch they agreed to this proposal but said that a time limit would need to be set.

Though the Library of Congress does not usually conduct scientific tests on material owned by private individuals, John Broderick, then the Assistant Librarian of Congress for Research Services, decided to make an exception in this instance. The fact that this broadside might be the only original copy of one of the fundamental American documents argued for such a course of action. The Library's mission is to preserve the country's cultural heritage—and identifying a national treasure like the genuine *Oath of a Freeman* would certainly qualify as part of that mission. Exposing a fake copy, of course, would also be appropriate. Consequently, on April 8, 1985, after discussing the matter with William Matheson, chief of the Rare Book and Special Collections Division, Raymond Wapner brought the *Oath* to Washington, and it was placed in the division's stacks. At the outset, there was no discussion about the broadside being offered to the Library for purchase. It was on deposit for thirty days of testing.

While Don Sebera prepared his equipment and cleared his calendar in order to be able to conduct the tests, the broadside received close scrutiny in the Rare Book and Special Collections Division's reading room by the division's staff and members of the Library's Preservation Office. Additionally, a few readers and members of the staff of the neighboring Folger Library, which is devoted to the study of Shakespeare and his times, were

18

invited to examine the broadside and contribute their expertise. The following conclusions were reached:

1. Staff members experienced with the seventeenth-century documents at the Folger Library agreed that the written inscription on the back of the *Oath* was done in a seventeenth-century style. Additionally, the iron gall ink used to write the notation had oxidized and at one point made a tiny hole in the paper. Iron gall ink is corrosive and over a long period of time can eat its way through a piece of paper, though some formulas are more corrosive than others. It is possible to age iron gall ink artificially, but usually the treatment will affect the entire document in other ways. For instance, heat will accelerate the oxidation of iron gall ink, but it will also turn the paper a shade of brown. Because the paper on which the *Oath* was printed was, if anything, unusually white, the ink could not have been aged with heat. At this time, no one knew any method of artificially aging iron gall ink without affecting the paper of the broadside in ways that were not consistent with the appearance of the *Oath* under study.

2. There are catalogues of watermarks used by various historical paper mills that are useful for dating pieces of old paper. However, there was no watermark on the *Oath*'s paper, eliminating this avenue of enquiry. It was an easy matter to determine that its paper was not machine-made, but all this meant was that it could have been produced any time before about 1810 when a machine-made paper came into general use. Karen Garlick of the Preservation Office was not able to match precisely the chain lines on the *Oath*'s paper to any in the Bay Psalm Book. However, she did determine that there was a great variety of types of paper used to print the Bay Psalm Book and that there were many different watermarks, indicating that Josse Glover may have gathered paper from several sources or from a batch of paper that was composed of samples from several mills. Therefore, the fact that the paper of the *Oath* did not match exactly any piece in the Bay Psalm Book was not significant since the different types of paper within the Bay Psalm Book did not match each other.

3. The unaided eye could not tell if the ink used to print the Bay Psalm Book was similar to that used to print the *Oath*. In fact, there was cause to indicate that the two inks should be different. At this early point in American history, Stephen Daye would necessarily have had to mix his own ink to print a document. The supply of printing ink made for the *Oath* would not have lasted the year between its production and the printing of the Bay Psalm Book. A new batch of ink would have been required, a batch that might have differed significantly from the earlier one. The presence of a modern alloy in the *Oath*'s ink would be conclusive evidence that the broadside was forged. But only a scientific test could detect the alloy.

However, one particularly important feature of the printing ink was discovered during the *Oath*'s initial examination at the Library. On the back or the verso of the document, a light golden-brown halo could be seen around many of the letters. Such halos are seen only on some older documents. They are caused by the binder in the ink leaching out slightly

19

into the paper around the edges of individual letters and turning light golden-brown over a significant period of time. That such a phenomenon occurs is not well known even among specialists. A thorough search of the literature and an informal poll among chemists and conservators acquainted with old paper and ink revealed that no one had ever heard of this phenomenon being artificially produced.

4. Extensive photography by Peter Watters of the Library's Preservation Office demonstrated two important things. The first was that the individual letters in the *Oath* cut into the paper at varying depths, confirming that the document had been printed from movable type rather than from a plate. The second was that the type of the Bay Psalm Book was not battered, as was commonly thought. Rather, the malformations were caused by the irregular absorption of ink on the surface of the paper along the edges of each letter. The irregularity may have occurred because the formula used for the ink did not allow it to be absorbed immediately into the paper, because the paper itself was sized in a way to cause the variations in the absorption of the ink, or because the type was overinked during the composition and there simply was too much ink to enter into the paper evenly. In those sections in the Library's copy of the Bay Psalm Book where the type had been lightly inked and the impression of the words was faint, the letters were as well-formed as those in the *Oath of a Freeman.*

5. None of the specialists from the Folger spotted anything in the spelling, punctuation, or usage of the words in the *Oath* that was inconsistent with early seventeenth-century practice.

6. Since the Schiller copy of the *Oath* was undated, the question of whether it was produced in England rather than in Massachusetts was raised. Peter Blayney, author of *The Texts of King Lear and Their Origins* and a student of seventeenth-century British printing-house practices, convincingly argued during several discussions that the *Oath*'s abnormal system of hyphenation would not have been tolerated in any London printing shop. The *Oath* had several hyphenated words that do not conform to standard practices of syllabification, which is also true of the Bay Psalm Book.

7. Several twentieth-century facsimiles of the Bay Psalm Book were intensively scrutinized to determine if letters, words, or phrases were cut out and rearranged to form the text of the *Oath*. The initial letter "I" in the *Oath* was particularly important since it appears in the same size only a few times in the Bay Psalm Book. Though the shape of the letter "I" in the *Oath* was clearly related to those examples of it found in the Bay Psalm Book, there were slight differences. If an exact match had been made with an "I" in the Bay Psalm Book, then the *Oath* would have been thrown under an immediate cloud of doubt and some kind of photoreproduction would have been suspected. Finding smaller individual letters that were common to both documents was not out of the ordinary since the possibility existed that the two were produced from the same type. The trick was to find some idiosyncratic letter or combination of letters that might link the two docu-

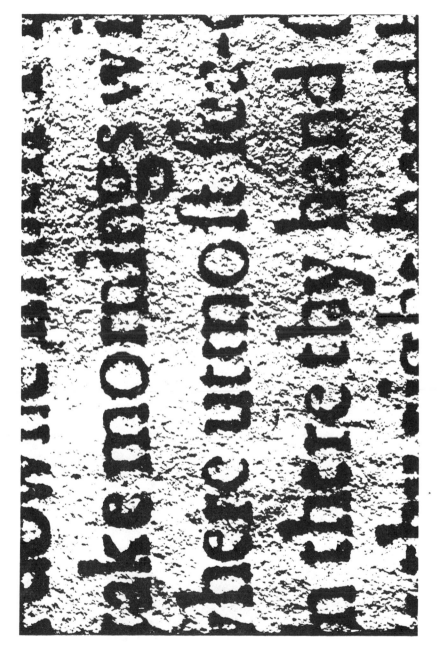

Fig. A. Section from a page in the Bay Psalm Book that shows the letter "g" in "mornings" interfering with two letters directly below it.

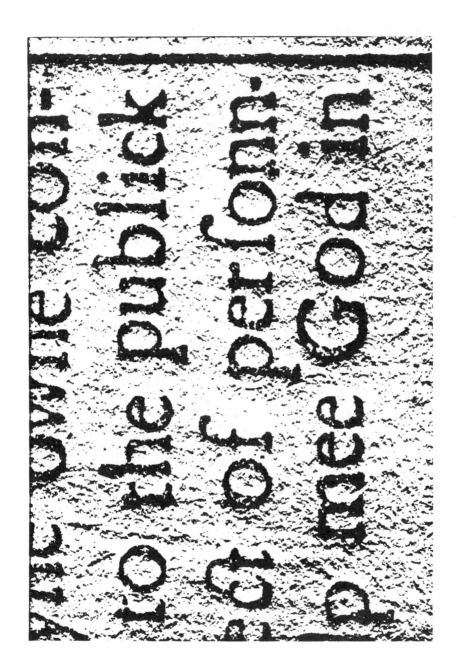

Fig. B. A section of the 'Oath of a Freeman' that shows the "p" in "personn," and the "G" in "God" entering into common space.

ments and could have been made only with a photograph. In the short time available to examine the *Oath*, I was unable to establish such a link.

8. We all quickly spotted the fact that in the *Oath* a few ascending letters, such as the "d" in "doe" in line five, came too close to descending letters from the line immediately above, such as the "j" in "subject" in line four. Some commentators have pointed to these juxtapositions as positive proof that the *Oath* was forged. In fact, in his interviews with the staff of the Salt Lake County Attorney's Office, Hofmann himself thought that he had made a mistake in this instance. However, in this Hofmann was luckier than he knew. Daye was not a good printer. He was a locksmith and clearly was not familiar with subtleties such as spacing. Not only was he unable to space his letters within a line in order that those lines needing a break could be finished at the end of a syllable, but he also kept his lines very near to one another. In the Bay Psalm Book there are numerous examples of ascenders and descenders closely impinging on each other's space. In some instances, it looks as if pieces of type might have been filed down in order to accommodate one another (see figures A and B). In effect, Hofmann's mistake made the *Oath* look even more credible.

As the investigation of the *Oath* in the Rare Book and Special Collections Division continued, we began to hear from various experts whom Schiller had contacted on his own. Nicolas Barker of the British Library, in a letter to William Matheson, wrote: "Since we spoke, I have seen a photocopy of the 'Freeman's Oath.' It is a poor thing to judge by, but there are a number of features about it that encourage the supposition that it may be genuine, and one or two that worry me a little. I hadn't realized that there was a handwritten inscription on it; this looks remarkably concordant with the purported date. Bob Nikirk has also sent me a clipping from the *Maine Antiques* (sic) *Digest*, which gives a good account of the whole business (except that it is headed 'The Ultimate Ephemera' (decline, as the Latin grammar used to say). At all events, I hope you'll keep me posted of further developments and let me know if I can help in any way." Katherine Pantzer wrote to Schiller saying that she could find nothing obviously wrong with the *Oath*. She made the most prescient remark of all by adding that it needed "to be seriously reconsidered, particularly in view of possible new technologies."

Under the terms of the agreement with Schiller and Wapner, the Library had custody of the *Oath* for only a short period. After about a week in the Rare Book and Special Collections Division, it was turned over to the Preservation Office for scientific analysis. We all hoped that these tests could provide a minute breakdown of the physical composition of the paper, printing ink, and manuscript ink of the *Oath*. Surely even the most careful forger might have made some small slip. Perhaps he used tap water to make the ink that would have left a trace of some modern alloy? Perhaps there was some tiny fragment embedded in the paper that could only have been manufactured at a much later time? Perhaps the iron gall ink had been artificially aged with some chemical that left behind an infinitesimal residue?

At the time the *Oath* left the confines of the Rare Book and Special Collections Division for its trip through the Library's system of tunnels to the Preservation Office in the new James Madison Building, my state of mind was similar to that described by Mark Twain when he visited what was said to be the grave of Adam just outside Jerusalem during the trip he depicted in the comic *The Innocents Abroad:* you can't prove that it is, and you can't prove that it isn't.

Preliminary Report on the Examination and Analysis of the 'Oath of a Freeman'

The Conservation Office and the Testing Office
of the Library of Congress Preservation Office

Editor's note: This is the Library of Congress report as it was originally issued with the exception of the following deletions: a list of Ektachrome color slides, photographs of magnified paper, the original graphs produced during the tests by the machines, and the list of the *Oath of a Freeman* type and word characteristics.

PRELIMINARY REPORT

ON THE

EXAMINATION AND ANALYSIS

OF THE

"THE OATH OF A FREEMAN"

Conservation Office

and

Research and Testing Office

Preservation Office

A B S T R A C T

Examination, full photographic and radiographic documentation, and technical and scientific analysis of the broadside entitled "The Oath of a Freeman" provide data that is consistent with that of the Bay Psalm Book, a known contemporary comparison. No evidence has been revealed that would contravene a mid-seventeenth-century date for the broadside.

Scientific analysis using x-ray fluorescence spectrometry and fourier transformspectrometry showed that the broadside substrate and the paper in the Bay Psalm Book were quite similar. Of particular note is the presence of zinc and manganese, which are not ordinarily found in modern papers, and FTIR spectra showing features that are consistent with old or oxidized cellulose.

Comparisons of color macrophotographs of the typography in the broadside and the Bay Psalm Book provide compelling evidence that the type came from the same matrices.

INTRODUCTION

On April 8, 1985, Raymond M. Wapner (representative for Justin G. Schiller, Ltd., New York, New York) and James W. Gilreath (Americana Specialist, Rare Book and Special Collections Division) delivered a printed broadside to the Conservation Office. The broadside is said to be an authentic printing of "The Oath of a Freeman", (Cambridge, 1638). It was brought to the Library of Congress for examination and analysis by the Conservation Office and the Research and Testing Office. The purpose of the study was to provide information through visual and optical examination, photographic and written documentation, and technical and scientific analysis that would help verify the authenticity of the broadside.

Previous scholarship had suggested that "The Oath of a Freeman" and the Bay Psalm Book (Cambridge, 1640), were printed by the same printer, possibly using the same paper and type. Therefore, the Library of Congress copy of the Bay Psalm Book (RBSC) was used as a known contemporary comparison for the broadside.

EXAMINATION METHODOLOGY

Methodology Employed by the Conservation Office

The Conservation Office visually examined the broadside and the Bay Psalm Book under reflected, raking, transmitted, and long-range ultra-violet light[1]. Optical examination under reflected light was conducted with a low power stereo microscope. The present condition and appearance of the broadside and Bay Psalm Book were documented with reflected, raking, and transmitted light photographs, reflected ultraviolet photo-graphs, and infrared luminescence photographs, and with beta radiographs.[2] Color macrophotographs were taken of selected typographical features in individual letters, sections of the text, and ornamental type in the broadside and the Bay Psalm Book.[3] In addition, the present condition and appearance of the broadside were fully described in a written report.[4]

----

[1] In this report, the word "light" is used generically to refer to the different spectra (ultraviolet, visible, and infrared) of radiant electro-magnetic energy.
[2] See Appendix B for this photographic and radiographic documentation as
[3] See Appendix C for color macrophotography.
[4] See Appendix A for full written documentation.

Methodology Employed by the Research and Testing Office

The Research and Testing Office employed the following analytical techniques:

(1) Optical microscopy utilizing Zeiss Photomicroscope.

Using transmitted and reflected light techniques, the fiber identity and paper structure are studied.

(2) X-ray fluorescence, (XRF) spectroscopy using Kevex 0700 spectrometer.

This technique determines the elements present in the sample by measuring the fluorescent x-rays produced when the sample is irradiated with higher energy x-rays. The technique only indicates the elements (primarily metals) present and not their form of chemical combination.

(3) Infrared spectroscopy using the Perkin-Elmer 1800 fourier transform infrared (FTIR) spectrophotometer.

This technique (with the present instrumental configuration) identifies organic compounds via the absorption of various frequencies of IR radiation by different functional groups in the compound.

(4) Chemical tests of printing ink.

The objective of these tests is to observe the solubility characteristics of the printing ink (which requires the deliberate removal of material from the object) and to identify, through FTIR techniques, the composition of soluble components of the ink.

Sample Preparation

During scientific examination the broadside was protected by polyester film (5 ml) encapsulation. Circular or oval windows were cut in the polyester film to allow access to various areas of interest on the document, i.e. unprinted area, printed area, manuscript ink area, adhesive area. These test areas are shown in Figure 1.

When the document was removed from the polyester film approximately 8-10 paper fibers that had become detached from the document remained affixed to the polyester film. Though the Library had permission to remove paper fibers for analysis, already detached fibers were mounted for microscopic examination.

The leaf, star3*, from the first section (*2-*4) of the Bay Psalm Book was used at the analytical comparison for the broadside. The middle printed and unprinted areas near the inner margin of the leaf were used for analysis. A leaf from the first section was selected because it contains the paper that is most similar to the broadside substrate, as determined from comparison of the spacing of the chain lines in both items. The Conservation Office examination showed that no exact match for the broadside substrate was found in the Bay Psalm Book.

DISCUSSION AND INTERPRETATION OF FINDINGS

CONSERVATION OFFICE FINDINGS

Characteristics of the Paper

Broadside

"The Oath of a Freeman" broadside is printed on a sheet of paper (hereinafter referred to as "substrate") that is continuous, i.e. that has no additions, laminar applications, false margins, or previous repairs. No surface coating has been applied that could disguise or obscure the presence of any kind of addition.

The substrate exhibits characteristics that are in accord with our knowledge of seventeenth century paper. Both beta radiographs and transmitted light photographs show a heavy deposition of the paper pulp along each side of the chain lines, typical of handmade Western paper produced prior to 1800.[5] The five evenly spaced chain lines exhibit minor irregularities. The upper two chain lines are wavy in contrast to the lower two chain lines which are relatively straight. The fifth, or lowest, chain line contains a break. The center chain line is difficult to interpret because of tears that coincide along the line. No watermark is visible.

Papermaking "flaws" revealed in the substrate include a thin spot in the lower third of the sheet, a slight variation in overall density and distribution of the pulp from the upper edge to the second chain line, and minor crimping of the substrate in the left half of the sheet.

----
[5]Such paper is commonly referred to as "antique laid".

Comparison of the Papers: Broadside and Bay Psalm Book

Examination of the broadside substrate reveals that it does not match exactly any of the leaves in the Bay Psalm Book. There is a similarity in the spacing of the chain lines in the leaves of the first section of the Bay Psalm Book (*2-*4) and the broadside substrate. However, the irregularities of the broadside's chain lines (the waviness and the break) are absent.

These disparities should not imply that the two papers are not contemporaneous with each other. The presence of at least 12 different watermarks in the Bay Psalm Book suggests that the printer did not have a sufficient stock of one type of paper from which to print this book.[6] If this assumption is correct, it would not be surprising that the broadside substrate and the book papers differ.

The relative whiteness and brightness of the broadside substrate may seem unusual for a document of this age and origin, especially when it is compared to the paper in the Bay Psalm Book, which is considerably darker. However, when viewed separately, the broadside substrate is not, in fact, strikingly different in color and tone from many other 17th century papers. In addition the surface tonality appears natural, not artificial or similar to a hue produced by chemical means.[7] The presence

---

[6]It is not known whether the other ten copies of the Bay Psalm Book have similar watermarked papers. A study of these copies could be informative.

[7]It has been suggested that the broadside substrate was bleached and that such treatment is responsible for the white color. If this were to be the case, the iron containing manuscript ink on the verso would ost likely have to be considered a later addition, since bleaching is known to change the color of iron containing inks.

of folds in the substrate, visible in raking light, suggests that the document may have been stored in various folded states and may have remained unused for a length of time. Furthermore, the brown discolored band across the lower part of the horizontal center fold of the broadside substrate, now partially torn, indicates that the document may have been hinged at one time onto a secondary support (possibly a scrapbook page). This brown discoloration could be related to the migration of colored decomposition products from the adhesive used on the hinge to the broadside substrate, a commonly observed phenomenon in hinged documents. The enclosed storage given to the document, if it had been hinged, would also have protected it from the hazards of use and the environment to which the Bay Psalm Book is likely to have been exposed. In fact, it is evident from the present appearance of the Bay Psalm Book that it has not only been used heavily, but has also been exposed to humid conditions and water damage.

Comparison of the Printing: Broadside and Bay Psalm Book

Cursory comparison of the printing in the broadside (which has a relatively clean type impression and has been lightly inked) and the Bay Psalm Book (which is generally over-inked and shows inconsistent press work) seems to indicate that at the time of printing, the type face of the former was new or little used while the type face of the latter was worn. In fact, close examination provides no evidence that points to one type face being more or less worn than the other. Further, detailed examination does reveal that the two type faces are identical. The differences that exist between the broadside and the Bay Psalm Book can be attributed to several factors, such as the surface quality variations in the papers

produced by the sizing and the inability of the printer to select a suitable ink for the paper. Such variations affect the letterpress printing
process and therefore the final appearance of the printing.

The surface of the paper in the Bay Psalm Book is less rough and
is stiffer than that of the broadside substrate. These qualities suggest
the paper was heavily sized during manufacture although the paper does not
now resist water as readily as could be expected of a heavily sized paper.
This lack of water resistance is similar to that exhibited by other seventeenth century book papers in which the protein size and related by-
products have broken down through oxidation, another explanation for the
overall discolored appearance of the paper in the Bay Psalm Book. Some
early printing inks were heavy and thick in composition and required a
paper that contained little or no size to create a good, clean impression.
To print cleanly on a heavily sized paper was difficult and required a
careful adjustment in printing pressure and selection of ink. In many
cases the printing ink would spread on the surface of the paper, but not
be absorbed by it, resulting in a fuzzy, imprecise delineation of
individual letters in words. The impression of the type in the paper
would be light and not as deep as was customary. Keeping this in mind, it
is not surprising that on initial examination the printing in the Bay
Psalm Book seems to lack sharpness and clarity and seems to be worn. This
view is reinforced when the heavy inking is also noted. However, examination using a low power stereo microscope and color macrophotographs
clearly shows that the type in the Bay Psalm Book is not worn and that
this illusion is created by the thickly deposited printing ink spread out
on the surface of the paper.

Clarity of the printing quality of the broadside also seems to be related to the degree of sizing in the paper and imprecise press work. Unlike the paper in the Bay Psalm Book, the surface of the broadside substrate is soft and the sheet is limp in handling, suggesting that during manufacture, it was more lightly sized. The more pronounced "felted" surface of a lightly sized sheet is conducive to receiving a sharp, clear impression from letterpress printing. This capacity is borne out by a close examination of the broadside which shows that while the inking is light, the printing is sharp and clean, and the type impression is deep.

Comparison of Typographical Features: Broadside and Bay Psalm Book

While the printing in the broadside and the Bay Psalm Book differ in appearance for the reasons just cited, several leaves of text in the Bay Psalm Book are more lightly inked than the others and lend themselves to comparison with the broadside.[8]

Three shared characteristics indicate that the type in both items came from the same matricies: the letter shapes, the letter counters, and the word setting. Many of the letters and letter ligatures reflect the telltale "earmarks" of the punch cutter's craftsmanship. Among the most significant are the "a", "d", "e", "f", "g", "m", "n", "r", "w", "ct", "sh", "sl", and "s". The lower case "o" is especially noteworthy because of the unusual reversed angle of the thick stroke slanting from lower left to upper right. This suggests that the punch cutter neglected to reverse the "o" when cutting the punch. In addition certain pieces of the type ornaments used in the border of the broadside and the heading of

---

[8]The variation in inking in the Bay Psalm Book supports the conclusion that the quality of the press work is erratic.

Psalm 42 in section I4 recto of the <u>Bay Psalm Book</u> match exactly. These traits are clearly illustrated in the macro color photographic comparisons of the two texts in Appendix B.

Finally, a comparison of the line spacing in both documents indicates that they are the same.[9]

The text measurements of the broadside are _____ and the text measurements of the <u>Bay Psalm Book</u> are _____. The slight variation in head to tail measurements in "x" height line spacing can be accounted for by the humidity and water damage to the <u>Bay Psalm Book</u> which has caused the paper to shrink.[10]

Manuscript Ink

The manuscript ink written on the back of the broadside along the left edge is more absorbent in ultraviolet than in infrared light and appears intense and dark under long wave ultraviolet examination in contrast to its almost transparent appearance in infrared luminescence photographs. This is consistent with the response to most aged iron gall inks. The strike through of the ink from the back to the front and the split in the substrate under the letter "h" in the word "Oath" is characteristic of the corrosive action of some aged iron gall inks.

----

[9]To measure the character count per line, the letters and punctuation marks in a full line setting were counted in both items. The spaces were not included in this count. In addition lines in the first section of the <u>Bay Psalm Book</u> (*2-*4) that had numerals were excluded.

[10]Shrinking and the resulting severe cockling is clearly shown in the raking light photographs in Appendix B.

RESEARCH AND TESTING OFFICE FINDINGS

Optical Microscopy

Unmounted Samples

Both the broadside and Bay Psalm Book papers were examined un-
mounted in transmitted and reflected light modes. Transmitted light was
most useful in characterizing fibers at the cut or frayed edges of the
documents and was limited to relatively low magnification (250X). Even at
that magnification the depth of focus was so shallow that viewing the
specimen required constant readjustment of focus and useful photomicro-
graphs could not be obtained. Reflected light (especially in the dark
field mode) showed much more of the overall paper structure and individual
fiber characteristics. It was particularly important to determine whether
or not wood fibers were present, since these would suggest a much more
recent date for the manufacture of the paper.

Both papers were very similar with long fibers with birefringence characteristic of cellulose. The majority of the fibers appeared to
be flax judging from their morphology (especially bast-like features), but
flat twisted fibers characteristic of cotton were also present in considerable number. Two short, smooth colored (red and green) fibers (silk?)
were seen in the broadside along the center tear.

The papers both had a certain amount of dirt or debris but in
addition many small ($<5\mu$) crystalline particles some of which showed
strong birefringence. Time did not permit further analysis, but taken
with the XRF data (vide infra) identification of the latter as calcium
carbonate is reasonable.

Figure 2 shows the paper and fiber morphology at low ($\sim$ 40X) magnification; Figure 3 ($\sim$ 250X) shows fiber structure in more detail and some of the small crystals.

Mounted Fibers

Some of the loose fibers from the polyester film encapsulation were removed and mounted in Aroclor 5442. Once again, no wood fiber-like objects were observed and the bast nature was more clearly in evidence. Figures 4 and 5 (250 x and 40 x with partially crossed polars) clearly show the bast and birefringent characteristics of the fibers.

Conclusions

The broadside and the Bay Psalm Book papers were very similar in appearance and consisted primarily of what appears to be long fibers of flax and cotton. Some debris which is probably dust and dirt was found in the papers as well as some crystalline material a portion of which had some optical characteristics of calcium carbonate. If time permitted additional tests could be conducted to confirm such an assignment and to characterize the other crystals present.

X-Ray Fluorescence Spectrometry

This technique can be very sensitive and can, under favorable circumstances, detect elements at the parts per million level. Its main applications in this study were to detect elements in the paper charac-teristic and uncharacteristic of its presumed age and to compare the ele-mental composition of the broadside and the Bay Psalm Book papers which may have come from a single source.

Under the influence of the exciting x-rays each element present in the sample will emit x-rays of energies characteristic of that element and in an intensity related to the excitation conditions and the nature of the sample. For comparison purposes it is usually sufficient to excite similar samples under the same excitation conditions. Such a procedure will show which elements are present and their relative amounts. The data reported here were obtained using a germanium secondary target excited by a 15 KEV/1.5 ma x-ray source and counted for 600 seconds. Several other excitation conditions were used in the analysis. All yielded consistent results. All XRF data are recorded in notebook 81-DKS-KEVEX and stored on computer disk.

In addition to the broadside and the Bay Psalm Book papers data were obtained under identical exitation conditions for a very pure (<0.006% ash) paper, Whatman 541, for the purpose of obtaining a background or control. Since the KEVEX spectrometer is constructed of lead and aluminum and the x-ray tube has a rhodium target, lines of these elements will be found in all measurements and should be subtracted from all observed spectra.

Data obtained for the various areas of the broadside and the Bay Psalm Book papers and the Whatman 541 paper are displayed in Figs. 6 to 15. Fig. 15 indicates the element assigned to each energy of the spectrum. Elements present at concentrations significantly above the Whatman 541 control are identified in each graph.

The elements found in both papers are: calcium (Ca), manganese (Mn), iron (Fe), copper (Cu), zinc (Zn), Potassium (K) and chlorine (Cl). Additional elements may be present at low levels but they are either masked by lines of other elements or of such low intensity, e.g. Titanium (Ti) , that their statistical significance is uncertain.

Iron and copper are nearly always present in paper as impurities. Calcium occurs as an impurity or sometimes is deliberately added Calcium Carbonate (as Ca CO_3) to make a more stable alkaline paper. Zinc is not a common high concentration impurity in modern papers but is sometimes added as a whitener. Manganese is not commonly found in modern papers at the levels observed here. However, both elements have been observed in older papers and have been attributed to the mineral content of waters in a particular region. The presence of these two elements may afford a clue to the identification of the papers as English or European in origin. Somewhat surprising, too, are the relatively high amounts of potassium and chlorine – particularly in the Bay Psalm Book paper. Once can account for the much lower potassium and chlorine concentrations in the broadside by assuming they are present as the water soluble salt potassium chloride which was washed out of the paper when the document was immersed in water to remove it from its mount. If time permitted, it would have been useful to determine if some of the small crystals observed microscopically are potassium chloride.

No significant differences were observed for a given paper between unprinted areas, printed areas, and areas where a residue of adhesive remains. However, when the area containing manuscript ink was studied the iron concentration increased several fold (Fig. 8) suggesting the ink is iron-based, probably an iron gall type.

Conclusions

The broadside has an elemental composition, except for significantly lower potassium and chlorine content, very similar to that of the Bay Psalm Book. There are two elements (zinc and manganese) which are not common to modern papers and which suggest a common source of manufacture.

No statistically significant amounts of aluminum were observed; the papers therefore were not alum-rosin sized. The lower potassium and chlorine content of the broadside may be associated with its immersion in water at some time in the past.

Fourier Transform Infrared Spectrometry(FTIR)

The FTIR spectra of various portions of the broadside and Bay Psalm Book were compared with each other and with Whatman 541 paper as a control. With the present configuration of the Perkin-Elmer 1800 FTIR instrument, analysis is largely limited to an analysis of organic functional groups. In older paper samples one might anticipate finding carbonyl and carboxyl functional groups associated with oxidation and hydrolysis of cellulose due to aging, amine and amide·groups associated with gelatin or glue size and ester groups associated with the drying oil medium of printing inks. Although greater sensitivity could be obtained utilizing the attenuated total reflectance (ATR) techniques, this mode was rejected in favor of transmission of the IR beam through the sample because of the vulnerability of the documents.

Most of the IR radiation impinging upon the sheet of paper is scattered and as seen in Figure 16, less than 1% of the analyzing radiation passing through the paper sample reaches the detector. It is only with FTIR techniques that useful information can be obtained from so small a signal. Figure 17 shows the spectrum of Fig. 16 expanded. Despite the noise in the signal, the various bands of cellulose in Whatman 541 paper are clearly evident even though the total transmission is only 0.4%.

Figures 18 through 29 are spectra of the broadside, Bay Psalm Book and Whatman 541 papers in various sampling areas. Fig. 18 through 21 show the higher noise level associated with 4 repetitions of the instru-

ment scan compared with 32 cycles for Fig. 23 through 28. Data and exper-
imental details are recorded in research notebook 77-DKS and on computer
disks.

Comparing the broadside spectra of unprinted, printed, manuscript ink, and glue areas, we find very few significant differences. The
manuscript ink area has a stronger absorption of 1740 cm -1 and a small
shoulder @ 1950 cm -1 and the printed area has absorption bands at 1960 cm
-1 and @ 1825 cm -1, absent in the unprinted area. The 1740 cm -1 band has been
associated with the carbonyl functional group of cellulose when the cellulose is oxidized. Iron is known to catalyze oxidation and so we may associate this with the iron containing ink. In fact, oxidation in the manuscript ink area has taken place to the extend that losses of paper have
occurred. The glue area was completely free of printing. Whereas the
manuscript ink area had a small amount of printing ink on the reverse
side. The bands at ca. 1960 and 1825 cm^{-1} appeared to be associated with
the printing ink on the broadside but have not been further identified. No
evidence was noted for functional groups associated with gelatin or animal
glue which may have been used as a paper size.

Comparing the printed areas of the Bay Psalm Book (Fig. 27, 28
and 29) with those of the broadside the 1960 and 1825 cm^{-1} peaks are
absent. This suggests another ink was used, or the broadside and the Bay
Psalm Book papers experienced different environments or treatments since
their printing.

Figures 24, 27 and 30 compare unprinted areas of the broadside
and the Bay Psalm Book. The broadside spectrum has a strong absorption at
1740 cm^{-1} absent in the Bay Psalm Book. Again, if one associates that
peak with more extensive oxidation of the cellulose, this may be evidence

that the broadside had at some time been subjected to oxidative bleaching. Additional evidence to support this hypothesis is: (a) the low potassium or chlorine content (which would have been decreased by aqueous bleaching followed by thorough washing), and (b) the whiter color. Bleaching would undoubtedly have some effect upon the printing inks and so may account for the differences noted between the broadside and the Bay Psalm Book printing inks.

Conclusions

The general features of the FTIR spectra of broaside and the Bay Psalm Book are consistent with old and/or oxidized cellulose. The broadside appears to be more extensively oxidized to carbonyl and carboxyl groups. The printing inks of the two documents differ significantly but reasons for the difference remain speculative. Additional analysis utilizing additional equipment (such as beam condensors) and a larger number of analysis cycles may reveal additional information now concealed in the noise and scatter.

Solubility Test on Printing Ink

The Research and Testing laboratory is not well equipped for nor is the staff very experienced in chromatographic analysis of inks. The analysis of older printing inks is particularly difficult since they are usually constituted of carbon black in a drying oil medium and vary little in composition. Only in relatively modern times have various synthetic dyes or pigments been incorporated into printing inks to improve their blackness. In lieu of chromatographic analysis, which in any case has been most fully developed for pen writing fluids and ballpoint pen inks, a solubility test followed by FTIR was employed.

A small cotton swab (about 1mm in diameter) was prepared, dampened with 1,2 dichloroethane and applied to a printed area (the second "E" of "Freeman" in the broadside). The white cotton was examined to see if any ink was removed; none was. Drops of solvent were applied to the damp swab and allowed to drip onto a sodium chloride (NaCl) disc. Soluble components removed from the ink would, upon evaporation of solvent, be concentrated on the NaCl disc which was then analyzed in the FTIR spectrometer. No difference was observed in the NaCL disc spectrum before and after deposition and evaporation of solvent.

Conclusions

Under the test conditions the printing ink is insoluble in 1,2 dichloroethane. A fresh carbon based oil medium ink might be expected to be at least partially soluble.

CONCLUSION

The Conservation Office and the Research and Testing Office examined, documented, and technically and scientifically analyzed the broadside entitled "The Oath of a Freeman" to determine whether or not it could be an authentic contemporary printing of the historic text issued by the Cambridge Press in 1638. The Library of Congress copy of the <u>Bay Psalm Book</u> (Cambridge, 1640) was used as a known contemporary comparison, since no contemporary printing of the broadside is known.

The study of the broadside focused on the paper substrate (elemental composition, organic function groups, fiber morphology, structural composition, surface character, and condition), the printing (quality and technique), the typographical features (the letter shapes, the letter counters, the word setting, and the line spacing), the printing ink (organic functional groups and appearance), and the manuscript ink (elemental composition, organic functional groups and appearance). The present condition and appearance of the broadside were documented with beta radiographs, a wide range of black and white photographs, and color macrophotography.

The <u>Bay Psalm Book</u> was studied by the same means as the broadside. Black and white photographs and color macrographs were limited to the first section (*2-*4), the type ornaments above Psalm 42 (I4), and leaf Hh.

The differences and similarities between the two items were studied and their relative significance weighed.

Scientific analysis suggested that the broadside substrate and the paper in the Bay Psalm Book were quite similar. Fiber analysis showed a composition primarily of flax, with some cotton. Elemental analysis using x-ray fluorescence spectrometry showed a close similarity. Data supporting a common manufacture was provided by the presence of zinc and manganese, which are not ordinarily in modern papers. Fourier transform infrared spectrometry spectra showed features that are consistent with old or oxidized cellulose.

The lighter overall color of the broadside substrate was considered to be typical of many mid-seventeenth century papers. It is possible that enclosed storage (evidence of which was supplied by folds and possible hinge adhesive discoloration) contributed to the preservation of the fresh appearance. The visual difference of the paper in the Bay Psalm Book (which is darker) was attributed to the effects of water damage, use, and oxidation of the original size. These variations between the broadside and the Bay Psalm Book relate to the history of the items after their production and are not fundamental differences.

Elemental analysis (x-ray fluorescence spectrometry) of the manuscript ink shows that it is an iron based ink. The ink is not absorbed by infrared and is absorbed by ultraviolet light, which is characteristic of the behavior of mostly aged iron gall inks.

Fourier transform infrared spectra of the printing ink in the broadside and the Bay Psalm Book show some differences. No conclusions can be drawn about the significance or meaning of these differences. However, solubility testing of the broadside printing ink suggests that it is not of recent origin.

The difference in the appearance of the printing on the broadside and in the Bay Psalm Book can be attributed to differences in paper sizing, composition of the printing ink (relative thickness), and press work. These factors alter the appearance of the printing so that the broadside is lightly inked, the letters are sharp and cleanly printed, and the type impression is deep while the Bay Psalm Book is generally over-inked, the letters have a fuzzy appearance, and the type impression is almost imperceptible. In addition, the quality of the press work in the Bay Psalm Book is erratic. When examined closely under a low power stereo microscope the type appears quite similar. Comparison of the type through color micrographs provides compelling evidence that the type came from the same matrices.[11]

'Finally, the studies of the broadside entitled "The Oath of a Freeman" conducted by the Conservation Office and the Research and Testing Office revealed no evidence that would contravene a mid-seventeenth century date for the broadside.

---

[11]This study was conducted over a brief period of time and was limited to the expertise and analytical techniques and tests presently available in the Library. Additional examination and further analysis of this and new data would be of great value in any further assessment of attribution of the broadside entitled "The Oath of a Freeman".

A P P E N D I X   A

CONDITION AND EXAMINATION REPORT

OF THE BROADSIDE

"THE OATH OF A FREEMAN"

Description

Item is a printed broadside on white laid paper of medium
weight. The sheet has an irregular rectangular shape and unevenly cut
edges. It measures in length, 14.9 cm on the right edge and 15.1 cm on
the left edge; in width 10.4 cm along the upper edge and 10.5 cm along the
lower edge.

The broadside text is surrounded by a rectangular printed border
composed of repeated pairs of ornamental type within a pair of line
segments. The border ranges from .6 - .7 mm in width, varying according
to the thickness of the line segments.

The printed text consists of 28 lines that measure as a block
13.2 cm (length) x 8.7 cm (width). Examination of the verso in reflected
light and under low power stereo microscopy reveals a heavy, clear impression characteristic of printing by letterpress. The printing ink for the

border and text is black. The inking of the text and border is uneven,
with interruptions clearly visible by direct visual examination as well as
under magnification.

The unevenly cut edges and the lack of any significant white
margin between the border and the edge of the paper provide evidence that
the broadside was cut down at some point in the past.

On the verso, a dark brown manuscript ink inscription reading,
"Oath of a Freeman" is written along the left edge, oriented from the
upper edge down, beginning 4 cm from the upper edge and extending down 6.6
cm.

Examination in transmitted light shows that the paper have five
(5) horizontal chain lines, approximately 1 1/16 inch apart, and approximately 27 chain lines per inch, as counted in a one inch area of blank
paper in the lower right quadrant, beginning 2.8 cm from the right edge
and 1 cm from the lower edge. The upper two chain lines are wavy in contrast to the lower two, which are relatively straight. The lower chain
line contains a break, 2.1 cm from the lower edge, 3.3 cm from the right
edge. (These characteristics of the chain lines suggest that the papermaker used an old or damaged mould to form this paper.) It is difficult
to interpret the chain line along the center because of the tears that
coincide at this point (see Tears below). The paper is slightly
glossy and has a moderate tooth. It is soft and limp to the touch, possibly a result of the aqueous treatment it has received (see Previous
Treatment below).

Transmitted light shows a heavier deposition of the paper pulp along each side of the chain lines than is evident through the sheet overall. This is typical of Western handmade paper before 1800, commonly referred to as "antique laid".

Papermaking "flaws" revealed in the paper include:

1. Semi-transparent spot (so-called "papermaker's tear") 5.5 cm from the right edge, 4.7 cm above the lower edge. (Measurement taken from the center of the tear.)

2. Uneven distribution of pulp from the upper edge to the second chain lines resulting in an area that is less dense than the overall sheet.

3. Minor crimping in the left half of the sheet, probably caused by prematurely moving the sheet before it was dry.

These defects when they are found together in a single sheet, are characteristic of paper known as "retree" or "first retree", slightly imperfect paper that is sold at a lower cost. Especially after printing, these minor imperfections can go unnoticed.

Examination in reflected light shows seven dark brown pinhead-sized holes in the paper, possibly from minor metallic contamination of the pulp, most notably:

1. 2 cm from the right edge, 1 cm above the lower edge.

2. 2.4 cm from the right edge, 1.1 cm above the lower edge.

3. 1.5 cm from the left edge, 1.7 cm above the lower edge.

4. 1.1 cm from the left edge, 1.5 cm above the lower edge.

5. 2.2 cm from the right edge, 2.7 cm below the upper edge.

6. 1.4 cm from the left edge, 7 cm below the upper edge.

7. 1.3 cm from the left edge, 7.2 cm below the upper edge.

Condition

Folds:

There are seven folds oriented throughout the paper, four of which are related:

1. A horizontal fold along the center chain line. This is visible in reflected light and is confirmed by examination under magnification. (See Tears below)

2. A set of four folds, visible only in raking light. The item was folded in half vertically (mountain fold) and then twice horizontally (mountain folds), 3.2 cm from the lower edge and 6.9 cm from the lower edge. Finally it was folded horizontally (valley fold) 2.5 cm from the upper edge.

3. Two diagonal folds, extending from the left edge to the right edge and visible only in raking light:

    a. 11.2 cm in length; beginning 6.2 cm from the upper edge and ending 2.5 cm from the upper edge.

    b. 15 cm in length; beginning .2 cm from the lower edge and ending 4.4 cm from the upper edge.

Tears

The broadside is torn in five places:

1. 1.5 cm above the lower edge, extending from the left edge: a .8 cm curved tear.

2. 1.2 cm from the lower edge, extending from the right edge: .2 cm horizontal tear that extends downward at the end .3 cm.

3. 1.2 cm from the left edge, extending from the upper edge: .3 cm vertical tear.

4. Approximately half way down the sheet (7.6 cm from the upper edge) two horizontal tears that run along the center chain line:

a. Beginning at the left edge and extending 7.7 cm from the left edge.

b. Beginning at the right edge and extending .7 cm from the right edge.

Under examination in reflected light the split extending from the left edge seems to have unusually sharp edges, suggesting that the paper may have been cut. However, examination of this area under magnification shows fibers that are teased out enough to support the opinion that the damage is the result of a tear. Further examination under magnification of the untorn area along this horizontal line (approximately 2.5 cm in length, beginning .7 cm from the right edge) shows that the paper is distorted and the fibers strained in a way that is characteristic of a fold.

Discoloration

Below this central horizontal fold is a discolored brown area (approximately .5 cm at it widest point) that is more clearly visible from the verso than the recto with diffuse edges, and tapered in shape. It begins .7 cm from the right edge and extends 6.5 cm from the right edge, where noticeable narrowing of the discoloration occurs and then continues (though less intense in color) to the left edge. It has been suggested that at one time the item may have been folded and attached to a secondary support (such as a scrapbook page) with a hinge adherred to the lower part of the fold on the verso. In aging, the adhesive or hinge could have become degraded and discolored, and discolored the paper through contact. This explanation would also account for the tearing of the paper as the paper would be weakened in the discolored area and could easily separate along the fold line in the course of handling.

From the verso, yellow hallowing is visible around each of the printed letters and elements that compose the border, possibly a result of an oil vehicle in the printing ink.

Losses

There are three small areas of loss:

1. A nick at the left edge, 5.1 cm below the upper edge.

2. The tip of the upper right corner.

3. An irregular area extending from the left edge, beginning 2.4 cm above the lower edge, 2.5 cm in length as diagrammed below. (The paper is slightly abraded at the beginning point of this loss.)

Previous Treatment

In a discussion with James W. Gilreath (American History Specialist, RBSC), it was learned that the broadside was previously mounted to a secondary support and was removed by the current owner in 19__ by immersion in tap water (Utah) for approximately 10 minutes. The temperature of the water is not known and the secondary support to which the broadside was mounted was not saved.

Residues

On the verso at each of the four corners is a small yellow spot of encrusted adhesive residue. The location of these residues suggests that the item was spot mounted to the secondary support from which it was removed. No microchemical testing of the adhesive residues was carried out at this time.

ADDITIONAL COMMENTS

1. The paper is generally in very good condition. It shows no evidence of insect damage, accretions (other than the adhesive residues mentioned), or surface dirt. It is not generally physically distorted. It retains good strength and flexibility and could be handled without risk of physical damage if the center tears were mended.

2. It is important to note that because of the combined length of the tears and the location of the intact area between the tears, the broadside is at serious risk of separating into two pieces even with careful handling. To minimize this risk the broadside has been placed into a 5 ml polyester folder and supported on a rigid surface when moved. Further, when removed from the polyester, the broadside has been gently slid on to another rigid support that is as thick as the rigid support under the polyester. The broadside has been replaced in the polyester folder in a similar way. Finally, the broadside has been turned over by rotating it between two rigid supports. The purpose of these procedures is to minimize direct handling and lifting of the item in an attempt to prevent creeping of the tears or separation of the paper into two pieces.

MACROPHOTOGRAPHS

TECHNICAL DESCRIPTION

Two hundred, sixty-four (264) ektachrome 50 35mm color slides were taken of the "Oath of a Freeman" and of random selections from the Bay Psalm Book. These selections were limited to the first section (*2-*4), ornamental type above Psalm 42 (leaf I4, recto) and the very light areas of printing found in and around Hh. A selection of the 264 slides have been reproduced in Cibachrome for our first report. Exact reproduction of color was felt to be of secondary importance to the keeping of a constant lighting, camera and enlarger exposure.

A low and constant angle of raking light was used throughout. The camera's automatic exposure system was used for the macro close-ups. In the printing of the Cibachromes a constant exposure value was used regardless of enlargement by measuring the light at the plane of the printing easel.

There was no "dodging" or any other kind of printing manipulation used.

Equipment Used:

1. 3200 Tungsten light single source
2. Light box for transmitted light
3. Om2n 35mm camera with 38mm and 50mm macro lenses
4. Typical exposure was from 20 seconds to 40 seconds at F22
5. Eight rolls of Ektachrome 50 processed in Kodak E-6 chemistry
6. Minolta Flash Meter III to measure the enlarger light falling on the plane of the printing easel. Setting of the meter was as follows:

        Switch set on ambient
        ASA 25
        Speed: 30 seconds

        Reflected reading for exposure with the image removed from the enlarger head was F11.7, exposure time was 5 seconds.

7. Cibachrome II delux CPSIK processed with P-3 chemistry; standard times for developer, bleach and fix

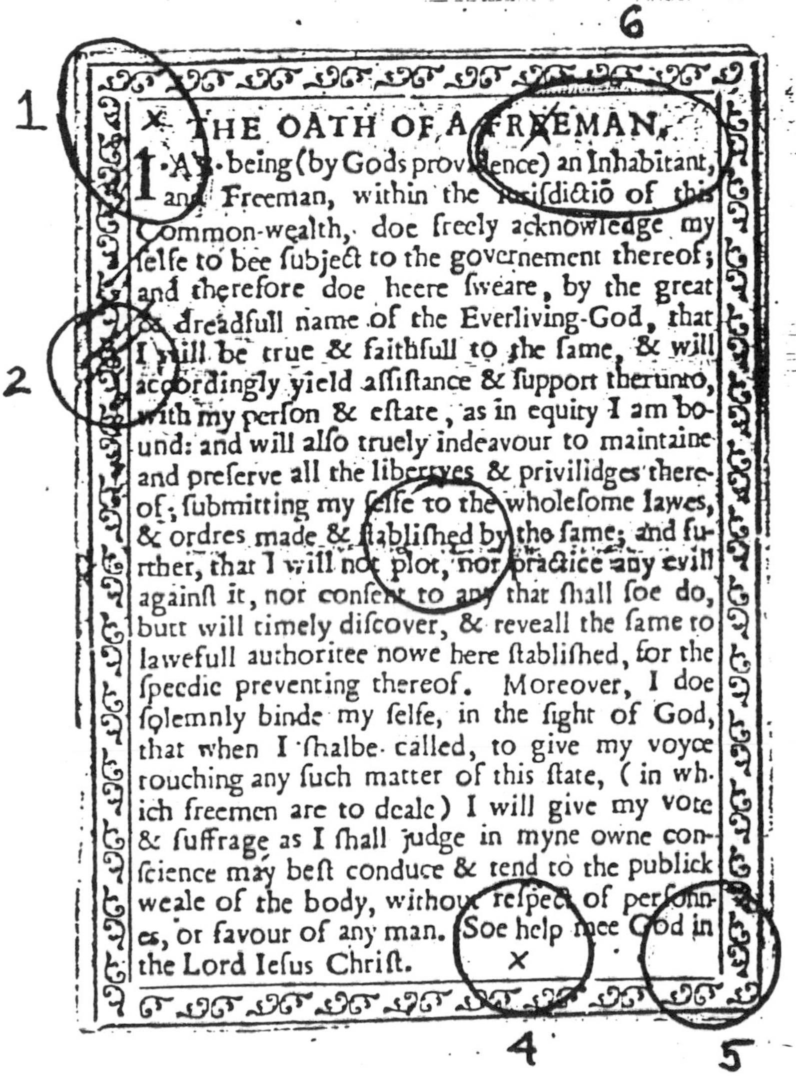

THE OATH OF A FREEMAN.

I. A.B. being (by Gods providence) an Inhabitant, and Freeman, within the Iurisdictiō of this Common-wealth, doe freely acknowledge my selfe to bee subject to the governement thereof; and therefore doe heere sweare, by the great & dreadfull name of the Everliving-God, that I will be true & faithfull to the same, & will accordingly yield assistance & support therunto, with my person & estate, as in equity I am bound: and will also truely indeavour to maintaine and preserve all the libertyes & privilidges thereof, submitting my selfe to the wholesome lawes, & ordres made & stablished by the same: and further, that I will not plot, nor practice any evill against it, nor consent to any that shall soe do, butt will timely discover, & reveall the same to lawefull authoritee nowe here stablished, for the speedie preventing thereof. Moreover, I doe solemnly binde my selfe, in the sight of God, that when I shalbe called, to give my voyce touching any such matter of this state, (in which freemen are to deale) I will give my vote & suffrage as I shall judge in myne owne conscience may best conduce & tend to the publick weale of the body, without respect of personnes, or favour of any man. Soe help mee God in the Lord Iesus Christ.

X

Figure 1 Windows in Mylar enclosure for *Oath of a Freeman*.

Schiller-Wapner Galleries Offers the 'Oath' to the Library of Congress

James Gilreath

Contrary to popular misconceptions in the news media and in several books about Hofmann and his forgeries, the Library's Preservation Office did not authenticate the *Oath of a Freeman*; its investigators merely stated that they could find no evidence of forgery based on their examination of the material used to make the document. There was no proof that the ink had been on the paper for almost 350 years, only that this ink was consistent with the types of ink that were used at that time. Nevertheless, the Preservation Office's report gave the *Oath of a Freeman* additional credibility, especially in light of other information gathered about the *Oath*. The thought of forgery was never far from our minds. However, we now realized that if it was a forgery, it was a very sophisticated one.

During mid-May, John C. Broderick decided to learn Schiller and Wapner's terms for selling the broadside and so invited them to make an offer. Both William Matheson and I not only agreed with this course of action but argued for it. This request for an offer from Schiller and Wapner was not a decision to buy the *Oath*, only a strategy to learn more about it. At this time, we had virtually no information about who owned the document, where and under what circumstances it had been found, or where it had been. Before the Library of Congress could take steps to acquire the *Oath of a Freeman*, a good deal more information was necessary. The Preservation Office's report was thorough and useful, but also inconclusive for the purpose of supporting a decision to purchase. Preeminently, a good provenance was as important—if not more important—than the Preservation Office's scientific findings and the historical conclusions drawn in the Rare Book and Special Collections Division. All three modes of investigation must work together in a synergistic way. A weakness in one weakened the others.

On May 8, 1985, William Matheson called Justin Schiller to ask for the terms of an offer to sell the *Oath* to the Library. He also requested information about the document's provenance. Schiller put him off for a day. On May 9, Schiller called to say that part of the group of investors who owned the *Oath* (later events revealed that the three anonymous owners were Hofmann, Schiller, and Wapner) was in Europe. No one wanted to set a price until all had seen the Preservation Office's report. I suspected that Schiller and Wapner owned some part of the broadside but did not know if still others were involved. Schiller then provided Matheson with some information about the *Oath*'s history. He said that the original owner bought the broadside as a decorative item "some time ago." When reading a recent Sotheby's auction catalogue that listed a copy of *New-Englands Jonas* for sale, he began to wonder if his *Oath of a Freeman* and the one described and reprinted in *New-Englands Jonas* were one and the same. According to Matheson's contemporary memo about the telephone conversation, Schiller told him that when the owner decided that his broadside might be the first thing printed in North America, he talked to "some local people" who convinced him to form an investment group. The original owner then contacted Schiller, because he had bought children's books from Schiller-Wapner Galleries in the past. However, Schiller reported a mysterious advisor was entering the picture who had the ear of the original owner and the investment group. The advisor threatened to derail negotiations by trying to market the *Oath* to corporations for $3 million. If the advisor was successful in making his case, the whole matter would be out of Schiller and Wapner's hands.

In response to Schiller's request for a copy of the Preservation Office's report, the Library of Congress sent a summary of the document that contained the conclusion that the tests could not find anything that would "contravene a seventeenth-century origin." Shortly thereafter, Schiller-Wapner Galleries sent a formal, written offer of the terms for the sale of the *Oath of a Freeman*. The price was $1.5 million; all communications about negotiations were to be kept confidential; Schiller-Wapner Galleries would produce a facsimile edition of thirty copies; there would be no warranty for authenticity; and the offer would expire on June 13 at 5:00 p.m. The offer clearly presented numerous problems.

Before any of us involved in the transaction had a chance to meet to discuss Schiller-Wapner Galleries' conditions, I set out to try to determine who owned the *Oath of a Freeman*. I had two pieces of information: the owner bought children's books from Schiller and Wapner, and he probably lived in Utah (based on Schiller's comment during lunch on the day I first saw the *Oath* that it had been soaked off cardboard in a city with hard water like Salt Lake City). These two leads proved adequate for my purpose. A few telephone calls to colleagues in the rare book trade in New York City turned up the fact that Schiller-Wapner Galleries had a very active collector from Utah during the last year by the name of Mark Hofmann. A few more calls to auction houses and rare book firms provided the information from their mailing lists that Hofmann lived in the vicinity of Salt Lake City. My checks of the Library of Congress's collection of telephone books and city directories for Salt Lake City did not show a listing for Mark Hofmann, which meant that his telephone number was unlisted. He appeared to be a secretive individual.

It was necessary to learn something about Mark Hofmann. I decided to call a midwestern bookdealer who I knew had excellent connections in Utah in order to use him to make discreet inquiries about Hofmann's reputation in his own state. Though Hofmann has usually been described as an unassuming individual whom no one suspected of being involved in illegal activities, the information that I received during May of 1985 painted a much different picture. The sources in the West claimed that he was an untrustworthy person with suspicious friends. There was even a hint of some sort of relationship with underworld figures west of Utah. I have never learned the basis for these characterizations. As Sillitoe and Robert's book *Salamander* indicates, Hofmann had a reputation at this time for bouncing checks and not returning telephone calls; and perhaps these practices were beginning to catch up with him. For these reasons, the caution light was on.

On May 22, 1985, John Broderick, Robert Sullivan (director for acquisitions and overseas operations), Robert Lincoln (assistant general counsel), Emma Montgomery (principal acquisitions officer), and I held a confidential meeting to discuss the Schiller-Wapner offer. Lincoln convinced the group that it was necessary that the sellers provide a detailed description of the chain of title in order for the Library of Congress to be certain that it would not face legal problems from disgruntled would-be owners. The consensus of the group was that we should express our significant difficulties with the price, title, and provenance of the *Oath of a Freeman* and in the meantime try to resolve the minor differences we had with the offer. Based on the great amount of reading I had done about authenticating documents during the past few weeks, I argued that we should ask for a one-year warranty in order to allow various experts to examine the broadside. Walter McCrone of Chicago and Thomas Cahill and Richard Schwab of the Crocker Nuclear Laboratory in California were just a few of the large number of experts around the country who, I believed, might be helpful. If during the warranty year the *Oath* were proven to be bogus, then the money would be returned. Though we did not know it at the time, taking this course of action necessarily led to the termination of negotiations. No document that had been recently salted in a New York City bookstore could provide the kind of provenance that would have satisfied us completely.

On May 30, Schiller and Wapner responded to the concerns expressed by the Library of Congress negotiators. They acceded to the one-year warranty for testing. But they offered no information about the chain of title and reiterated their decision to guard the owners' anonymity until after completion of the sale. We were puzzled by the reluctance of Hofmann and his agents to reveal his name. His secrecy and the reports from our sources in the West about his reputation fueled our suspicions. What was he trying to hide? The nebulous origins of the *Oath*, questions about who owned it, unnamed groups of investors, mysterious, secret advisors, the high price, unfavorable information about Hofmann himself, and his reluctance to be publicly identified were all factors that convinced us not to proceed. This was not a situation in which a public institution could become involved.

On June 5, Robert Sullivan wrote to Justin Schiller to advise him that he could pick up the *Oath of a Freeman* at the Library of Congress on June 13. At that time, we would provide him a complete copy of the Preservation

Office's report. Raymond Wapner arrived on the morning of June 14 to take the *Oath* back to New York. We informed him that providing all information about the broadside's ownership and provenance was an essential first step to resuming discussions.

Though Hofmann was able to manufacture a very realistic copy of this historic broadside, he was unable to fabricate a credible history for it. Ironically, it was history itself that thwarted Hofmann's plans to sell the *Oath of a Freeman* to the Library of Congress. When Raymond Wapner left the Preservation Office on the morning of June 14, all formal negotiations between Schiller-Wapner and the Library of Congress ended, never to be resumed.

Found at Last? The 'Oath of a Freeman,' the End of Innocence, and the American Antiquarian Society

Marcus A. McCorison

Some thirty-five or forty years ago, the librarians of the American Antiquarian Society and the John Carter Brown Library were stirred with excitement. A book scout had located a copy of the *Oath of a Freeman* and had offered it for sale! Clarence Brigham and Lawrence Wroth were ecstatic. Was it possible after three hundred years that a copy of the first printed document issued from a press north of Mexico, the first entry in Charles Evans's *American Bibliography*, had actually turned up? No, it was not possible, and it had not. On inspection, the ascenders and descenders were found to impinge upon one another, proving that the text had been printed from an electrotype plate of a paste-up of types from a facsimile of the Bay Psalm Book. (Two solid objects, such as two characters of printing type, cannot be in the same place at the same time.) In the early spring of 1985, when the Americanists' world was electrified again by the news that a copy of the *Oath* had surfaced, the recollection of that event made the staff of the Society cautious, but, as events unfolded, not sufficiently suspicious.

On March 28, 1985, I received a telephone call from Justin Schiller of Schiller-Wapner Galleries, that a customer of the firm (not identified to AAS) had brought to his establishment an impression of the *Oath of a Freeman*, which, against all odds, appeared to be genuine. He and Michael Zinman, a collector of Americana living in Ardsley, New York, had compared it with the copy of the Bay Psalm Book at the New York Public Library. The chain lines of the paper used by the printer of the *Oath* and that of a gathering of the Bay Psalm Book were very similar, but not identical. That same day, Schiller cooperatively sent a photocopy of the *Oath* with a letter describing these events to Worcester, which arrived appropriately enough on April Fool's Day.[1] In the meantime, I had talked with Zinman, who was torn, as we all were, between wanting to believe that the little printed document was genuine and having to maintain a highly critical

---

1. The date should have brought to mind an incident of a few years earlier when I received from the Houghton Library a set of library catalogue cards on which was typed a description of a copy of the *Oath of a Freeman*. I was green with envy at the good fortune of my friends in Cambridge for having captured the veritable Black Swan of American printing, until I had the wit, for some reason, to fish the torn envelope from my waste basket, on which I read the date, April 1.

attitude toward it. In the next few weeks I received any number of telephone calls from Zinman, Schiller, and others. Rumors were rife. During one conversation, I suggested to Schiller that before everyone's expectations were raised too high or before establishing a buyer or price, the actual document should be examined by a number of people who were well versed in the practice of seventeenth-century English and American printing. To this Schiller assented, and I sent a call for a meeting on May 21 at AAS, enclosing a photocopy of the *Oath*, to the following people: Schiller and Zinman, James Gilreath of the Library of Congress, Roger Stoddard and Katherine Pantzer of the Houghton Library, Paul Needham of the Pierpont Morgan Library, Roderick Stinehour, and Keith Arbour of the AAS staff. However, on April 5, Schiller telephoned me to say that the *Oath* had been offered to the Library of Congress and that the proposed meeting was to be canceled, as I then did. Through these and other telephone calls, I learned that the *Oath* had been purchased for $25 at Louis Cohen's Argosy Book Store in New York City where a "coin dealer" from Salt Lake City had found it in a bin of prints and broadsides; that the sheet had been pasted to a piece of cardboard and had been immersed in tap water to separate it from its backing; that it was rumored a partnership in the ownership had been formed; ad infinitum. At some point during all this, although it may well have been later in the summer, Kenneth Nebenzahl, the well-known rare book dealer of Chicago, telephoned me and identified the owner as someone named Hofmann, a person whose name meant nothing to me. Later, I realized that the newspaper accounts that I had earlier read of discoveries of highly significant historical Mormon documents had pertained to him.

The Library of Congress was given an option to buy the *Oath* until the middle of June, and, as you have read in previous chapters, the document was subjected to a variety of very intensive tests under the aegis of the Library. By the end of May, it was clear to Schiller that negotiations with the Library of Congress were breaking down, and he informed us that we would have the next chance at it. On June 6 and 17, I sent Schiller-Wapner Galleries a series of conditions under which AAS would consider the purchase of the *Oath of a Freeman*, namely:

1. that the firm and the owner(s) warrant the authenticity and genuineness of the document, its provenance, and in all other respects;

2. that the document be offered to AAS with the final selling price and other conditions of sale indicated in full;

3. that a terminal date of the offer be established that would allow AAS to thoroughly examine the document and to raise the funds for the purchase, if AAS decided to buy the document;

4. that the name of the owner(s) be divulged to AAS, with full proof of ownership, as well as all known details pertaining to the history of this example of the *Oath*;

5. that the results of the tests made by the Library of Congress be exposed to AAS;

6. that AAS be given permission to subject the document to various tests in locations other than the AAS library, AAS to be held harmless should some accident befall the document while in our keeping;

7. that the owner provide independently developed evidences of authenticity, based on something other than personal opinion.

Raymond Wapner, Schiller's partner, delivered the original *Oath* to AAS on June 27 or 28 in a case made for it at the Library of Congress and further protected in a Mylar envelope. It arrived at a most propitious time, for on June 24 AAS began a ten-day seminar sponsored by our Program in the History of the Book in American Culture, bringing to AAS a number of knowledgeable bibliographers—Roger Stoddard, Michael Winship, Katherine Pantzer, among them. We held a rump session in my office to examine the *Oath.* It did not look right, we thought. It was set as a vertical rectangle rather than as a horizontal one—we had in mind the image of the *Oath* published in 1939 by the Press of the Woolly Whale with Lawrence Wroth's historical essay. Kitzi Pantzer corrected us by pointing out that contemporary English printed oaths looked like this one, and she later sent us copies of examples to prove her point. Was the easy telltale there: the overlapping ascenders and descenders? There were three instances where one might detect possible impingement: between lines 4 and 5, where "j" of "subject" on line 4 and "d" of "doe" on line 5 are very close, but they are not juxtaposed against one another; between lines 9 and 10, where "p" of "person" on line 9 and "ill" of "will" on line 10 are very close, but, again, they are not juxtaposed; and between lines 20 and 21 where "y" of "my" on line 20 and "(" of "(in wh" are extremely close, but not quite juxtaposed against each other. I believed that these examples were not conclusive because the ascenders and descenders are not adjacent to one another and because the lines of type were not precisely straight. The latter condition might be explained by the forme not having been locked up securely by the neophyte printer, Stephen Daye, thus allowing types to shift within the chase.

Did the types and ornaments look right? Well, yes, they appeared to be those of the Bay Psalm Book, although, because the border ornaments had been set sideward, they looked a bit odd, but certainly not impossible. Why did the printed image of the *Oath* look sharper than that of the Bay Psalm Book? Was it because the type page was relatively small and the printer had been able to produce a better impression than when he was hurriedly printing the book? We were nonplussed. At first blush, we could find nothing to indicate definitively that this *Oath of a Freeman* was a fabrication intended to deceive.

Shortly thereafter, AAS was made privy to the extensive reports prepared by the Library of Congress. I did not believe, given the expertise and facilities available to us at AAS, that we could make any useful addition to the information that LC had extracted from the physical document itself during the investigations in Washington. The import of the LC reports was that it had not been possible to find evidence that "would contravene a mid-seventeenth-century date for the broadside." In fact, to my mind the

64

most significant opinion of the LC staff was that "the type in both items [the *Oath* and *The Whole Booke of Psalmes*] came from the same matrices." A further conclusion was drawn from the impressions of the types in the paper in examining many precise photographs taken of them. We concluded that the document had been printed from individual types.

Here was a conundrum indeed! To those of us who are not forensic scientists, the problem lay in the printing types. If the document was fabricated in recent times, how and where could the perpetrator obtain foundry types that matched those of the Bay Psalm Book. There was no satisfactory answer. The Bay Psalm Book types, except for a half-dozen sorts dug up a few years ago at the site of the privy of the president of Harvard College, do not exist. Is it conceivable that a fabricator could or would cut and cast a new font of types that exactly match those of the Bay Psalm Book? Not likely, if not impossible! Ergo, if printed in separate sorts from the same font of type used to print the Bay Psalm Book in 1639 and 1640, how could *not* the *Oath of a Freeman* lying before us have been printed in Cambridge, Massachusetts, in 1638/39? Because forgers of older printed matter usually are unfamiliar with the craft of printing, it did not occur to me that the fabricator would know enough to alter the printing surface of his printing plate, thereby obliterating the clue we looked for: a flat impression from a level line cut. However, as we learned later, the manufacturer of the 1985 *Oath* had applied a file to many letters, thereby giving them casts different from their neighbors and giving the printed document the appearance of having been printed from individual types.

The perpetrator's perspicacious act also produced the riddle that I confronted when I first saw the original of the *Oath of a Freeman*. I was troubled by the appearance of the relatively precise definition of the image of its types. The impression of the type in the Bay Psalm Book often is not clean and sharp; in fact it can be rather sloppy, because the inking of the forme had not been skillfully performed. Had the *Oath* been printed from a line cut of a pasteup of types or words extracted from a facsimile of the Bay Psalm Book, the impression of the *Oath* should have resembled that of its imprecise parental images. We now know why it did not and how our eyes were fooled.

What about paper and ink? I contended that evidence from the paper on which the document was printed must be inconclusive, so long as it was a sheet intended for printing and of a seventeenth-century European origin. Who can say now from what source the Reverend Mr. Josse Glover, or President Dunster, or Stephen Daye obtained paper of whatever make? Obtaining such in 1985 (or 1989) is not difficult because books, large and small, of the period exist in large numbers at bookshops and in libraries everywhere. Recipes for printing inks exist in books and manuals that are readily available, and the ingredients for inks of the period are commonly found and easily combined. Without the instruments for chemical analysis and knowledge of Roderick McNeil or the long experience and techniques of the most skilled of forensic experts, such as George Throckmorton, it was not possible for us to even hazard a guess about the ingredients of the ink or when it had been impressed into the paper. Those questions, we later told Schiller, had to be answered by specialists at the expense of the owner of the document.

A manuscript docket on the verso of the document, "Oathe of Freemen," presented yet another problem. Of course, it did not have to be contemporaneous with the printing of the *Oath*. Thus, the handwriting did not have to match the manner of the mid-seventeenth century, for it could have been written fifty years later. It appeared to have been written in iron gall ink, the kind commonly used in holographs of the time, and it appeared to be in a style consistent with seventeenth- or early eighteenth-century documents, of which AAS has many examples. Here, too, chemical analysis was needed to substantiate appearances.

Unable to satisfy ourselves that the *Oath* physically was not what it purported to be, I asked Keith Arbour of our staff to investigate the historical and textual matters surrounding its use in the 1630s in Massachusetts Bay. We understood that the oath was administered by governmental officials to men who qualified as voters of the colony. I had long assumed that the Oath of a Freeman had been printed so that it could be circulated to officers in the several towns surrounding Boston in order that a correct version of the oath could be administered by them. Arbour's researches showed that I was in error.[2] To qualify as voters, men had to travel to Boston or Cambridge, where the General Court met, to take the oath, after which their names and the date of their admission as freemen were entered in the records of the Company. Thus, there was no need that the oath be printed and circulated.

In fact, as Arbour pointed out, the entire enterprise was fraught with danger. The oath that Gov. John Winthrop devised was seditious, and he gave it a title that was intended to mislead officials in London. Freeman's oaths were administered by each trade guild to their newly admitted members, who then received the privileges of trade accorded by their fellow guild members; and, like most English legal documents, from deeds to patents, each began with an acknowledgment of the Crown's authority. Winthrop took this innocuous title, coupling it to articles of fidelity to the government of the Massachusetts Bay Company. However, the 1634 version of the oath, which remained in force with minor changes until 1665, contains no reference to the king's authority or to his laws.

Arbour went on to explain that the revolutionary nature of the oath has an analogue in the importation of a printing press to Massachusetts in 1638. The Puritans undoubtedly were aware of the royal charter of the Stationers' Company, which prohibited anyone who was not a member of the company from printing anything anywhere in the kingdom without specific leave. Similarly, they must have known of the Star Chamber decree of 1637,

---

2. The information given below is in large part taken from a paper Mr. Arbour prepared for presentation before the Philobiblon Club of Philadelphia in July of 1986.

which imposed severe penalties on printers who broke the various licensing acts and which occasioned the writing of John Milton's *Areopagitica*.

Printers and the press must have been smuggled out of England to New England under the management of the Reverend Mr. Glover, who died en route to the Bay colony. In 1641, one of Glover's shipmates, Stephen Daye, was given 300 acres of land by the Massachusetts General Court for "being the first that set upon printing." It is possible that Daye's sons, Stephen, who died in late 1639, and Matthew, aged about eighteen in 1638, had learned the printer's craft in Cambridge, England, and immigrated to America without revealing their training because craftsmen were strongly discouraged from leaving England. They worked the press after it had been set up in the house of the president of Harvard College, Henry Dunster, who had the wit to marry the wealthy Widow Glover. Matthew died in 1649 and was succeeded at the press by Samuel Green, who later wrote that printing was "the employment I was called unto when there was none in the country to carry it along after the death of him that was brought over for that work by Mr. Jose Glover."

Thus, the Oath of a Freeman was a subversive document issued through means of no little risk to the owners of the press. Why, then, was it chosen as the document to be the first thing printed in English America? I have no satisfactory answer. It was not selected on official or utilitarian grounds. Perhaps it was chosen because of its brevity and lack of typographical complexity. But those associated with the press were fully aware of the symbolic significance of their initial imprint. Governor Winthrop wrote in his journal for March 1639: "A printing house was begun at Cambridge by one Daye, at the charge of Mr. Glover, who died on sea hitherward. The first thing which was printed was the freemen's oath."

During July, Arbour and Barbara Trippel Simmons, also of our staff, went to the archives of the Commonwealth to examine the official manuscript version of the text, comparing it with the printed versions of 1647 and 1648 and the recently found *Oath*, then before us. Arbour and Simmons examined and analyzed the texts of four authoritative versions, viz.: that adopted by the Governor and Company of Massachusetts on May 14, 1634, and recorded on page 114 of volume 1 of the Company's manuscript records; a contemporary copy of the same, entered on page 5 of the same volume; the text of a printed pamphlet demonstrating the disloyal tendencies of Massachusetts inhabitants, *New-Englands Jonas Cast up at London* (London, 1647), p. 9, by Maj. John Child; and the version printed in the Massachusetts *Book of the General Lawes and Libertyes* (Cambridge, 1648), p. 56. Arbour reasoned that, based on variations in wording, punctuation, and scribal alterations, there existed two lines of descent of the text. One passed from the original version of the text, found on page 114 of the Company's records, to the holograph copy in the same volume inserted at page 5, to the version printed in 1648 *Lawes and Libertyes*. The other line passed from the text found on the page 114 of the records to Child's *New-Englands Jonas*. He believed that the text of the oath under examination could not have been printed before 1634, when its text was approved, nor after 1648 when the text of the oath was altered. He reasoned further that the text of the oath on the printed broadside, if actually issued in March 1638/39, was intermediate between the text on page 114 of the Company records and that of *New-Englands Jonas*. Later, he was to conclude that the use of the contraction "stablish" (in a prose context rather than metrical), instead of "establish" indicated that the fabricator of the broadside oath had erroneously repeated that usage, thereby condemning the broadside as a fraud.[3] Our acceptance of this particular point has since been disputed by another textual scholar.

On August 6, Prof. Robert Mathiesen of Brown University came to AAS. He and Arbour spent some time carefully examining the original, printed document. They puzzled over the question, for example, whether the dirt on the page lay under or over the inked image. Mathiesen's report to us of his conclusions is printed later in this volume. Then, on August 13, Arbour went to the Library of Congress to review the LC reports with Peter Watters and Karen Garlick of the LC conservation laboratories.

At the end of all this, we were no better off than when we had started. Our examinations as well as those of the Library of Congress, both of which were conducted at the expense of the two libraries, did not definitively confirm or refute the authenticity of the printed document offered by Schiller and Wapner as being the only known copy of Evans 1, the *Oath of a Freeman*, printed on the first press in northern North America in March of 1638/39. We were willing to accept it as being of a seventeenth-century American origin, and would further consider its purchase, provided that

1. the sellers, without expense to AAS, subject the document to the most rigorous scientific examinations available, including tests in the cyclotron at Davis, California, to analyze the text, inks, and techniques used to produce the *Oath of a Freeman*, finding no anomalies therefrom;

2. they commission a thorough canvas of papers used in seventeenth-century Cambridge imprints to determine if an exact match exists between the paper used to print the *Oath* and other Cambrige imprints, finding no anomalies therefrom;

3. they identify the owner, completely revealing his background, as well as a full provenance for the document that is satisfactory to AAS;

4. they convene a meeting, such as I had recommended earlier, to assess the evidence compiled by all parties and ascertain the correctness of the attribution of this copy of the *Oath* to a seventeenth-century Cambridge, Massachusetts, press.

Schiller and Wapner agreed to the above, but put the question to us: If their tests were to provide satisfactory answers to AAS, would AAS purchase the document at the asking price of $1,500,000. The answer to that

---

3. See Mr. Arbour's letter to Detective Kenneth Farnsworth, dated April 3, 1986, and the letter from this writer to Nicolas Barker, dated December 23, 1986, both reproduced in Appendix E of this volume.

was, No! I do not believe that the *Oath of a Freeman* can be realistically valued at a million and a half dollars. The Bay Psalm Book, as a principal monument in American intellectual and cultural history, if offered for sale now, surely would be valued at about that level or more. I do not think that this "souvenir," if that is what it is, merits or commands the regard of the Bay Psalm Book, nor a price in the same range as that of its vastly more important sibling. We offered $250,000, expecting that if the *Oath* was finally proved to be "real," we might be able to negotiate a price of about a half to three-quarters of a million dollars. This was unacceptable to Schiller and Wapner. They asked for the return of their copy of the *Oath of a Freeman*. So, Georgia Barnhill of our staff gingerly took it to New York City on September 11, obtained a receipt for its safe delivery, and we concluded negotiations.

The bombs went off in Salt Lake City early in the morning of October 15, 1985. The terrible light from those explosions ultimately exposed the darkest corners of an edifice built of greed and wishful thinking. This episode and the more recent discovery of forged and fabricated Southwestern documents surely have signaled the end of our innocence. No doubt, rare book and manuscript dealers who have been plagued with sharpers and their thefts and frauds, are more cynical about such matters. However, in thirty-five years of buying and looking at rare materials, until recently I have not been exposed to so much deceit in our community, one that is dedicated to the advancement of knowledge through the veracity of historical evidence.

I, like others who are part of the community of collectors and curators of Americana, became part of the enthusiasm (perhaps even near-hysteria) that surrounded the "discovery" of the *Oath of a Freeman*. Thus, all of us involved must bear a portion of the responsibility for this dreadful event. And, who wants the following as an epitaph?

Lawyer's question: Hypothetically, if the American Antiquarian Society had been able to, and did vote to purchase your "Oath" on October 15, 1985, for about a million dollars, what would that have done to the financial hole that you had dug yourself into by that time?

Hofmann's answer: It would have relieved me from it. Hence, . . . the bombings would not have taken place.[4]

The veteran Boston bookseller, George T. Goodspeed, who never laid eyes on the purported *Oath of a Freeman*, and who always has the last word, was right then, when, from the very beginning, he declared it a fraud, saying, "Provenance, Provenance, Provenance!"

4. I must reiterate that AAS returned the *Oath* to Schiller on September 11, and report that a vote on the purchase of the document was not on the agenda of the AAS Council when it met on the afternoon, E.D.T., of that fateful October 15.

Preliminary Report on the 'Oath of a Freeman'

Robert Mathiesen

Preliminary Report on the <u>Oath of a Freeman</u>

Having examined the copy of the <u>Oath of a Freeman</u> for several hours on 5 August 1985, I have noticed the following points which bear further investigation.

1. Although there is no watermark on the paper on which the <u>Oath</u> is printed, the pattern and spacing of chain lines is sufficiently distinctive so that one might hope to match it with paper used in some other product of the first Cambridge press. I have not yet been able to find any such match.

The paper of the <u>Oath</u> does **not** appear in any of the following:

Bay Psalm Book, 1640 (Evans 4, AAS and JCBL copies),

Bay Psalm Book, 1647 (Evans 20, JCBL copy),

Cambridge Platform, 1649 (Evans 25, AAS and JCBL copies),

Bay Psalm Book, [1658? 1669?] (Evans 49, Brown Univ. copy),

Norton's Heart of New-England, 1659 (Evans 56, JCBL copy),

Eliot's Indian New Testament, 1661 (Evans 64, both JCBL copies),

Propositions Concerning Baptism, 1662 (Evans 68, JCBL copy),

Eliot's Indian Old Testament, 1663 (Evans 73, JCBL copy),

Davenport's Discourse, 1663 (Evans 79, JCBL copy),

Higginson's Cause of God, 1663 (Evans 80, JCBL copy),

Shepard's Church-Membership, 1663 (Evans 82, JCBL copy).

In the above list, Evans 20 and Evans 49 may have been printed in England.

The JCBL copy of Winthrop's Declaration [1645?] (Evans 17) could not be found, probably because of misshelving.

I have not yet found the time to examine the Brown University copy of Eliot's Indian Bible (Evans 64 and 73).

It is probably safe to assert that the <u>Oath</u> is not printed on paper belonging to the supply which Mr. Glover imported to New England in 1638 for the use of the first Cambridge press.

If anything, the paper of the <u>Oath</u> more resembles (in the spacing of its chain lines and in its coloring) that found in the Cambridge imprints from the early 1660's, although there is no exact match here either. These Cambridge imprints are on paper imported in 1660 and subsequent years.

If the <u>Oath</u> is authentic, it most likely was printed on paper from some other supply, for example, a hypothetical supply available to the General Court for its own business. In this case, one might expect to find an exact match among the early manuscript records of Massachusetts Bay Colony.

2. The printer's ink in the <u>Oath</u> appears (under an inexpensive 30x monocular microscope) to be less viscous and less dark than the ink used to print the Bay

Psalm Book of 1640, and the inking appears to have been better done. It is difficult to be certain here, for the Oath may have been cleaned at some time with some soft abrasive such as Trace Clean, with the observable result that much of the ink is now missing from the individual letters of the Oath.

3. The type of the Oath, while apparently cast from the same matrices as the Bay Psalm Book type, displays a larger twenty-line measure. Twenty lines of type in the Oath measure 95 mm, whereas twenty lines in the AAS copy of the Bay Psalm Book measure 92 mm. This difference is probably within the limits of variation due to different rates of paper shrinkage.

4. The docketing inscription ("Oathe of freemen") appears to have been written while the document was unfolded, for there is no trace of ink on the other half of the sheet, despite the presence of a small hole under the inscription. (Yet the hole may be later than the inscription.) Moreover, the fold itself does not fall exactly in the middle of the Oath (in its present dimensions), but seems to fall along one of the chain lines. Each of these points is more compatible with the Oath's being a forgery than with its authenticity, although neither is conclusive.

5. There seems to be some small amount of dirt in the fold, and this dirt may lie under the printer's ink, rather than over it (as expected if the Oath is authentic). It is impossible to tell for certain with the 30x monocular microscope whether the ink truly lies over or under the dirt in the fold. If the ink is above the dirt, then the Oath was printed after the paper had been folded, and is almost certainly a forgery. If the ink is beneath the dirt, no conclusion can be drawn from that fact as to the Oath's authenticity.

* * *

It may be instructive to consider how such a document as the Oath might be forged. A forger would need seventeenth-century paper, printer's ink, writing ink, and the means to replicate the type and ornaments of the 1640 Bay Psalm Book, as well as considerable knowledge about the printing of the period, and a plausible text of the document to be forged.

A blank piece of seventeenth-century paper could be purchased in the form of a blank leaf in a seventeenth-century imprint, or perhaps even stolen from a loosely secured library or archive (yet why multiply risk by an unnecessary theft?). A forger would surely try to procure a leaf without a watermark (like the leaf on which the Oath has been printed). This paper probably would not match the paper of the Bay Psalm book. Again, a forger might not know just how precisely paper stocks can be matched even in the absence of a watermark, or he might reason that a failure to find an exact match would not constitute proof of forgery. If the Oath is a forgery, the forger knew enough to get the chain lines right (i.e. horizontal). This might be done by cutting down a pair of conjugate leaves from a volume in folio, but only at the cost of a fold in the middle of the resulting piece of paper (see point 5 above).

There are a few extant seventeenth-century recipes for printer's ink; it is not known whether any of them match the ink of the 1640 Bay Psalm Book. A forger might not know that one could detect such minor discrepancies, or he might reason that they would not constitute proof of forgery, even if detected.

Various photographic processes exist by which one might manufacture a replica of the Bay Psalm Book type font (spaces and all) and its ornaments. One might also construct a paste-and-scissors replica of the entire Oath, and then make a plate from which that replica could be printed. To do so, however, one would need very precisely taken photographs from one of the eleven extant copies of the 1640 Bay Psalm Book. It may not be possible any longer to ascertain whether such photographs were ever made, since one of the eleven copies (the Library of Congress copy) was in private hands until 1961, and not all libraries keep equally detailed records of photocopies.

A plausible text (such as the one in the document under examination) could be constructed with little effort, in view of the four attested earlier and later versions of the Oath. The present text of the Oath seems to me to be compatible with either hypothesis, that the Oath is a forgery or that it is authentic.

* * *

I am as yet unable to reach any firm conclusion about the Oath's authenticity. I recommend further examination along the following lines:

1. The Oath should be examined under a binocular microscope of high power, to settle whether the dirt in the fold is above or below the printer's ink of the letters which cross the fold. This **may** settle the matter, as noted above (point 5). We have the facilities for this examination at Brown, and they are at your service.

2. One might have the printer's ink of the Oath and the printer's ink of the 1640 Bay Psalm Book chemically analyzed at the Crocker Nuclear Laboratory, Davis, California.

> See R.N. Schwab, T.A. Cahill, B.H. Kusko & D.L. Wick, "Cyclotron Analysis of the Ink in the 42-Line Bible," *Papers of the Bibliographical Society of America* 77(1983), 285-315. This analysis is "rapid, non-destructive and inexpensive." I have visited this facility, and have every confidence in the method as well as in the personnel.

If there are great discrepancies in the composition of the ink, the authenticity of the Oath becomes less certain. If these discrepancies are such that the ink of the Oath may have been compounded according to one of the extant early recipes, while the ink of the Bay Psalm Book does not follow any extant recipe, then the suspicion of forgery becomes even stronger. However, this would not be conclusive by itself.

3. One might make a detailed typographic comparison of the Oath and the 1640 Bay Psalm Book using the composite imaging process developed by Paul Sternberg and John Brayer at the University of New Mexico, in hopes of detecting traces that the Oath derives from a paste-and-scissors composite prepared from photographs of the 1640 Bay Psalm Book. In particular, one might compare the less common words (such as "stablished") in the Oath with every occurrence of the same words in the Bay Psalm Book.

> See P.R. Sternberg & J.M. Brayer, "Composite Imaging: A New Technique in Bibliographic Research," *Papers of the Bibliographical Society of America* 77(1983), 431-445.

This method **might** yield conclusive evidence of forgery; it could hardly yield conclusive evidence of authenticity.

4. One might search all the extant early manuscript records of the Massachusetts Bay Colony (and the other extant pre-1660 imprints from the first Cambridge press, to be on the safe side) for a precise match to the paper on which the Oath has been printed; and if such a match is found, test it by chemical analysis at Crocker Nuclear Laboratory. If an exact match could be found, it would strongly favor authenticity. Yet even this would **not** be conclusive proof of authenticity, for a single blank sheet of such paper might conceivably have been obtained by purchase or theft.

* * *

At this juncture the balance of evidence may tip **very slightly** towards the Oath's being a forgery. I would have expected an authentic Oath to have been printed on paper from the supply imported in 1638, and this does not seem to be the case. I would also have expected the dirt in the fold to lie above the printer's ink, and this may not be the case, either. Each of these points should be settled conclusively, however, before one passes judgement on the Oath.

If further examination bears these two points out, the burden of proof will then fall on those who want to posit authenticity.

If the Oath is a forgery, it is a brilliant one, a product of real scholarship created at considerable expense. This fact, of course, is not evidence that the Oath is authentic. A forger could expect to recover his or her expenses, if the forgery remained undetected; and forgers are not necessarily motivated by considerations of profit alone.

Robert Mathiesen

Robert Mathiesen
Department of Slavic Languages &
   Committee on Medieval Studies
Brown University

Compositional Comparison of the Mark Hofmann 'Oath of a Freeman' and the 'Whole Booke of Psalmes'

T. A. Cahill, B. H. Kusko, R. A. Eldred, and R. H. Schwab

Mark Hofmann's *Oath of a Freeman* and the *Whole Booke of Psalmes* were analyzed by the external proton milliprobe at the Crocker Nuclear Laboratory, University of California, Davis, for the elemental constituents of their paper and ink. These analyses were supported by Mr. Justin Schiller of Schiller-Wapner Galleries in New York, with the collaboration of Ellen Dunlap, director of the Rosenbach Library, Philadelphia, who supplied an original copy of the *Whole Booke of Psalmes*. The purpose of these analyses was to compare the documents in order to extract compositional data with which to judge the authenticity of the *Oath*. In this article, we will give a little background on the analyses, reproduce the original report in its entirety, and then comment on the results with the benefit of knowledge of subsequent events.

Proton Milliprobe Technique

The proton milliprobe technique at Davis is a refinement of the technique called Proton Induced X-ray Emission (PIXE), designed to generate quantitative composition data on fragile objects without any harm. The 4.5 MeV proton beam for the Crocker Cyclotron passes through the paper and ink, generating characteristic X-rays that reveal the mass and type of all elements with an atomic weight equal to or greater than that of silicon (figure 1). Sensitivities are generally about one part per million, while accuracy and precision are about ±5 absolute. Each analysis covers an area of between 0.5 mm^2 and 3 mm^2, depending on the task.

A few points must be noted. Since the data reveal only elemental composition, chemical states are not revealed. Thus, the iron in Fe_2O_3 (ferric oxide) cannot be told from the iron in FeO_2 (ferrous oxide). Secondly, the ink must be analyzed with the substrate, as shown in figure 1. Thus, to obtain the composition of the ink, one must subtract the result of the "substrate only" from that of "substrate plus ink." (In this instance, "substrate" means the unprinted paper of the broadside.) For some elements, this procedure is easy; but even in the best cases, a severe loss of sensitivity ensues. In the worst case, in which there is a large amount of a given element in the substrate, the "ink-alone" values are very insensitive. Finally, all results are

75

merely comparisons. No dates can be assigned when examining any single document. We can only say that any questioned book, manuscript, or broadside is either similar or dissimilar to another item of the same kind that has a known date of production. Thus, for those periods from which many documents are available for comparison, such as pre-1500 printed books, a high degree of confidence can be attained. For others, such as the first years of the Stephen Daye Press in Cambridge, Massachusetts, few documents survive to be used for comparison's sake. This problem is compounded by the diverse sources of Stephen Daye's paper, originally from England in multiple batches, which make paper comparisons quite complicated.

Knowing this background about the methodology is necessary to understand how the CHAPS team at Davis tested both documents during the afternoon and early evening of April 17, 1986. The preliminary report of those analyses follows.

April 28, 1986

Preliminary Report on the Comparison

of the Oath of a Freeman

and the

Bay Psalm Book

by

B. Kusko, T. Cahill, R. Schwab and R. Eldred
The Crocker Historical and Archaeological Project
Crocker Nuclear Laboratory, University of California, Davis, CA 95616

On April 17, 1986, two documents, the Oath of a Freeman,
from J. Schiller of the Schiller-Wapner Galleries, NY and the Whole
Book of Psalms, F. Dunlap, Rosenbach Library, Philadelphia, were
analyzed by PIXE on the external proton milliprobe of the CHAPS group,
Crocker Nuclear Laboratory.

For a description of the procedures and quality assurance
protocols, see Appendix 3. For this run, several standards were used:
1) lead foil, copper sulfite foil (both from Micromatter, Inc., WA);
2) NBS thin film standard 1607, and the 1180 AD Manuscript (TAC)
previously analyzed on almost every CHAPS run since 1978. Agreement

was excellent, and no normalization correction had to be applied (RE NORM - 1.000). The beam spot was set to 1.5 x 1.5 mm, giving a 1.5 x 2.1 mm spot on the documents.

Twenty analyses were made on the Oath of a Freeman (see Appendix Figure 1). Since the paper, ink, and verso manuscript inscription were very similar at all points, we proceeded to analyze the Bay Psalm Book.

Twenty-two analyses were made of the Whole Book of Psalms. These included a paper and paper-plus-ink analysis for the five major paper types, the facsimile pages, the two end papers, and front and back covers of the book.

An early analysis of the paper and ink is shown in Appendix Table 1. All data have been corrected for X-ray attenuation by the code IPAPA (REA), and results are given in absolute units (ng/cm^2). The data are presented for the major paper types, for comparison with the Oath of a Freeman. As can be seen, the Oath, while appearing to contain old (pre-1830) paper similar to other analyzed at Davis, differs sharply from every type of paper in the Bay Psalm Book.

The lack of sulfur, chlorine, potassium, and mercury in the Oath paper are significant, as is the presence of lead. The Bay Psalm Book paper contains large amounts of sulfur, chlorine, and potassium, and does not contain lead but has mercury. The elements silicon, calcium, magnesium, iron, copper, and zinc are found in varying but comparable amounts in the two documents.

The printing inks of both documents were similar in having only trace amounts of any element above silicon on the periodic table, and therefore mostly carbon-based. Both inks showed significant amounts of lead (100-200 ng/cm^2) and traces of iron.

The manuscript ink on the verso of the Oath of a Freeman contained large amounts of iron, as well as phosphorus, potassium and chlorine. This is typical of iron-gall ink, a common manuscript ink used since the 1100's.

Summary

The dramatic differences in the papers of the Oath of a
Freeman and Bay Psalm Book clearly indicate a different paper type.
The very low values of sulfur, chlorine, and potassium are unusual but
not unique in our studies of pre-1830 papers. Some examples of other
papers are given in the appendices, but none is particularly relevant
to the present papers.

We do not mean to imply that the Oath is either a forgery or
authentic, just that different paper was used. The printer may in
fact have used different paper when printing this broadside as opposed
to the book, and we have only a very limited number of documents to
compare.

The ink used in both documents appears to be carbon-based,
containing small amounts of lead. The ink used in the Oath may also
have titanium. They are neither unusual nor statistically different

from each other, and it is possible they are from the same source.
Again, we have very few inks of the period for comparison, and carbon-
based inks with trace impurities are found routinely in many
documents.

1. 1981 Cahill, T.A., B. Kusko and R.N. Schwab. Analyses of inks and papers in historical documents through external beam PIXE techniques, Nuclear Instruments and Methods 181 205-208.

2. 1981 Schwab, R.N., T.A. Cahill, B.H. Kusko. "The Cyclotron and Descriptive Bibliography: A Progress Report on the Crocker Historical and Archaeological Project at Davis" The Quarterly Newsletter, The Book Club of California, 42 3-12.

3. 1981 Cahill, T.A., C.G. Higgins and S. Howard. Accelerator-based methods for fingerprinting marble: A preliminary report. The 83rd General Meeting of The Archaeological Institute of America.

4. 1983 Eldred, R.A. External beam PIXE programs at the University of California, Davis. IEEE Transaction on Nuclear Science, NS-30:1276-1279, Seventh Conference on the Application of Accelerators in Research & Industry, North Texas University, (invited paper).

5. 1983 Schwab, R.N., T.A. Cahill, B.H. Kusko, and D.L. Wick. Cyclotron analysis of the ink in the 42-line bible. The Papers of the Bibliographical Society of America. 77:3 285-315.

6. 1984 Cahill, T.A., B.H. Kusko, R.A. Eldred and R.N. Schwab, Gutenberg's inks and papers: non-destructive compositional analyses by proton milliprobe. Archaeometry, 26:1 3-14.

7. 1984 Eldred, R.A., B.H. Kusko and T.A. Cahill. The external PIXE milliprobe at Davis: Laser alignment, PIXE calibration, and quality assurance, Nuclear Instruments and Methods, B3, 579-583.

8. 1984 Kusko, B.H., T.A. Cahill, R.A. Eldred and R.N. Schwab. Proton milliprobe analyses of the Gutenberg Bible. Nuclear Instruments and Methods, B3, 689-694.

9. 1984 Howard S., T.A. Cahill, N. Herz, C. Higgins, E. Kinmoth and B.H. Kusko, Computer-assisted accelerator-based methods of determining the provenance of ancient marbles, presented at the second Conference on Automatic Processing of Art History Data, Pisa, Italy.

10. 1984 Bliss, A.S. Cyclotron analysis and a fake gospel lectionary of 1328. Scriptorium, International Review of Manuscript Studies XXXVIII, 2.

11. 1985 Schwab, R.N., T.A. Cahill, R.A. Eldred, B.H. Kusko and D.L. Wick, New evidence on the printing of the Gutenberg Bible, Papers of the Bibliographical Society of America, 79:3, 375-410.

12. 1985 Almquist, H.J., Color of the Ledger Lines of the Large Numerals issue of Mexico, 1887. The American Philatelist, vol 99, pp.241-2.

13. 1985 Kusko, B.H, Proton milliprobe analysis of the hand-penned annotations in Bach's Calov Bible, in The Calov Bible of J.S. Bach, Howard H. Cox, ed. Studies in Musicology, No. 92, UMI Research Press, Ann Arbor, p 31-106.

14. 1986 Schwab, R.N., T.A. Cahill, B.H. Kusko, R.A. Eldred, D.L. Wick, Ink patterns in the Gutenberg New Testament: The proton milliprobe analyses of the Lilly Library copy, Papers of the Bibliographical Society of America, 80:3, 305-331.

15. 1986 Cahill, T.A., D.W. McColm, B.H. Kusko, Control of temperature in thin samples during ion beam analysis, Nucl. Instrum. and Methods, B14. 38-44.

16. 1987 Cahill, T.A., R.N. Schwab, B.H. Kusko, R.A. Eldred, G. Möller, D. Dutschke, D.L. Wick and A.S. Pooley. The Vinland Map, revisited: new compositional evidence on its inks and parchment. Analytical Chemistry, 59, 829-833.

17. 1987 Kusko, B.H., and R.N. Schwab, Historical analyses by PIXE. 4th Int. PIXE Conf., Tallahassee FL, 9-13 June 1986. Nucl. Instrum Methods B22, 401-406.

18. 1987 Cahill, T.A., The Nuclear Bibliophile: Cyclotron studies of rare documents. Transactions of the XIVth Congress of the International Association of Bibliophiles, ed. Stephen Tabor Los Angeles, 1987, 37-50.

19. 1987 Schwab,R.N., The history of the book and the proton milliprobe: an application of the PIXE technique of analysis. Library Trends, Summer 1987, 53-84.

20. 1988 Kusko, B.H., Cyclotron analysis of paper and ink reveals secrets of the written and printed word. Presented at a special seccion of the 1987 convention of the Modern Language Association of America, December 28, 1987. To be published in Literary Research.

21. 1988 Cahill, T.A., Gutenberg and the Cyclotron. Accepted for publication, The Library Associates, UCD.

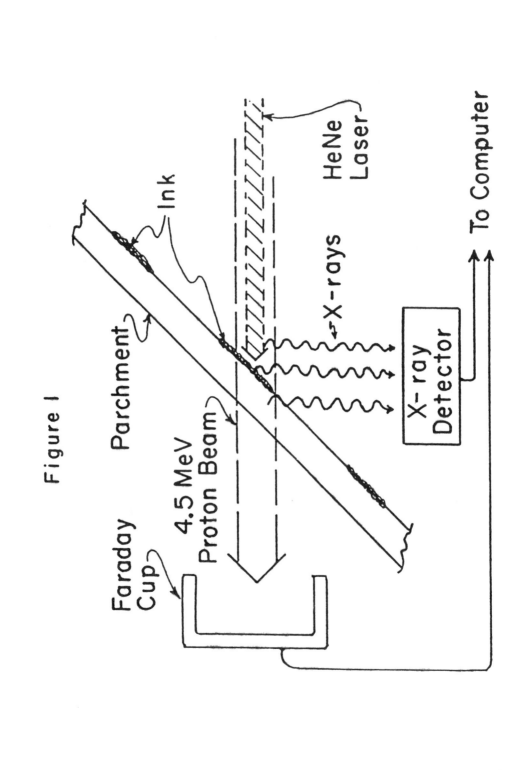

Figure I

Appendices

1. Original record of analyses for the Oath of a Freeman and Bay Psalm Book

2. Results of Elemental analyses for both documents

3. Description of the Davis PIXE milliprobe from "the Calov Bible of J.S. Bach." [This appendix, included in the original report, is not included here. See Howard Cox's The Calov Bible of J.S. Bach (Ann Arbor, Michigan, University of Michigan Research Press, 1985)].

4. Examples of various papers--

    a) 18th through 19th century
    b) Incunabula period, 15th century
    c) the Calov Bible of J.S. Bach, German 17th century (this appendix is not included in this reproduction of the report).

Appendix 1

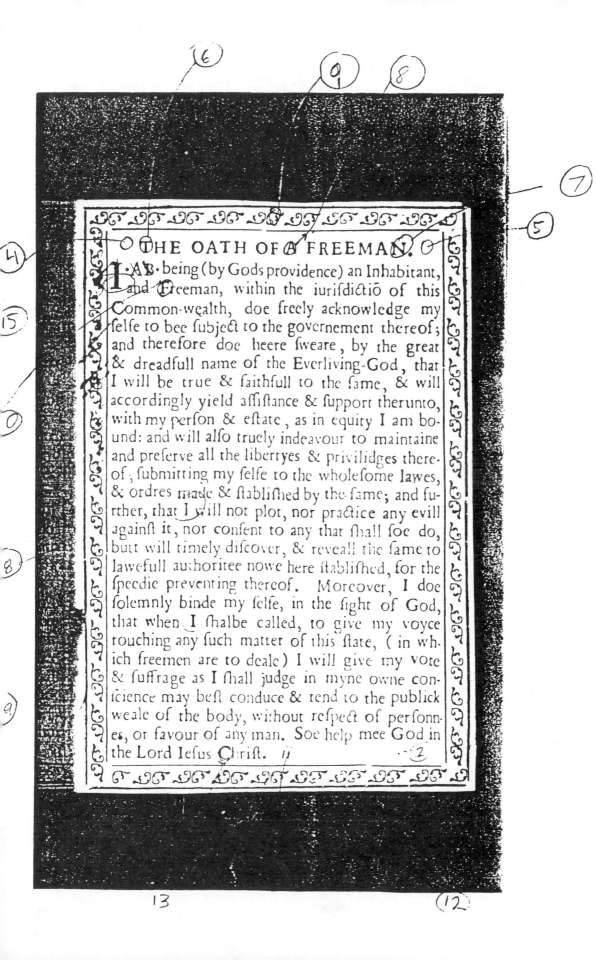

THE OATH OF A FREEMAN.

I. A.B. being (by Gods providence) an Inhabitant, and Freeman, within the iurisdictiō of this Common-wealth, doe freely acknowledge my selfe to bee subject to the governement thereof; and therefore doe heere sweare, by the great & dreadfull name of the Everliving-God, that I will be true & faithfull to the same, & will accordingly yield assistance & support therunto, with my person & estate, as in equity I am bound: and will also truely indeavour to maintaine and preserve all the libertyes & privilidges thereof; submitting my selfe to the wholesome lawes, & ordres made & stablished by the same; and further, that I will not plot, nor practice any evill against it, nor consent to any that shall soe do, butt will timely discover, & reveall the same to lawefull authoritee nowe here stablished, for the speedie preventing thereof. Moreover, I doe solemnly binde my selfe, in the sight of God, that when I shalbe called, to give my voyce touching any such matter of this state, (in which freemen are to deale) I will give my vote & suffrage as I shall judge in myne owne conscience may best conduce & tend to the publick weale of the body, without respect of personnes, or favour of any man. Soe help mee God in the Lord Iesus Christ.

CHAPS ANALYSIS   FILE *84171*   (CAVE) COMPUTER

Description Oath of a Freeman   1

Substrate: paper, vellum, or _____ Helium: Yes   No

Comments:

RUN DATE ___/___/___ OPERATORS _____ BEGIN TIME _____ END TIME _____

RUN#	POSITION	DESCRIPTION	
9	1	paper verso	
10	2	paper verso	
11	3	paper verso	
12	4	paper recto opposite 1	
13	5	paper recto opposite 2	
14	6	ink	
15	7	ink	
16	8	ink	
17	9	ink (fleuron)	
18	10	ink "F"	
19	11	paper recto	
20	12	paper recto (pinhole #1 - see LC Appendix A, p.3)	
21	13	ink	
22	14	adhesive verso	
23	15	ink I	
24	16	recto interfold up w/ fleuron?	
25	17	inscription	
26	18	ink I	
27	19	ink I	
28	20	paper verso, in pinhole #1	
29	21	Paper Fac D-1	Bay Psalms
30	22	Ink at bottom of page D-1	
31	23	—	no charge
—	24		
32	25	Ink recto p D2	paper D2
33	26	Paper FF1 - FF4 verso	Ink recto p D2
34	27	ink	paper FF1-FF4 V
	28		
	29		
	30		
	31		
	32		
	33		
	34		
	35		
	36		
	37		
	38		
	39		
	40		

Appendix 2

Table 1

COMPARARTIVE ELEMENTAL COMPOSITIONS OF PAPER AND INK

(ng/cm2 ; corrected for absorbtion by IPAPA)

	PAPER		INK		
	Oath of a Freeman (Mean ± σ)	Bay Psalm Book (Max/Min)	Oath of a Freeman (print)	(writing)	Bay Psalm Book (print)
Silicon (Si)	14,300 ± 4,500	29,700/ < 4,500	–	–	–
Phosphorus (P)	< 1,500	< 1,700 *	–	4,900	–
Sulfur (S)	<400	48,500/ 19,000	–	–	–
Chlorine (Cl)	<500	22,500/ 2,080	–	830	–
Potassium (K)	<200	7,490/ 3,520	–	2,815	–
Calcium (Ca)	13,190 ± 2,640	13,600/ 8,710	–	–	–
Titanium (Ti)	< 75	NA	~ 140	190	–
Manganese (Mn)	235 ± 109	2,280/ 236	~ 60	–	–
Iron (Fe)	1,225 ± 310	3,720/ 1,290	~ 400	19,600	~ 300
Copper (Cu)	27 ± 12	102/ 18	–	–	~ 16
Zinc (Zn)	199 ± 45	261/ 83	–	–	–
Mercury (Hg)	< 25	3,130/ 298	–	–	–
Lead (Pb)	268 ± 291 (365 ± 140) *	155/ < 25	~ 270	–	500

* 1 analysis deleted   ** 5 out of 7 analyses when lead was found
Values marked with a ~have a standard deviation as large as the values given.

Appendix 4

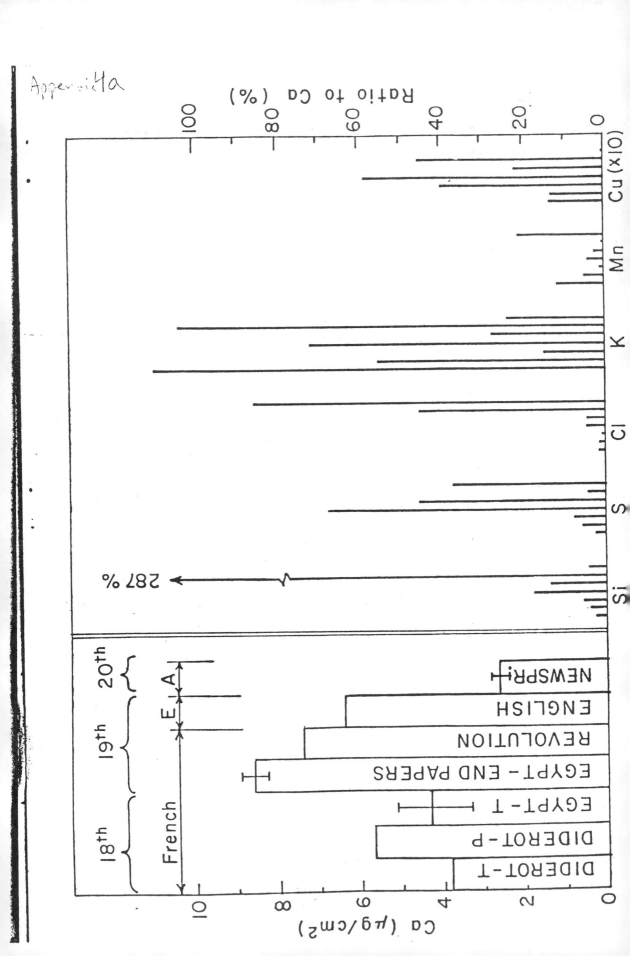

Appendix 4a

~~Table 3~~

Example of Results on a Guntenberg Bible Leaf

Description: Gutenberg Leaf, "Ezekiel", from U.C. Santa Barbara; Vol. I, pg. 134

Comments: No visible alterations in visible light (transmitted or reflected) or ultra violet light (long or short wave).

Analytical Results: Date 7/17/81; Tray 80703

Mass: 10.7 mg/m^2 Ca = 0.75 $\pm$ 0.3

(Ratio to Ca - %)

Element	Paper (8)	Inks (3)	Rubric (1) Red	Rubric Blue	Other Markings
Na	–	-	-	None	None
Mg	–9	-	-		
Al	–6	-	-		
Si	65+8	-	-		
P	16+3	-	-		
S	9+1	-	-		
Cl	Variable a)	-	-	a) Upper left to lower right diagonal;	
K	Variable a)	-	-	UL= High Cl 45+11	
Ca	(=100)	(=100)	(=100)	K 29+1	
Ti	1.4+0.1	-	-	LR = Low Cl 11+4	
V	–0.2	-	-	K 16+3	
Cr	–0.2	-	-		
Mn	1.2+0.1	-	-		
Fe	5.6+.5	-	-	b) Inks (black)	
Co	–0.07	-	-	1. Mass of Pb 0.17%+0.05%	
Cu	0.14+0.04	17.1+2.0	1.0	to paper	
Zn	0.17+0.04	-	-	2. Ratios to Pb (%)	
Ga	–0.06	-	-	Cu 88+3	
Ge	–0.06	-	-	Pb =100	
As	–0.01	-	-		
Se	–0.01	-	-		
Rb	–0.02	-	-	c) Rubrics (red)	
Sr	–0.2	-	4.3	1. Mass of Hg, 2% to paper	
Zr	–0.2	-	-	186% to Ca	
Mo	–0.4	-	-		
Ba	–0.4	-	-	2. Ratios to Hg	
Au	–0.7	18.8+1.5	-	Cu 0.52%	
Hg	–0.7	-	186.0	Sr 2.3%	
Pb	–0.7	-	.44	Pb 0.26%	

Upper limits for elements not observed (i.e. less thans) are given by minus values (Rb, -0.2, was not observed but was surely less than 0.2).

Appendix 4C

The Calov Bible

Table 4a. PIXE Results: Paper, Title Pages (File 10)
(Amounts in nanograms per square centimeter)

ID	Run No.	S	Cl	K	Ca	Mn	Fe
1	1	5770 ± 665	4630 ± 490	3540 ± 360	2590 ± 265	14*	222 ± 25.0
2	7	4800 ± 605	3210 ± 360	2940 ± 305	2290 ± 235	25.5 ± 12.2	197 ± 23.5
3	107	13000 ± 1400	1590 ± 215	3980 ± 405	2170 ± 225	17.2 ± 10.3	301 ± 33.5
4	133	13400 ± 1450	4200 ± 465	3790 ± 390	2790 ± 285	14*	169 ± 21.5

ID	Run No.	Cu	Zn	As	Sr	Hg	Pb
1	1	19.9 ± 4.3	11.0 ± 3.3	18*	30*	52*	57*
2	7	14.6 ± 4.0	10*	18*	30*	52*	134 ± 38.8
3	107	10.6 ± 3.3	10*	18*	30*	52*	57*
4	133	30.9 ± 6.5	10*	18*	30*	52*	57*

*Denotes minimum detectable limit; element not found.

Table 4b. PIXE Results: Paper, Other Pages (File 11)
(Amounts in nanograms per square centimeter)

ID	Run No.	S	Cl	K	Ca	Mn	Fe
1	15	6390 ± 755	406 ± 128	1760 ± 185	3240 ± 330	15.7 ± 12.1	212 ± 25.3
2	18	6000 ± 810	270 ± 118	1300 ± 145	2890 ± 295	14*	227 ± 26.5
3	21	3390 ± 940	977 ± 163	1460 ± 160	3145 ± 320	22.3 ± 13.3	164 ± 21.7
4	24	6320 ± 720	183 ± 110	1190 ± 130	2860 ± 290	12.6 ± 12.2	153 ± 19.3
5	26	6210 ± 725	986 ± 160	921 ± 105	3520 ± 360	18.4 ± 9.6	148 ± 18.7
6	28	7600 ± 855	662 ± 141	915 ± 105	4560 ± 460	30.6 ± 10.9	224 ± 26.3
7	111	8600 ± 1040	627 ± 145	732 ± 88	4740 ± 480	14.1 ± 12.5	203 ± 24.3
8	114	8170 ± 965	250*	1980 ± 210	1910 ± 195	14*	215 ± 25.2
9	117	6400 ± 795	438 ± 133	1320 ± 145	3200 ± 325	26.2 ± 11.7	232 ± 27.9
10	139	8770 ± 1010	1225 ± 193	1370 ± 150	4900 ± 495	14*	126 ± 17.5
11	142	7390 ± 380	530 ± 143	1650 ± 175	3370 ± 345	14*	136 ± 18.6
12	145	7720 ± 905	591 ± 142	1020 ± 115	4510 ± 460	14*	124 ± 17.2

ID	Run No.	Cu	Zn	As	Sr	Hg	Pb
1	15	13.2 ± 3.9	10*	18*	30*	52*	57*
2	18	10*	10*	18*	30*	52*	57*
3	21	10*	10*	18*	30*	52*	57*
4	24	10*	10*	18*	30*	52*	57*
5	26	10*	10*	18*	30*	52*	57*
6	28	10*	10*	18*	30*	52*	57*
7	111	10.6 ± 3.5	10*	18*	30*	52*	57*
8	114	10*	14.3 ± 4.4	18*	30*	52*	57*
9	117	15.4 ± 4.7	10*	18*	30*	52*	57*
10	139	10*	10*	18*	30*	52*	57*
11	142	10*	17.5 ± 5.5	18*	30*	52*	57*
12	145	12.6 ± 3.9	10*	18*	30*	52*	57*

*Denotes minimum detectable limit; element not found.

The compositional uniformity of the Mark Hofmann *Oath* is clearly evident in the results for the paper and ink. Thus, good average values were obtained, especially for the paper. The inks were harder to evaluate, since the mass of elements heavier than silicon was so low that the ink was clearly carbon-based. The minor trace elements in the *Oath*'s ink, derived as we now know from the combustion of seventeenth-century paper, were of the same magnitude as those in the printing ink of the Bay Psalm Book. The iron-rich manuscript ink looked a little too clean (i.e., see our results on the "Tartar Relation" (number 16 in our bibliography), but we now know that Hofmann added pure (modern) tannic acid to the inks for the verso inscription. Processing from oak galls would have added additional trace elements, yet the results were not outside of the range of other inks of the period (16).

The clear and consistent differences between the two documents' papers were the strongest evidence against the *Oath*. As was stated in the report, the *Oath* "differs sharply from every type of paper in the *Bay Psalm Book*." Yet, without better knowledge of the paper sources, who could say definitely that such paper was impossible? (In fact, we know that the paper dated from the seventeenth century, England, but thirty or fifty years later. Why were the papers of the Bay Psalm Book so chemically complex?) Unless we discover and examine more examples of paper from this period, we may never know.

In summary, the choice of a subject for forgery by Mark Hofmann had a touch of genius, because materials able to be compared to the *Oath* were not available for the kinds of tests that we do at Davis. His techniques of forgery guaranteed the kind of "messy" trace elements usually found in old documents, and even the carbon-14 dating would have shown the broadside to be close to the purported age. Only the paper proved to be a serious handicap, and his solution was not adequate to avoid glaring (if hard-to-interpret) differences. We can only wonder what he could have done if he had been turned loose in England for six weeks with a sharp razor blade! Fortunately, we shall never be put to this test.

Acknowledgments

We want to acknowledge the support and encouragement of Mr. Justin Schiller for his cooperation under what must have been trying circumstances.

Walter C. McCrone's January 19, 1987,
Letter to Justin Schiller

McCRONE RESEARCH INSTITUTE
2678
2508 SOUTH MICHIGAN AVENUE
CHICAGO, ILLINOIS 60616 USA
TELEPHONE 312/842-7105

A NOT-FOR-PROFIT CORPORATION

TEACHING:
MICROSCOPY
CRYSTALLOGRAPHY
ULTRAMICROANALYSIS

19 January 1987

Justin G. Schiller, Ltd.
1 East 61st Street
New York, NY 10021

Dear Mr. Schiller:

I appreciated the opportunity to examine the "Oath of a Freeman", thought to be the first press-printed document in North America, probably in 1638 in Cambridge, Massachusetts.

I did not repeat any of the sophisticated tests carried out by the Library of Congress. I did repeat some of the simple observations already made such as examination by reflected and transmitted light at magnifications of 1X to 50X. I also used visible and ultraviolet light. I confirmed the linen fiber composition, absence of watermarks (presence of chain lines) and uneven loose texture of the paper. I note no disagreement between my observations and the report from the LC.

I did concentrate on the possible evidence for soaking of the ink medium into the paper since this is an age-related effect. The absence of such an effect along the ink lines would indicate a modern document. We were once able to unmask an alleged copy of a Christopher Columbus letter by the un-stained linen fibers immediately adjacent to any of the ink lines. The Oath of a Freeman, on the contrary, shows readily visible evidence of unusually wide ink media borders. The borders are easily detectable using the stereo microscope by top light because the ink medium in soaking into the paper cuts down the reflectivity (whiteness) of the paper surface. [We can remember the fact that in, at least, Revolutionary War days log cabin windows were covered with oiled paper in lieu of glass to allow more light (and less cold air) to enter.] The oil ink medium has the same effect though to a much lesser degree. The oil cuts down light scatter and makes the paper more transparent to light and darker by reflected light. It is not difficult to observe this effect around the ink lines on "The Oath of a Freeman". Furthermore, the use of reflected ultraviolet light shows that this ink medium quenches the fluorescence of the paper and makes the dark borders much easier to see.

I believe these effects I have observed are indications of old paper, old ink and old printing. The degree to which the medium has soaked into the paper is quite consistent with a 350-year-old document. It is quite impossible to observe such effects on any printed document even 50-100 years old.

It may be hard for some to believe such a weighty conclusion could be drawn from such relatively simple observations. However, examination of a number of printed documents covering the past 100-200 years has led me to accept as real the effect of slow migration of ink components away from the ink line as a function of age. Some impressive work has recently been done to quantitate this effect (Roderick J. McNeil in Archeological Chemistry III, Joseph B. Lambert, Editor, pp. 253-269 [1984]) using a physical analytical method to detect the migration of iron in iron gallotannate inks from the ink line.

It is difficult because of variations in ink formulas, paper nature and conditions of storage to expect this to be a general method for exact ageing. It may not be necessary with "The Oath of a Freeman" to do more than make qualitative observations since surely the question is 17th vs. 20th Century. On this basis I would have a high degree of confidence in accepting the 17th Century as correct in this case.

Sincerely,

Walter C. McCrone

WCM:gaf

Microscopy and Authentication

Walter C. McCrone

A forger of any object almost inevitably makes a mistake that can be detected by scholars or scientists. However, some objects are more difficult than others to forge without detection. The methods of detection also vary with the object but generally embrace the following areas. A successful forger must:

— match the style of the period during which the object is supposed to have originated;

— match the style of the alleged craftsman, artist, sculptor or scholar;

— match the chemical composition of the materials available at the alleged time;

— match the physical form of that material during the alleged time period;

— match the actual date of production of those materials when they can be dated.

Few forgers are knowledgeable enough or sufficiently skilled to meet those challenges; and often proper materials are not available. It is increasingly important, however, that scientists and scholars become more alert to the possibility of forgery and more sophisticated in the methods used to test for forgery.

Because there are almost no means for detection, the easiest object to forge is an inscription in or a figure made of stone. No one can ever be certain that the Kensington Stone is or is not a forgery. Still, I think it odd that even a Viking, upon discovering his companions murdered by Indians, would stick around long enough to find a two hundred-pound flat stone and then chisel a communiqué describing the event before fleeing home. Likewise, because of its lack of provenance, the Venus de Milo could be a forgery, although I know of no reason to suspect it is. Still, I know of no way to prove it is authentic.

It is, in fact, almost impossible to prove that any object is authentic. One can say when examining an object that he can't find any mistake a forger made, but perhaps that time the forger didn't make a mistake. An oil painting is one of the most difficult objects to forge because of the number of components: support, ground, media, and perhaps a dozen different pigments. All must be chemically correct, be made by the proper process, exist in the proper physical state, and date from the proper period.

The tests for analyzing a printed document follow the above outline of the tests that any object must pass. The paper must be of the correct composition, and its process of manufacture must be consistent with the alleged time and place. We once found man-made viscose rayon fibers intimately mixed with linen fibers in an alleged Revolutionary War letter. There were only a few artificial fibers, but even one would have been sufficient to declare the manuscript false. Skip Palenik of our laboratory once found polyester fibers in the label of a jacket "once owned and worn" by Adolph Hitler. Of course, polyester did not come into widespread use in clothing until long after Hitler's death.

A printed document is much easier than many other items to forge—though doing so is not by any means easy. The paper must be both characteristic of the alleged time *and* datable to that time. The ink must be chemically and physically correct, and its age correct in those instances when a date can be assigned. The style of writing or printing must be convincing. The ink/paper combination must demonstrate the proper age. All inks undergo physical changes over time, and these are detectable as changes in solubility.[1] Concomitant with the solubility change, the vehicle or other components of the ink slowly migrate into and diffuse through the substrate. In general, inorganic elements of the ink diffuse into the fibers of paper much more slowly than the ink's organic compounds. The latter are most useful for dating modern documents and the former for documents aged between 100 and 1,000 years.

Organic components that diffuse along the ink lines and letters darken over time just as does the varnish on a painting. Eventually, they become visible microscopically as a yellowed border next to the black ink. Around 1920, one enterprising forger of the Vinland Map, who knew about the gradual yellowing of organic material in ink but was unable to wait six hundred years, decided to paint the yellow borders.[2] He very carefully drew the entire map with broad yellow ink lines. He then, even more carefully, placed a black line down the middle of all the yellow lines. It was a superb effort, but one fatal to his purpose, because he incorporated a pigment called anatase titanium white, invented in 1917, in his yellow ink.

Another famous artifact, the Shroud of Turin, represents another object unmasked because of a forger's mistake.[3] If the forger had used body fluids to create the image of a crucified man on the linen, I probably would have been fooled and unable to detect the forgery. However, being an artist, the forger felt safer painting the image with a very dilute red ochre and lacing the blood-stained areas with vermilion. A polarized-light microscope was able to correlate the presence of paint media and pigment with the image areas and thus confirm the Shroud to be only a marvelous painting.

I feel confident that science and scholarship will continue to become more sophisticated in detecting forgeries than will the forger in perpetrat-

1. See the description of Dr. Antonio A. Cantu's test for analyzing this change in Richard L. Brunelle and Robert W. Reed's *Forensic Examination of Ink and Paper* (Springfield, Ill.: Charles C. Thomas, 1984), pp. 130-37.

2. Walter C. McCrone, "The Vinland Map," *Analytical Chemistry* 60 (1988): 1009-18.

3. Walter C. McCrone, "Microscopical Study of the Turin 'Shroud,' " to be published in *Wiener Berichte über Naturwissenschaft in der Kunst* 4/5 (December 1988).

ing more sophisticated forgeries. I believe this in spite of being fooled by Mr. Hofmann and his *Oath of a Freeman.* I felt sure that I saw evidence of migration of an ink medium into the linen paper. I saw this as an apparent increase in transparency of the paper in the *Oath* along the inked letters. This would happen if any colorless liquid component diffused along the fibers into asperities on the fiber surface, cutting down light loss by scattering and increasing transparency. I still believe I saw such an effect on the *Oath,* but I think I should have insisted that the diffused liquid also yellow slightly before I professed the document to be early seventeenth century. If Mr. Hofmann used a fluid ink containing a soluble but nonvolatile component, it would readily diffuse into the substrate fibers, especially if aided by a low-temperature oven treatment for an hour or so. Mr. Hofmann claims to have aged the ink on the *Oath* with ozone gas. More research is needed on this relationship between inks, paper, time, and ozone.

Forensic Document Examination and the 'Oath of a Freeman'

Marvin G. Rennert

I n April 1986, I was contacted by the resident agent in charge of the Salt Lake City office of the Bureau of Alcohol, Tobacco, and Firearms (ATF) with a request to assist in a bombing homicide investigation. Although he only briefly described the facts of the investigation, it became immediately clear that he was embroiled in an unusual case. He related a story of three bombings that resulted in two deaths and a serious injury. The evidence led to a suspect, Mark Hofmann, who had been injured in the third explosion. Investigators believed that Hofmann was responsible for the first two murders and had accidentally injured himself while transporting the third explosive device. The motive for the bombings was to cover up fraud involving the forgery of a large number of historic documents.

My agency, ATF, is a law enforcement arm of the U.S. Treasury Department whose name is not always recognized by the public and perhaps deserves an introduction. Our bureau actually has a two-fold responsibility: we serve a regulatory role for the alcohol, tobacco, and firearms industries; and we are a law-enforcement agency charged with the investigation of criminal violations. We have a long history. For most of our existence, we were part of the Internal Revenue Service. Eliot Ness was one of our investigators when we were called the Bureau of Prohibition, and there have been many name changes since then. The ATF system of laboratories can trace a continuous history back more than 100 years, making it one of the oldest in the federal government. Many people are surprised to find that the agency's enforcement responsibilities include the investigation of many serious criminal violations, such as trafficking in narcotics when firearms are used and making bombs.

At the time of the bombings, I was one of four forensic document examiners at the agency's National Laboratory Center in Rockville, Maryland, a suburb of Washington, D.C. Almost all federal law-enforcement agencies—such as the Customs Service, the IRS, the Secret Service in the Treasury Department, the FBI, the Immigration and Naturalization Service, and the Drug Enforcement Agency in the Justice Department—have their own crime laboratories, generally referred to as forensic laboratories. The ATF Forensic Science Laboratories provide services to our agents such as identifying fingerprints, chemically analyzing explosive and arson debris, examining trace evidence like hairs and soil at crime scenes, and examining firearms and documents. As a forensic document examiner, I would most commonly be referred to as a handwriting expert. Although identification of handwriting was the most common kind of examination that I conducted, I actually was responsible for all analyses of documents that would not require the work of an analytical chemist. My tasks included the physical matching of papers and inks, restoring charred or water-soaked documents, deciphering obliterated entries, and identifying typewriting, printing, and handwriting.

When I was first contacted about the Salt Lake City bombings, I was given the telephone number of Detective Ken Farnsworth of the Salt Lake City Police Department, who served as a liaison between the city police and the local ATF agent. I was told to call him for more details. When I reached him, Detective Farnsworth laid out the situation. Among the many documents in Salt Lake City that were suspect was one titled the *Oath of a Freeman*. This was actually a second copy of the *Oath*. The first had originally been offered for sale through a firm in New York City. If either document were authentic, it would be the first document printed in the United States and would be of tremendous historical and cash value. The investigation had uncovered a photographic negative that had been used to manufacture a printing plate. The printing plate was strikingly similar to the *Oath* that was being held as evidence in Salt Lake City. My task was to attempt to determine whether the *Oath* had in fact been printed using a printing plate produced from this negative.

The request for our laboratory to examine evidence in the Hofmann case turned out to be unusual in several ways. First, it is not normal for forensic document examiners to be called upon to examine historical documents. Although examiners receive training in the general history of documents and the evolution of handwriting and printing, the purpose of this training is to serve as a background for their mission of examining evidential documents that are almost always modern, usually connected with illegal financial transactions or a crime of violence such as threatening letters or robbery notes. When historical documents are submitted to a forensic laboratory, they fall into two groups. Either the examiner is asked to do a comparative examination, or he and a chemist at the laboratory are asked to conduct an analytical examination.

A comparative examination is the method often used by forensic examiners when they work with modern documents, for example, comparing a signature on a questioned document with the same signature on an item that was unquestionably authentic in order to determine if the first is genuine. On the other hand, when a disputed document has nothing with which to be compared, and its authenticity must be determined solely by looking at it, then an analytical examination is necessary. This requires an enormous amount of research on the part of forensic specialists. Chemists must establish the norm for paper and ink composition for the particular time period during which the questioned document was allegedly printed or written. The forensic document examiner must research the physical properties of documents from the time period—what writing instruments were in use, how paper was being made, from where writing materials originated. He must learn to recognize these physical properties on sight through experience with a wide variety of similar documents—and only then make a judgment about the questioned item's authenticity. In the case of the *Oath*, it was extremely fortunate that the examination requested was a comparative one. The time constraints for working with the evidence, dictated by the circumstances of the investigation and pending criminal prosecution, became an important limitation in the examination.

A second unusual factor about this case was that there were forensic document examiners with access to the *Oath* already assisting the local investigators. Detective Farnsworth gave me the telephone numbers of two examiners who were deeply involved in the examination of other questioned historical documents. One was George Throckmorton, who was at the time on loan from the attorney general's office and who also had a private practice. The other was Bill Flynn, an examiner for the State of Arizona who was privately consulting with the county attorney's office in order to assist Throckmorton with the large number of exhibits involved in the case. Normally, examiners working in the public sector attempt to avoid getting involved in one another's cases. The practical reason for this is that, in most instances, using too many government examiners results in the duplication of effort. It is especially troublesome when several examiners have to devote time to appear in court to provide information that could be established by one. In fact, one of our examiners from our San Francisco laboratory, Mary Riker, had already examined handwriting on the packing materials that had been used to conceal the bombs, with inconclusive results.

Flynn and Throckmorton had already done a tremendous amount of work, and they had identified a significant number of demonstrably fraudulent documents. The most significant contribution was the development of a microscopic technique to detect the many forged handwritten letters. Because of a dearth of verifiable, authentic manuscripts by the purported authors that could be used in comparison with the disputed documents, it was not possible for any examiner to make definitive handwriting comparisons. However, the inks of all of the disputed documents, when examined under a microscope, showed a curious cracking, but the inks on authentic documents of the same time period and area of the country did not. This observation, though not at that time conclusive evidence of fraud by itself, was damning when considered with the other circumstances surrounding the documents.

I called George Throckmorton to see if my presence was, in fact, appropriate to the ongoing analysis. Throckmorton was very encouraging and gave several reasons why my involvement was useful, the first of which was that the prosecution knew that the defense was seeking experts to authenticate the suspect documents, including the version of the *Oath* that was being held in New York. The defense already had one authority who was prepared to testify that the New York *Oath* was authentic and prosecutors feared the possibility of a "battle of the experts." If either *Oath* were fraudulent, as suspected, it would be better to have as many different authorities testifying about as many different pieces of evidence as possible. This did not mean that we were all to examine the *Oath*. Although we all were willing to exchange our findings, the idea was that we each would specialize in one particular analysis, mine being the *Oath*. Throckmorton also believed that my being on the East Coast was an advantage. There was a tremendous legal struggle between the prosecution and the custodians of the New York *Oath*, with the prosecution trying to get access for analysis and the custodians denying it on the grounds of the climate in Salt Lake City—both the dry air and the politics. The feeling was that my location in Washington might make it possible to get access to the New York *Oath*.

A third unusual circumstance of the request for my intervention in the Hofmann affair was that the New York version of the *Oath* had been analyzed by some rare book experts who, although reserving final judgment, were holding out high hopes that it was authentic. Already they had carefully measured type designs and even made some analytical examinations. They had the advantage of being able to compare the *Oath* directly with copies of the Bay Psalm Book, an authentic standard that was prepared on the press that would have printed the *Oath*. Although they had found examples of misaligned type characters in the broadside, these were things that the original printer, Stephen Daye, might have done. There was no evidence that could be used to establish that the New York version of the *Oath* was a forgery. The type design, paper, and ink all were consistent with the *Oath*'s purported age.

The morning after speaking to Detective Farnsworth, I went to Salt Lake City. Farnsworth met my plane and during the drive from the airport gave me an excellent briefing on the status of the investigation. It is not essential that a forensic specialist know a great deal about a case in which he is involved. Some prefer to know nothing, on the theory that it makes them less likely to be biased. After fifteen years of experience, however, one is not likely to be swayed by such details. Rather, understanding a bit about the investigation can sometimes lead to insights about where evidence could have originated, what could have changed its condition, and why something that is seemingly unimportant could become critical.

From the airport, we went to the home of examiner George Throckmorton. Bill Flynn from Arizona was there. Throckmorton had been on the case for some time. He was working from his home because of a recent change in employment, and there were no appropriate facilities at his new position. The laboratory space in his basement was very small but fairly well equipped and allowed Throckmorton and Flynn briefly to demonstrate their prior findings about some of the fraudulent documents that they had examined. The materials were a curious mix: a copy of the first edition of *The Call of the Wild*, which had a printed impression of what was supposed to be Jack London's signature; an old letter that had been altered to include a Betsy Ross signature; Spanish Fork notes and Deseret currency issued by Mormons during their early years in Utah that were poor reproductions made with stamp-pad inks; promissory notes from Jim Bridger; deeds; and numerous handwritten documents.

I took brief custody of the *Oath* and a negative that the police had recovered from an engraver whom Hofmann had used to make a printing plate of the *Oath*. Also, I had a contact print that the printer had made from the negative for the investigators to facilitate the examination. The *Oath* had been relief-printed on a coarse, hand-made paper. The printing on the broadside clearly had the look of an unsophisticated hand-set type and had been lightly inked, giving the characters a gray rather than a black appearance. If the *Oath* had been prepared with an etched printing plate, as investigators alleged, the original artwork that had been a model for the negative must have been made by hand.

I spent several hours comparing the *Oath* with the contact print and the negative. Superficially, the contact print and the printed *Oath* were the same. I briefly examined the *Oath* under slight magnification using a microscope light set at an oblique angle to observe the embossing effect of the print into the paper, a characteristic of relief printing. I then started the comparison part of the analysis by using a transmitted-light table, superimposing the negative onto the printed *Oath*. This method can be surprisingly subjective. Paper can shrink or expand dramatically depending on the temperature and humidity. Such changes frequently present problems for document examiners when they look at typewritten manuscripts, in which critical measurements are important to detect identifying characteristics. Examiners use grids etched into the surface of glass plates or printed on overlays to make these measurements. In this instance, the potential expansion rate of the negative retrieved from the engraver was quite different from that of the paper on which the *Oath* was printed, so there was no assurance that the two would superimpose exactly. But there was no problem. The negative and the broadside matched as closely as could be wished for.

Next, I made a side-by-side comparison, using a microscope to view features of the contact print and the *Oath* alternately. I occasionally used the microscope to inspect the negative on the light table in order to ensure that the features in the contact print were accurate representations of the negative. A comparison microscope, usually available in a crime laboratory, would have made the examination easier. However, because Throckmorton's laboratory was designed for documents that did not require a comparison microscope, he did not have one. This meant that during this examination I had to rely on visual memory, moving back and forth from one item to the other. There were many repetitions and careful confirmations. The purpose of this part of the examination was to find identifying characteristics. These are unique formations that occur through accident or wear, but they would be unique to this negative and, if the printed *Oath* had been produced from the negative, the characteristics would appear there as well.

When I looked at the *Oath* under the microscope, it was like a low-altitude aerial view of the Grand Canyon. The individual fibers in the coarse paper stood up like mountains with great canyons in between. The high-contrast negative showed the letters as clean solid areas (actually clear spaces in the negative with light showing through), and on the contact print they translated into solid black areas. The lightly inked printing had not filled in the gaps as it would have in modern lithographic printing. The black ink lay like snow only on the mountain tops. I found many flaws in the negative; but when I attempted to locate them in the *Oath*, there were only disrupted white patches. I finally located several such characteristics, however. The most significant of them, because of its clarity, was a break in a letter "M." In the printed *Oath*, it appeared as if the letter had been cut. There was a long white streak through the left-center side of the letter that looked like a line (although strictly speaking it was not a line but a long thin gap in the ink). I found the same line on the negative; but, of course, it appeared as a black streak on the clear transparent letter.

The identifying features common to both the printed *Oath* and the negative established without a doubt that they were of common origin. The question remained, which came first? At face value, that question could be quickly answered. The negative had a typewritten notation on the bottom below the image of the *Oath*, whereas the printed *Oath* had no such message. Thus, it would seem that the negative could not have been made from the printed broadside, because there was no notation on the broadside. That simple observation was not, of course, sufficient to prove that the negative was not made from the broadside; and it was necessary to develop additional proof to ensure that the negative had not been altered, perhaps by superimposing the legend over the *Oath* during photography. A close examination under magnification of the printed *Oath*, of the negative, and of the contact photograph provided the confirmation. The film used for the negative was very high-resolution and high-contrast. The *Oath*'s poor-quality, lightly printed text showed low resolution and low contrast. Resolution is the image's ability to show fine details; contrast means the difference between black and white. High-contrast film records blacks as totally black (completely clear areas in the negative) and records white as completely white (nontransmitting areas on the negative). Faint shadows or marks would not show at all in this film. The *Oath*, however, had no totally black or white areas. The paper was far from bright white and the print was gray. Even the uneven paper seemed to cast shadows. Had the negative film been a photograph of the printed *Oath*, it would have turned the grays into black, because it had the ability to record even the finest detail. The letters that were recorded in the film were solid black; but the letters in the *Oath* were gray, broken by fine unprinted areas. Had the negative been a photograph of the *Oath*, the individual letters would have appeared in the negative as black broken by white. One example of this is what I called "the islands." The *Oath* had a black border made up of solid, thick segments of line. On the right side of the negative there was a cluster of cavities in a part of this line. In the contact print, under magnification, they were white islands in the sea of black border. The edge of one of the islands was very close to the inside edge of the border. In the printed *Oath*, the fine line of the border that separated this island from the interior white spaces had disappeared, making the island a peninsula. The high-resolution negative had recorded the island from the original artwork; but during the process of acid etching the printing plate or while printing the *Oath*, that separating line was lost. The sequence of production was clear. The negative could not have been a photograph of the *Oath*, because it could never have added that black line to turn a peninsula into an island.

The negative had been made from some unrecovered artwork and was used to manufacture an acid-etched relief printing plate. The unrecorded original plate, with the legend at the bottom removed, had been used to print the Salt Lake version of the *Oath*. There are theoretical possibilities that there might have been intervening plates and documents (i.e., that the plate was used to make a print, that was used to make another plate, etc.). The forensic specialist must allow for such possibilities, but realistically the artwork that produced this negative led to the *Oath*.

One more question remained. If the Salt Lake printed *Oath* was a forgery, was it a copy of the New York version, which still might be authentic? There were only photocopies of the New York *Oath* available for scrutiny in Salt Lake City. Although clearly the printing was similar, it would have been a serious error to form any conclusions or assumptions about that document based on a reproduction from a commercial copier.

Before leaving Salt Lake City, I made one more effort to develop additional evidence that the *Oath* was a counterfeit. The morning on which I was scheduled to depart, I went to the library at the University of Utah to examine facsimile reproductions of the Bay Psalm Book, taking the contact print and a small magnifier with me. Facsimiles from two different publishers were available for viewing. I had to return to Washington in only a few hours, but I was anxious to try to find the source of the letters and ornaments used to manufacture the *Oath*. Others who had carefully examined the New York version of the *Oath* had compared the size and design of the printed type with originals of the Bay Psalm Book. I certainly was in no position to duplicate that time-consuming examination, given my limited access to the *Oath* and the near impossibility of trying to get timely access to an original of the Bay Psalm Book.

My interest was served by examining the facsimiles themselves. It was almost impossible that a forger would have had unrestricted access to an original Bay Psalm Book to use as a model for the type design, and so I thought a facsimile of the Bay Psalm Book was the likely source. I had a hope that a letter or combination of letters in the *Oath* might have identifying characteristics that could be found in the facsimile. If I were able to locate a printed character in the *Oath* that could have been attributed to the facsimile because of a printing anomaly, it would have been strong proof of forgery. Alignment characteristics of individual hand-set pieces of type would not recur in another printed document. If the printing anomaly had originated with the original Bay Psalm Book and was only faithfully reproduced in the facsimile, this evidence would have very little value.

Because of my limited time, I concentrated on the larger letters and the ornamental designs around the border of the *Oath*, because their counterparts were easier to find in the Bay Psalm Book. I was not able to match the *Oath* with either of the facsimiles. There was one interesting observation of the ornaments around the border, however. In examining the facsimiles, I discovered that the ornaments had the appearance of an ivy vine, curling around with leaves extending on very fine stems into the interior of the curl. In the *Oath*, the leaves were slightly deformed and the stems connecting the leaves to the vines had frequently not printed, leaving the leaves disconnected. I felt that it was possible that these unprinted features could have been caused by the very light printing on rough paper; however, the characteristic was common with most electrostatic copies. I had seen it produced many times by copy machines such as those put out by Xerox, Savin, Canon, etc. Electrostatic copiers frequently fail to record fine detail like the stems and deform small shapes like the leaves, because of the way toner is attracted to the image areas and fused onto paper. The similarity to an electrostatic copy was so striking that although I did not feel that the conclusion was demonstrable at that time, I did feel strongly that a copy machine, rather than a photographic technique, had been used as a part of the counterfeiting effort.

It was also interesting to note that in the lower right corner of the *Oath* the ornament came very close to the outer black border and that the black border appeared too narrow to accommodate the extra space being demanded by the ornament. It certainly seemed possible that this was a coincidence or that an unskilled printer might have narrowed the malleable material of the border to accommodate this last type character. However, it struck me that I had seen this kind of thing many times when cut-out letters were photocopied. If one character inadvertently overlaps another when they are copied, the overlaid letter appears in the photocopied image as if it had had a notch taken out of it.

I later continued an examination of the Bay Psalm Book facsimiles at my laboratory but was never able to match them to the *Oath*. This, of course, did not change my original finding, but it was troubling that the Bay Psalm Book was the only readily available source of the type design. It appeared that the letters may have been changed or overwritten. Perhaps this was not done deliberately to alter the shapes of the letters, but only to make them more reproducible in the most likely copying process.

Upon my return to Washington, I began trying to find out information about the history of the *Oath*. I had a library search done to get more information about the Cambridge Press, Stephen Daye, the *Oath of a Freeman*, and the Bay Psalm Book. I also interviewed the staff of the Library of Congress, who had been able to examine the New York version of the *Oath*. They could not have been more cooperative. Jim Gilreath briefed me on their observations about the *Oath* and showed me an authentic Bay Psalm Book. He also introduced me to Karen Garlick, a paper conservator at the Library, who had made a minor repair to the New York *Oath*, placed it in a protective cover, and arranged to have it photographed. She also had a beta radiograph made.

I had an opportunity to make a very thorough examination of the photographs that had been made. The New York version of the *Oath* was different in several ways: it had been folded and subsequently cracked along the fold; there was evidence of glue in the corners, as if the document had been posted for display; and there was old-style handwriting along one edge of the back.

The quality of the Library of Congress photographs was excellent and illuminating. It was possible to make a very thorough examination using these photographs and the contact print from Salt Lake City. The identifying characteristics, including the line through the "M," were present. The evidence of sequence between the negative and the *Oath* in Salt Lake City was also present in the photograph of the New York *Oath*, including the "peninsula." I was close to preparing a report based just upon the examination of the Library's photograph, but this would have caused problems in "chain of custody." It is likely that if I had prepared a report based upon the photographs that a large number of technicians from the Library of Congress would have had to testify to authenticate the photographs in the event the issue went to trial. It seemed likely that negotiations might soon give me direct access to the New York *Oath* in any event, so I decided to wait.

In the meantime, I was able to conduct another indirect examination of the New York *Oath*, which regrettably was inconclusive. The existence of a beta radiograph of the New York *Oath* held out the hope of being able to match the *Oath*'s paper to a source in a book in Salt Lake City. Everyone suspected that Hofmann had ripped out a blank sheet of paper from some seventeenth-century book available to him in the Salt Lake City area. Police investigators in Utah had, in fact, during their searches of Hofmann's property, recovered such a book in which the front and back blank fly leaves had been removed. The Library of Congress beta radiograph, which was a picture of the chain lines of the paper on which the New York *Oath* had been printed, revealed a broken chain line. If the same break could be found on one of the pages in the seventeenth-century book in the custody of the Salt Lake City investigators, then the evidence would point to the New York *Oath* being a forgery. The paper of the *Oath* would have to have been manufactured in the same mold as the paper in the book in order to have the same broken chain line.

The beta radiograph is an excellent tool. Relatively harmless to people, it emits energy that passes through paper, recording on X-ray film the different densities of the paper caused by a watermark, laid lines, or chain lines without recording any printing or writing that might be on the paper. I borrowed a beta radiograph from the United States Secret Service and recorded about fifty sample pages from the Salt Lake City book. Comparing these beta radiograph pictures with the Library's beta radiograph of the New York *Oath*, I searched for a similar break in a chain line. It was a very

111

time-consuming process; and, unfortunately, I was unsuccessful. There were very subtle differences in the spacing of the chain lines that suggested that this particular book was not the source of the paper for the *Oath.*

Finally, arrangements were made to examine the New York *Oath.* After considerable pressure, the bookstore holding the *Oath* consented to allow its examination in New York, agreeing that we could use the facilities of the U.S. Postal Service Laboratory. I flew to New York City on the morning of the examination, June 25, 1986, and proceeded directly to the laboratory, the staff of which was extremely helpful in setting up the examination. At the laboratory, I met George Throckmorton, who brought the negative from Salt Lake City with him. The representative from the firm that had the New York *Oath* was quite late and was again reluctant to turn over the broadside. For a while, it appeared that the trip was going to be for nothing. I, however, emphasized my prior meetings with staff of the Library of Congress. For some reason, this seemed to mollify him, and he turned over the *Oath* for examination. Regrettably, given all of the delays, there were only two hours left for examination.

Throckmorton first inspected the writing on the back of the *Oath* and found the same cracking that had been common to the other handwritten forgeries. The negative brought from Salt Lake City lined up on the light table with this version of the *Oath* as nicely as it had done on the Salt Lake City *Oath.*

My examination was sped by my prior familiarity with the Library of Congress photographs; and, fortunately, everything fell into place, paralleling the examination which had taken place in Salt Lake City.

The New York *Oath* was also a forgery.

The examinations conducted were certainly adequate to support the conclusion of forgery; yet, it is regrettable that there was not more time available to follow up on some other approaches that could have been made. There are computerized techniques that permit the very precise measurement of typeface designs. Because it is likely that a copying machine was used as a part of the counterfeiting process, it is quite remarkable that the *Oath* duplicated the size of the print in the Bay Psalm Book. Most copy machines either very slightly enlarge or reduce the copied image. Random chance makes the selection of a machine that produces one-to-one images unlikely. Perhaps variations in sizes of type could have been detected by computer measurement.

Digital imaging systems are also available that allow microscopic features to be overlaid to detect differences or similarities that should not exist. Perhaps such a system could have detected a consistent pattern in type or ornaments that could have established the source of the type designs in the *Oath* beyond what the eye can detect using only magnification.

The forensic specialist is always seeking confirmatory tests to remove subjectivity from examinations. Had all additional tests, proposed or still unthought of, failed to develop additional proof of forgery, my original finding of forgery would not have changed. The *Oath of a Freeman* that I examined in Salt Lake City and the *Oath of a Freeman* that I examined in New York City both originated from a photographic negative that was used to produce a printing plate.

Forensic specialists are always reluctant to describe the work they have done as easy. Such a description seems frequently to be taken to mean that the analysis did not require skill and training. Of course that is not the case, but my examination of these documents was easy because of my years of experience in this field. It was a straightforward comparative examination of a limited number of samples in a basic medium. The only complicating factors were the limited time involved, the travel required to get to the documents, and the inordinate attention given to the work as a result of the importance assigned to the disputed documents. The credit attributable to the solution of this case certainly belongs to the investigators who followed long and complicated leads to run down the evidence that incriminated Mark Hofmann as the bomber and who finally followed the financial trail to the printing plate maker, still in possession of the negatives that had been used to create the *Oath*. There was a lot of good forensic work done in this case; but if any should be singled out, it was the observations made of the inks by George Throckmorton and Bill Flynn, and the work that Flynn did to prove that the inks were not consistent with inks of the period. Developments of this kind were important to the criminal investigation at a very critical time.

As a forensic specialist who must normally be concerned about the impact of a careless word on the results of a criminal investigation, I seldom have opportunities to make an editorial comment. Since this case is over, I feel that I can offer some necessary observations. First, Mark Hofmann has been referred to as a master forger. I have some doubt about that. Having seen some of the very primitive forgeries attributed to him, I feel that only the handwritten material deserves any note; and there were even flaws in these. As for the *Oaths*, Hofmann was just lucky that he had picked an area where so many variations from the norm were within acceptable tolerances. Misaligned type and faint printing were acceptable because Daye was a poor printer. Paper that could not be matched to the other paper used by Daye was acceptable, because it was known that Daye had used scrap paper. And the simple ink, made from materials that are still readily available, was a formulation that was as variable as the person mixing it.

Secondly, the attention that finally unmasked the *Oath*s resulted from murder bombings and the fact that an authentic *Oath* would have been one of the most significant and expensive pieces of Americana. I believe that the study being focused on the New York *Oath* by rare book specialists who were methodically and steadily testing its authenticity would have eventually revealed this document to be a fraud. There should, however, be great concern over less significant documents that are offered for sale. Not only are Hofmann's techniques quite satisfactory for fabricating documents that are not going to be subjected to close scrutiny, but there are now computerized tools that can be used to record and digitize any kind of visual image in extremely high resolution. Once an image is recorded, it can be reproduced in any desirable form. The letter designs in the Bay Psalm Book could be recorded and called up at any time and in any form to create a printing plate. Although these instruments are quite expensive, the print and advertising shops that most commonly use them are not likely to be exercising a lot of security over after-hours creative efforts. Currency is not the only candidate for sophisticated forgery efforts used in order to reap great financial gain.

Finally, I found the prosecutors, investigators, and technical specialists who were a part of this investigation to be highly motivated individuals, dedicated to solving two terrible murders and insuring that the man responsible was punished under the law. In future such investigations, I hope that everyone can recognize the importance of that purpose and lend his support.

Scanning Auger Microscopy for Dating Two Copies of the 'Oath of a Freeman'

Roderick McNeil

My involvement with the *Oath of a Freeman* began simply enough; I was asked to meet with the staff of the Salt Lake County attorney's office to give a detailed review of the dating technique I had developed for documents. That meeting was held in July 1986 and they decided that the technique might be of value to their case. In September 1986, I was retained to examine a large series of documents purported to be forgeries.

I began working with George Throckmorton (special agent, documents examination) to categorize the importance of each of the hundreds of documents related to the case. George had made an initial priority list of twenty-eight documents to be reviewed. We planned to conduct EDAX (Energy Dispersive Analysis by X-ray) analysis on all twenty-eight using the equipment at Brigham Young University in order to sort further the test documents to find candidates for SAM (Scanning Auger Microscopy) technique.

While we were waiting for the tests to begin in October, George and I discussed the various ink formulations suspected of being used on the documents in question. George had noted that many of the documents he thought were forgeries had ink that cracked in what he referred to as an "alligator" pattern. George had worked long and hard on reproducing some of the aging effects noted, basing his work on reference material found in the Hofmann home.

I noted that the gum arabic used in some of the formulations is a protein used as an organic binder. Because of the highly substituted nature of the chemical bonds in gum arabic, exposure to UV (ultraviolet) radiation would cause the protein configuration to contract, producing the cracking. With gum arabic solutions prepared in George's basement, we were able to observe the rapid development of the so-called alligator cracking on paper exposed to UV light under a video-enhanced stereo microscope. I had observed ink cracking in many older documents but the crazed-cracking effect produced by the use of aging accelerants was unique in my experience. George also felt that ammonia may have been used in aging the documents. I explained that this would only further stimulate cracking, as the ammonia

The author wishes to express his sincere gratitude to Dr. Tony Cantu, George Throckmorton, Gerry D'Elia, and Ken Farnsworth for their unwavering support and suggestions for the research described in this report.

would act as a denaturing agent causing the organic binders to contract even before UV exposure.

To better understand the nature of the tests I was to conduct from October to December 1986, a brief historical review of the method's development might be helpful.

The hypothesis that secondary ion migration might take place in textiles dyed with inorganic dyes was suggested while Alan D. Adler (professor of chemistry at the University of Connecticut), John H. Heller (forensic medicine consultant), and I were discussing the chemical testing of the Shroud of Turin. The discussion had turned to the retting process for linen and the selective absorption of inorganic species into the cellulosic base material. It seemed possible that if such secondary migration took place, the process would also occur on cellulosic-based manuscripts when inorganic inks are used.

The basic concept is that the migration of ions from the ink is in direct proportion to time elapsed. This would allow dating the application of ink rather than dating the writing support (i.e., the paper), which seemed to have merit. Although good destructive (C14 carbon dating) and non-destructive (particle accelerator) techniques exist for dating the support, neither technique addresses the question of when the ink was applied to the writing surface. The hypothesis, if valid, would have value in detecting forgeries and for dating. As an analytical biochemist, I saw the challenge in document examination to be the development of an objective scientific test to determine the authenticity of a document rather than the accumulation of large amounts of subjective expertise in numerous historical areas.

Preliminary Experimentation

As a preliminary experiment, I evaluated several documents from my collection spanning the period 1272-1972 by using X-ray energy dispersive analysis as well as scanning auger microscopy (SAM). A literature survey had shown that iron gall was likely to be the most prevalent ink in the 1200-1600 period; I therefore believed that elemental iron would be a good atomic species for investigation.

Although a number of unique elements, including phosphorus, calcium, potassium, iron, and zinc, were present to some extent, only iron was present in sufficient quantities (greater than 1 percent) and had high enough atomic weight ($Z\pm20$) to make auger spectroscopy feasible. A survey of twelve additional documents on vellum, parchment, and paper showed similar results.

In order to detect the small amount of ionic migration suspected at the periphery of the ink margin, I employed SAM to improve spatial resolution and elemental specificity. Auger spectroscopy differs from electron spectroscopy for chemical analysis (ESCA) in that the former uses electrons instead of X-rays for specimen excitation.

Both electron microprobe analysis and SAM use an electron beam for

116

excitation of the specimen. The microprobe technique allows the detection of emitted X-rays, while SAM measures emitted electrons. For both techniques, the energy of any detected particles can be linked to a characteristic energy level of a particular parent atom, thus identifying the atomic species present. The lateral spatial resolution in SAM is superior to other techniques because of the much shorter mean free path of the emitted energy (electrons). The escape depth of auger electrons is approximately 10 A° (Angstrom) versus 1000 A° in microprobe analysis. This phenomenon makes SAM a highly specific surface-analysis technique. Auger electrons are caused by the ejection of an electron in an outer shell of an atom to a state in the continuum. If a primary vacancy exists in the K shell, the vacancy is filled from the L_2 shell, and the energy released in this transition results in the expulsion of an electron from the L_3 shell; the ejected electron will be denoted as an Auger electron of the KL_2L_3 type. Thus, there are nine forms of radiationless transition in the KLL group, each with a specific energy unique to the element.

In figure 1 we see the relative energies of various Auger transitions versus Z, the atomic weight of the element. Obviously, the transition Auger line may be selected to yield maximum sensitivity. In the case of iron, the L_1L_2 line at 5.519 KeV and the L_2L_3 line at 5.619 KeV were monitored. An initial low resolution (1.0 um) lateral scan of the ink profile in sample MS3-4 yielded the results shown in figure 2. Note the parallel valleys created by the nibs of the quill pen and the shoulder at either side that represent the diffusion by capillary action on the surface in the parchment.

If the area count is normalized to 100 percent at the capillary shoulder, a "tail" becomes evident (see figure 3). The area integration of this tail was found to vary with time. Seven paper documents dating from 1272 to 1972 were then run by the same technique to confirm the relationship of area increase with time. An averaging of three replicate measurements from five different sites on each document is shown in figure 4. Because the phenomena seemed to lend credence to the secondary ion migration hypothesis, a detailed study of a number of documents began.

During 1982 and 1983 over 100 documents were borrowed from the Beinecke library at Yale University and more than 200 additional documents of "known date" were borrowed from the privately held Bishop collection, the Redemptarist Monastery, and a variety of rare book dealers in the Boston and New York City areas. These documents were used to confirm the predictability to the time-curve relationship and analyze sampling problems associated with various inks, writing media, and site selection on the document. The time span covered by these samples covered 1000 B.P. (before present) to the present. A far more limited set of illuminated manuscripts (36) was studied, covering the time period from 3400 B.P. to 500 B.P. As will be discussed later in the text, the use of heavier metals, particularly lead and mercury, allowed considerably more sensitive dating analysis for the later samples.

A detailed discussion of the development of the final sampling protocols

117

is described in my "Scanning Auger Microscopy for Dating Manuscript Inks" in volume 205 of the Advances in Chemistry Series.[1] In summary, the sampling protocol has been standardized in the following manner over the past five years.

Although the Auger technique itself is nondestructive, the requirements of degassing documents to 1×10^{-7} Torr is too time-consuming for all but the most valuable documents. Typically, at least two hours per page are necessary to provide an adequate electron-free path for the Auger technique. With the exception of two instruments in the country, there is a sample-size limitation of 4 to 9 square inches per item. My instrument has been modified with two turbo-molecular pumps and a custom sample chamber to allow samples up to 36 square inches. Third-generation Auger instruments from PHI (Physical Instruments, Inc., a division of Perkin Elmer Corp.) now have optional sample chamber and pump configurations capable of handling samples up to 144 square inches.

If it is at all possible to take samples from the document, an eight-gauge hypodermic is ground flat and used as a punch to remove tiny pieces from the document. This has the advantage of providing an unequivocal location mark for the sample site and dramatically reducing degassing time (typically fifteen minutes for five samples). Because rental time on commercial instruments costs $3-5,000 per day, this is a significant consideration.

The sample punch must bisect the ink line and include fibrils that run on the surface of the document perpendicular to the ink line. A longitudinal scan along the perpendicular fibril must be conducted on three fibrils per punch and five samples per document in order to assure adequate accuracy in dating.

A detailed history of the document in question is necessary in order to determine if acid neutralization techniques have ever been used. If prior document treatment is unknown, an EDAX scan of the paper (in an area where ink is not present) for high background counts of iron, calcium, zinc, or any other cations will determine if the Auger technique will work for a particular sample. EDAX should be undertaken for each sample proposed for dating. Initially, the quantitative assay for all inorganic cations should be made to determine which is most suitable for the Auger scan. Databases exist for iron, lead, and mercury. The relative concentration of the inorganic cation to be used for measurement should exceed 10 percent of the total cation count and exceed the paper background count by ten times. If these two basic parameters are not met or one of the three metals is not present, the document cannot be dated without establishing a timeline database for those metals that are present.

Once EDAX confirms that the document meets minimum concentration requirements, the sample is evacuated to 1×10^{-9} Torr, imaged, and scanned along the selected fibril at the maximum resolution of the Auger instru-

1. Roderick J. McNeil, "Scanning Auger Microscopy for Dating of Manuscript Inks," *Archaeological Chemistry - III*, ed. Joseph B. Lambert, Advances in Chemistry Series, vol. 205, pp. 255-72.

ment, which will vary between 1500A° and 700A°, depending on the age of the instrument. The instrument used in the majority of work to date is a modified PHI 560 with a maximum spatial resolution of 1500A°. Of the more than 450 documents analyzed so far, 82 percent have used the KL_1L_2 at 5.519 KeV and the KL_2L_3 at 5.619 KeV of iron to make age determinations. The remaining documents were illuminated manuscripts in which the paint pigments provided a variety of alternative inorganic cations to develop alternative time datelines.

A series of controls, established in 1982, to determine the effect of environmental variables on ion migration rate has been monitored for six years and has begun to show signs of ion migration using the most sensitive Auger instruments available (PHI 610, 700A resolution). The initial control set evaluated only temperature and relative humidity; a second set of controls was added in 1985 to evaluate the effects of acid neutralization on the paper itself. Whatman Paper Co. has maintained control samples of paper produced at various steps in pulp neutralization for many of its paper lots produced since the 1780s. In order to maintain continuity with the first control lots, Whatman kindly provided samples of Whatman Elephant-grade writing paper produced in 1926 at all stages of pulp neutralization. These five samples had pH's of 4.52, 5.34, 6.02, 7.20, and 7.54, respectively.

In the past eight years the database for the iron timeline has been increased from 22 to 240 paper documents and from 8 to 124 samples for parchment. The number of vellum samples (a parchment of calfskin) has been increased from 7 to 44. Although parchment samples are more difficult to work with (selection of collagen or cellulosic fibrils perpendicular to the ink line occur far less frequently than cellulosic fibrils in paper), the larger sample database has reduced the inter- and intra-sample error to virtually the same limits found in paper.

Applications

My technique was originally developed with the thought that a nondestructive dating analysis technique that determined when ink was placed on the writing material would be of value to the literary and historical communities. In fact, more than 90 percent of the samples submitted to me so far have been historical documents of interest to private collectors, investors, or libraries. The remaining 10 percent have been samples involving criminal prosecutions ranging from fraud to murder.

Some of the collections submitted are limited to a single historical period or family. The Collins collection of Medici letters in private hands included eighty-seven documents acquired over a forty-five-year period. Two major questions were addressed during the testing: the authenticity of the documents and the chronology of the undated documents. All of the documents purportedly date from 1427 to 1527, but several contained information that was highly contradictory. Testing revealed that nine of the manuscripts were forgeries produced after 1940. The elimination of these from the collection resolved most of the historical contradictions. And establishing the chronology of later documents was of value in understanding the politics associated with Giuliano dé Medici's influence on his brother's ascension to the papacy.

The majority of documents submitted to me are from the American Revolutionary and early Republic period, between 1760 and 1820. A surprising number of forgeries have been detected. Of the 122 documents submitted so far, twenty-six were forgeries. While these might have been detected by some other subjective technique, all of these documents had been authenticated by handwriting analysis and/or paper/historical analysis. One of the most surprising aspects of this work has been the ready availability of old paper produced as early as the late 1600s. Clearly, paper of the proper date is readily available to the well-informed forger, making establishment of the age of paper a poor choice in document authentication.

Another technique of interest to the forensic community is stroke sequence. In the case of a will or another legal instrument, the issue of who signed first can be of pivotal interest. The Auger instrument can be used to record the total inorganic composition of each ink type in the overlaid area. Then another electron microscopy technique, Electron Spectroscopy for Chemical Analysis (ESCA), is used to do a depth profile to determine which is on the bottom. In some cases, one of the documents involved contained a questionable signature. An optical microscopy examination showed paper roughness consistent with erasure but no ink was visible with infrared or unaided examination. A digital image reconstruction has been used first to subtract the signature from the site and the chemical composition of the ink formulation from the main text stored in memory. Using Auger and ESCA, the suspected area was rescanned for the same chemical ink composition, and the original signature was restored as clearly as the main body of text.

In documents when suspected of being traced to restore image quality or information, the tracing can be readily detected by a double staircase effect in the Auger scan. Using the digital image reconstruction available on later Auger instruments, it is possible to "subtract" all areas of an intact document that have been altered.

The 'Oath of a Freeman' Documents

I first examined the Salt Lake City copy of the *Oath* in October of 1986 in Provo, Utah. The site selections on the broadside were based on what visually appeared to be two of the highest ink-concentration areas. Sampling was by the hypodermic procedure previously described in this report. Each document was examined at 10X to 70X using a Bausch & Lomb stereomicroscope. Areas were selected where ink concentrations appeared as high as possible in order to maximize elemental detection sensitivity. A sample approximately 1 millimeter in diameter was excised from the parent document in such a way that one half of the sample consisted of the ink line and the other half extended into the background area surrounding each letter.

In those documents about which there is some conjecture that a portion of the document might be genuine, multiple samples are taken from "genuine" and "nongenuine" areas to allow comparison of ink chemical composition and, if sufficiently high-atomic-weight (z) materials are present, to allow the utilization of SAM to date ink samples from varying areas on the same document.

Three or four samples from the Salt Lake City *Oath* were mounted on each stub to minimize the number of stubs used and the variation between gold-coating runs. The Polaron coating unit used was capable of coating ten stubs simultaneously, and a total of two runs were made. Coatings were made for thirty seconds at 0.001 Torr, 1.0 KV, and 20 Ma current load. Samples were evacuated in an AMR 1000A to 1x10-5 Torr and observed at 30 KV in the backscatter mode. Initial EDAX runs were made from two to twenty KV for 100 seconds to determine which elements were present.

Higher-resolution runs were then made from two to ten KV for 200 seconds with the eight most common elements automatically background-corrected in the quantitative mode. The system used was the Edac Corp. Model 7000 unit. For those samples that showed other than the most common eight-element matrix in the initial scan, two quantitative runs were made: the first for the common matrix and a second run to incorporate all those elements excluded in the first run in addition to the most common elements from the first standard run.

Of the initial twenty-eight documents in the Hofmann case considered for dating, the list was whittled down to seven, one of which was the Salt Lake City *Oath*. EDAX clearly showed that insufficient iron was present on the broadside to allow accurate dating. However, lead levels were quite high and the MNN transitions were used to perform the dating. Unfortunately, the available database for lead is significantly smaller than that for iron and the relative standard error is therefore greater.

The seven samples selected in late December of 1986 for SAM were stripped of gold by reverse fielding with steel electrodes at 1.2 Kv, 10 mA, for 90 seconds and then were evacuated to 1x10-9 Torr for two hours. The most common emission lines monitored for the *Oath* were the MNN_1N_2 line at 1.620 KeV and the MNN_2N_3 line at 2.19 KeV. A lateral scan resolution of 0.01 um was used with a drive rate of 0.1 um per 1,000 seconds. Date calculations were based on the average of five independent measurements from three different sample sites. For those samples (of the seven) on which the quantitative element constituted less than 5 percent of the total inorganic or for which a metal lighter than iron had to be used (such as copper), was a total of ten samples was taken before date calculations. The correlation data for iron-ink documents now consists of more than 1,200 samples with a fit correlation of 0.996. There are far fewer documents dated using lead (147), and the regression fit is 0.928. Thus, the accuracy of a potential timeline fit is poorer with metals such as lead until such time as more samples have been run. The SAM showed that in the Salt Lake City *Oath* virtually no ink migration had taken place and a date of 1920 plus or minus seventy-five was obtained for the lead. The confidence interval of 90 percent created a relatively wide time window, but the document missed the validity period by two whole centuries at a minimum.

The second copy of the *Oath* was in the possession of a private dealer in New York. The district attorney's office had requested that I not deal with other parties concerning the Hofmann documents until my final report was submitted to them. My report was completed on January 7, 1987, and I obtained the second copy of the *Oath* for immediate testing. Since the owner did not want the document harmed in any way, it was impossible to destructively test it in exactly the same way as the Salt Lake City *Oath*.

Two of the sample sites used on the New York City *Oath* were in common with the test sites used on the Salt Lake City copy of the *Oath*, sites 1 and 2. The general condition and quality of the printing (in terms of the ink concentration) were superior on the New York City copy, and the remainder of the sites selected were in the margin areas to allow easier manipulation of the Auger stage (see figure 5). Due to the size of the document surface, charging was a significant problem. I used modified 3M silver grounding tape beneath each sample site as data was collected. This type of information is important to any future archeometric evaluations, since other researchers may well wonder why there are square silver patches on the back of their questioned documents. The locations of all grounding tape used in the New York copy of the *Oath* are also indicated in figure 5. The surface adhesion properties of the 3M grounding tape were highly modified on one side (the side in contact with the document) by washing the tape with methylene chloride and then adding an almost dry paste of silver paint to the tape prior to placing the document in contact with the support block. Once the measurements were completed, it was fairly simple to remove the dried paint from the back of the document.

The concentration of lead in all of the sample sites was sufficient to allow a dating accuracy of plus or minus fifty years back to 950 B.P. with a 90 percent confidence interval based on five samples run three times. A survey of the paper background showed elevated zinc readings that may be indicative of acid neutralization in the paper.

The ink on the back of the document contained 1,200 ppm of iron, so this was used as the test medium for the handwriting. The concentration of iron at all ink sample sites was sufficient to allow dating accuracy of plus or minus thirty years back to 900 B.P. with a 70 percent confidence interval, using three samples measured three times. I reasoned that a greater confidence measurement was not necessary if the print proved not to come from the proper time period. The grounding problems associated with the ink samples were even more severe, because I did not want to use any grounding adhesive on the face of the document in case it was genuine. I used the virtually dry silver paint again on the face of the document for grounding the writing on the reverse of the document. Though not visible to the naked eye, these silver spots might well show up under EDAX or SAM.

For the New York *Oath*, the print was dated at 1940, plus or minus fifty years, and the writing on the reverse was dated at 1955, plus or minus thirty years. The slightly higher accuracy of the measurement for the New York *Oath* printing results from the use of five as opposed to three sample sites to complete the statistical measurements.

Discussion

The past eight years have greatly expanded the database for this technique and have eliminated some of the sampling errors associated with its early development. The use of computerized inflection detection with the Golay fused peak technique has improved the sensitivity of the technique to provide accurate relative dates from seventeen years B.P. to 1200 B.P. If a third-generation Auger instrumentation is available, the standard error can be reduced to twelve years.

The current results associated with the controls suggest that the minimum theoretical detection limit for the ion migration process is six or seven years. Thus far, no environmental effects have been found that affect the accuracy of the technique. With the much larger sample populations, the relative standard error associated with inter-sample and intra-sample techniques have been reduced to 4.5 plus or minus .2 percent for date-dependent errors and 3.3 plus or minus .2 percent for date-independent errors in both paper and vellum. Mostly because of the variability in hide preparation and tanning techniques, the relative errors associated with sampling are significantly greater for parchment. The intra-sample errors were 10.2 plus or minus .3 percent and 11.1 plus or minus .3 percent for date-dependent errors. The date-independent RSE values were reduced to 5.9 plus or minus .2 percent for intra-sample and 4.7 plus or minus .3 percent for inter-sample errors.

The use of SESD (Scanning Electron Stimulated Desorption) has shown that the phenomenological explanation for the ion migration process is related to the presence of carboxyl groups for a form of "dry" lateral ion exchange with a concentration gradient. If the carboxyl groups are saturated with cations, then the migration process does not take place and the Auger technique is of no value in dating. This often occurs in acid-neutralized paper or dyed paper lots. Chromic and some forms of organic tanning also saturate the support with cations. A rapid determination of the suitability of a document for Auger analysis can be made by doing an EDAX scan of the area immediately adjacent to the writing area for cation concentration. All of the acid paper neutralization techniques of which I am aware stop the ion migration process. However, the neutralization process does not affect the ion migration that has already taken place.

Conclusions

I hope that this brief article has piqued interest in the use of this technique in the antiquarian community. Though the Auger dating technique has some limitations associated with the support and the ink formulation, the technique is generally applicable to a wide variety of documents and allows an objective determination about the authenticity of a specific sample. Additionally, for those documents that do not bear dates, this technique may allow the historical relevance of a piece to be placed in context. For documents that have been altered, it is possible, using Auger and ESCA in conjunction with digital image reconstruction, to restore a document to its original format.

I will make the database used in preparing this report available to anyone interested in implementing the technique on an Auger instrument. The more widespread use of this technique will further improve its accuracy and usefulness to the literary and forensic community. I am aware of two academic and two commercial labs offering the so-called McNeil dating technique. Further expansion of the database for metals other than iron, lead, and mercury, as well as more samples from differing support media, will reduce the standard error in the technique.

The original goal of providing the scientific community with an objective dating technique based on the time of application of the ink onto the support has in large part been met. Though some limitations of the technique exist, the vast majority of documents seem to be candidates, although the cost of testing is very high because of the capital equipment costs involved. Readily available EDAX can be used as a powerful screening tool to test the suitability of a document for the more expensive SAM testing.

In the case if the *Oath of a Freeman,* the cost of not testing was very high indeed.

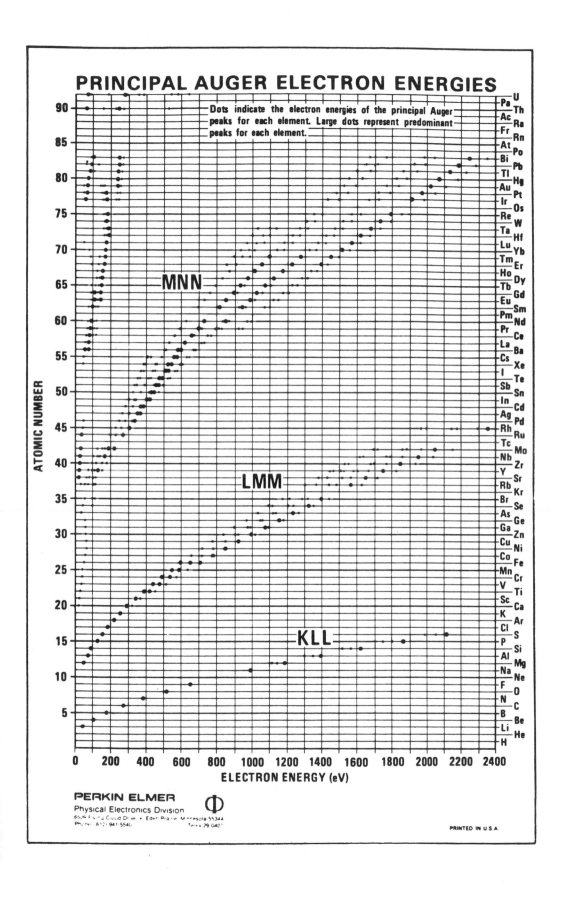

PRINCIPAL AUGER ELECTRON ENERGIES

Dots indicate the electron energies of the principal Auger peaks for each element. Large dots represent predominant peaks for each element.

MNN

LMM

KLL

ATOMIC NUMBER

ELECTRON ENERGY (eV)

PERKIN ELMER Φ

Physical Electronics Division

6509 Flying Cloud Drive • Eden Prairie, Minnesota 55344
Phone (612) 941-5540   Telex 29-0407

PRINTED IN U.S.A.

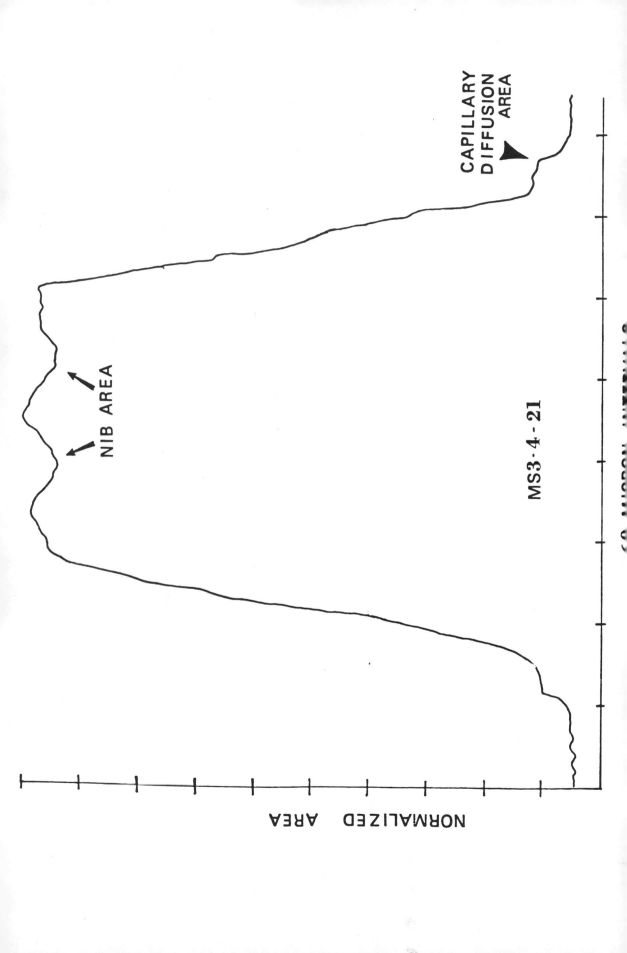

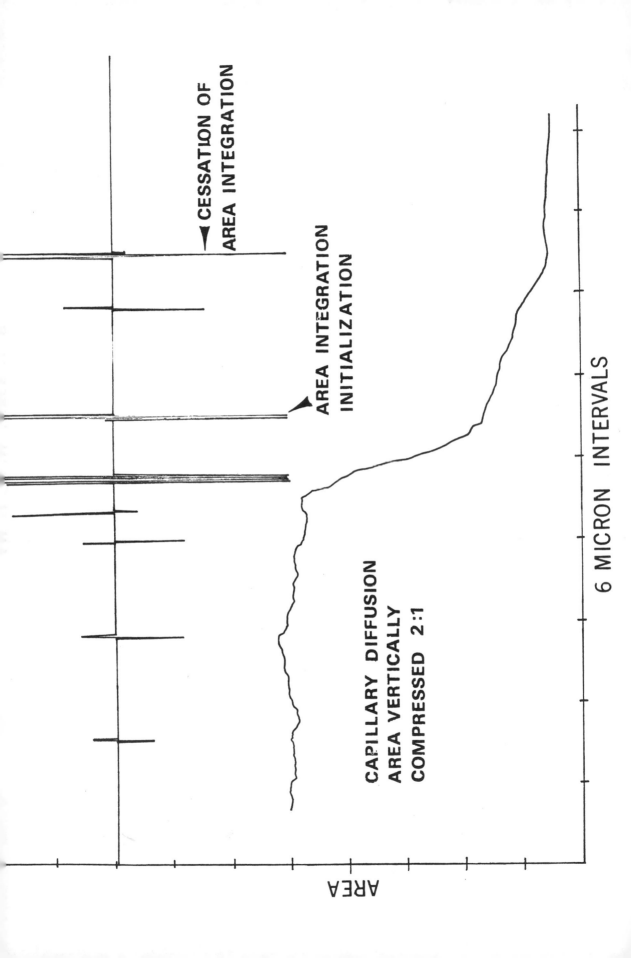

CESSATION OF
AREA INTEGRATION

AREA INTEGRATION
INITIALIZATION

CAPILLARY DIFFUSION
AREA VERTICALLY
COMPRESSED 2:1

6 MICRON INTERVALS

AREA

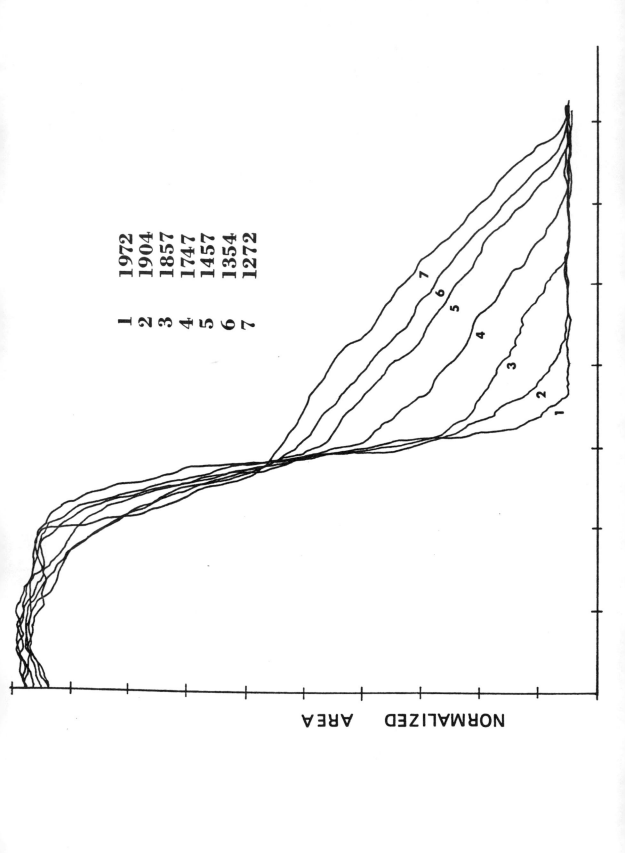

NORMALIZED AREA

1   1972
2   1904
3   1857
4   1747
5   1457
6   1354
7   1272

THE OATH OF A FREEMAN.

I·AB· being (by Gods providence) an Inhabitant, and Freeman, within the iurisdictiō of this Common-wealth, doe freely acknowledge my selfe to bee subject to the governement thereof; and therefore doe heere sweare, by the great & dreadfull name of the Everliving-God, that I will be true & faithfull to the same, & will accordingly yield assistance & support therunto, with my person & estate, as in equity I am bound: and will also truely indeavour to maintaine and preserve all the libertyes & privilidges thereof, submitting my selfe to the wholesome lawes, & ordres made & stablished by the same; and further, that I will not plot, nor practice any evill against it, nor consent to any that shall soe do, butt will timely discover, & reveall the same to lawefull authoritee nowe here stablished, for the speedie preventing thereof. Moreover, I doe solemnly binde my selfe, in the sight of God, that when I shalbe called, to give my voyce touching any such matter of this state, (in which freemen are to deale) I will give my vote & suffrage as I shall judge in myne owne conscience may best conduce & tend to the publick weale of the body, without respect of personnes, or favour of any man, Soe help mee God in the Lord Iesus Christ.

The Investigation of the 1985 Mark Hofmann Forgery of the 'Oath of a Freeman'

Kenneth C. Farnsworth, Jr.

Mark Hofmann was known in the Mormon history community as a discoverer of rare, valuable, and controversial historical documents relating to the history of the Mormon Church. He also dealt in other kinds of Americana. In March 1985, he claimed to have discovered the *Oath of a Freeman*. It was his crowning achievement. Much effort was put forth by Justin Schiller and Raymond Wapner, both book dealers in New York City, the Library of Congress, and the American Antiquarian Society, to determine the authenticity of Hofmann's *Oath*. The Salt Lake City Police Department became involved in that investigation because of the murders of two people in the Salt Lake City area. This paper addresses the investigation by the police agencies, evidence developed by expert witnesses employed by the police task force, and contributions of other antiquarian document experts to the police investigation.

My involvement in the investigation was one of my duties as a police officer of the Salt Lake City Police Department, where I have been employed for more than seventeen years. At the time of the investigation of the murders and of the *Oath of a Freeman*, I had been assigned to the homicide squad as a detective for about eighteen months. I had very little background in forgery investigation, and none in antiquarian documents. I learned much in both those fields by the time the case was over.

I could tell the story of the investigation of the *Oath* in a number of ways. I have chosen to tell it in the chronological order of the investigative events so that the reader will in effect become the detective doing the investigation. The reader will also appreciate the difficulties faced by our group during the investigation and will understand how we resolved the case and came to the conclusion that the Hofmann *Oath* was a forgery.

To set the scene for the investigation of the forgery of the *Oath of a Freeman*, I would like to note the key dates of this incredible tale. On Tuesday, October 15, 1985, at 8:10 a.m. Steven Christensen, a thirty-one-year-old Utah businessman and father of three, with a fourth on the way, was killed in his downtown Salt Lake City office by a bomb that exploded in his hands. Kathleen Sheets, the fifty-year-old wife of Christensen's former business partner and mother of four, was killed at her home in Salt Lake City by a bomb cradled in her left arm at approximately 9:45 the same morning. On the following day at 2:45 p.m., Mark Hofmann was seriously injured by a bomb that exploded in his car on a downtown Salt Lake City street. By that night, police officials stated publicly that Hofmann was the suspect in all three bombings. The police believed that Hofmann's bombing was accidental and that the bomb had been meant for a third victim.

The bombings of Christensen and Hofmann occurred in the jurisdiction of the Salt Lake City Police Department. Mrs. Sheets was killed outside the city in the jurisdiction of the sheriff's office. My involvement in these events began at 8:30 a.m. on October 15, when Detective Jim Bell and I were called to the scene of the crime at Christensen's office. I was assigned the investigation of Steven Christensen's murder. The next day, Bell was assigned the responsibility for the Hofmann car bombing. A task force of investigators was created from the staffs of the Bureau of Alcohol, Tobacco, and Firearms (ATF), the Federal Bureau of Investigation (FBI), the Salt Lake County Sheriff's Office (SLCSO), the Salt Lake County Attorney's Office, and the Salt Lake City Police Department (SLCPD). We then played out various roles in this real-life drama.

I will focus this narrative on how the *Oath of a Freeman* became a significant part of the investigation and a solution to not only the two murders but also the numerous frauds and forgeries credited to Hofmann. From time to time throughout the narrative, I will explain the context in which certain information surfaced, and how we regarded it in light of what else we knew at the time. I will comment on other parts of the investigation only to provide a context for the reader to understand the importance and timing of certain events in the murder investigation in relation to the investigation of the *Oath.*

Based on ATF bomb technician Jerry Taylor's observations about the three bombing scenes and about the recovered bomb components, some of which he said were sold exclusively by Radio Shack stores, SLCPD officers went to the company's nineteen Salt Lake stores on October 18 in the hope of determining who had purchased similar components. At a store near Hofmann's home, officers found a receipt for a mercury switch and a battery pack like those in the two bombs' components. The switch and battery pack had been purchased on October 7, 1985, by "M. Hansen," who gave a nonexistent address in the same neighborhood.

The first significant event in the investigation that related to the *Oath of a Freeman* also occurred on October 18. The task force made the second of three searches of Mark Hofmann's home in order to obtain documents, papers, pictures, diaries, devices, tools, or machines that could have been used for the alteration or production of documents. During the search, many cardboard boxes of property were taken from Hofmann's private, locked office in the basement. The more than ten thousand separate items found included personal notes, books, catalogues, financial records, magazines, newspapers, chemicals, a duplicating tool, and a quantity of stampless covers and other antique papers and documents. I was not present during the search, but I was informed that several boxes of materials remained in

131

Hofmann's office. Undoubtedly, materials related to the forgeries were left behind, because we had no expertise in forged antique paper documents. And it would be two months before forgery became factual evidence used to explain part of the motive in the case.

However, a number of pieces of paper taken during this search did become important evidence in the murder and forgery cases. Four of these bore the name "Hansen" or "Mike Hansen." Three days after the murders, we had developed enough evidence to be convinced that Mark Hofmann used aliases and that Mike Hansen was one of them. We also found evidence about the forgery of the *Oath*, but its importance was not clearly understood.

The Radio Shack receipt, with the information about the Hansen alias discovered in Hofmann's house, and other factors formed a pretty good circumstantial case against Hofmann. As I saw it, Hofmann was guilty and our next goal was to determine if he had worked alone.

By this time, the *Oath of a Freeman* had been mentioned in police interviews by Hofmann's friends and business associates. Neither I nor the other investigators knew what it was historically or textually. We didn't even know what it looked like, nor were we aware that he had used this *Oath* and a second one that he had printed to defraud several people. Those who spoke to us about the *Oath* did so with a great deal of respect and awe for its importance in American history and for its monetary value.

At the time, we were too busy to deal with the *Oath*. We had bombing evidence from three scenes, enough boxes of old papers and books from Hofmann's car and house to fill a small room stacked to the ceiling, and even a couple of pieces of papyrus. We were so ignorant of this world of antiquarian documents that a piece of papyrus was formally listed on Salt Lake City Police evidence files as a board. With more than one hundred investigators from various agencies working on the case and bits and pieces of information coming in from all over the country, the *Oath* was the last of my worries. Forgery was only one of many side issues at this time. The focus was on the investigation of the murders.

On October 21, an East Coast Americana collector, Michael Zinman, called the Salt Lake County Sheriff's office and spoke to Robert Jack, captain of detectives, who had also been designated as the task-force commander. (The SLCSO was responsible for the investigation of Kathleen Sheets's murder.) Jack sent me a memo stating simply that Zinman had information about Hofmann.

My next activity related to the *Oath* came on October 23. That morning I found Hofmann's Toyota van at his parent's home. We had obtained a search warrant for the car based on an eyewitness account of one of Kathleen Sheets's neighbors who had seen an identical van at Sheets's house the night before the bombings. This information had been obtained the day before, and a search warrant was immediately issued. When Hofmann's wife, Doralee, came out to leave in the vehicle, we told her we were impounding the van for the search. She asked for permission to retrieve a manila envelope from the van, saying it was very important because it contained the provenance for the *Oath of a Freeman*. Inside the envelope was a copy of a receipt from Argosy Bookstore dated March 13, 1985. The receipt listed, among other things, the *Oath of a Freeman* for $25. Another antique document, dated 1602, written in a handwriting that I could barely read, was with it. (See Appendix A.) My notes, which reflect my lack of knowledge at the time, say that this second document appeared to be the *Oath*. The documents were seized with the van.

On November 5, 1985, Deputy Salt Lake County Attorney Gerry d'Elia, Special Agent David Cummings of Alcohol, Tobacco, and Firearms, and I went to Justin Schiller and Raymond Wapner's gallery in New York and interviewed them. They told us of their deal with Hofmann for the purchase and resale of Charles Dickens's *The Haunted Man* manuscript and their investment in it. Schiller also told us of Hofmann's discovery of the *Oath of a Freeman*, and how they had become involved. Hofmann had made them partners in the ownership of the *Oath*, and they were now fifty percent owners with the marketing rights to it. They told us of a possible plan to sell the *Oath* to a large investor or a corporation that could use it in a marketing campaign by displaying it at the upcoming anniversary of the Statue of Liberty. They said that Hofmann owed them a great deal of money. Even so, and to my dismay, they said they would continue to deal with him as a customer if he walked in that day. An important point made by Schiller was that any sale of the *Oath* would have been a warranted sale and that Hofmann would not receive any money for a year after the transaction. Schiller and Wapner seemed to be very candid in the interview. We came away much better informed about the *Oath* and its status. We learned much later from Thomas Wilding, a Utah investor who will figure importantly in later events in this story, that Schiller and Wapner held back an important fact during the visit: they knew of and had seen a second copy of the *Oath*.

I was next contacted about the *Oath* on November 6, 1985, via a phone call from Michael Zinman, who explained that Justin Schiller had called him in the spring of 1985 about the *Oath*. Going to Schiller's gallery in New York City to look at the *Oath of a Freeman*, Zinman met Hofmann there with Schiller. (See Appendix B for the firsthand account by Zinman of the event, contained in a letter that he wrote to Keith Arbour of the American Antiquarian Society on November 25, 1985.) The letter was sent to me on December 5, although Zinman had already attempted to explain everything to me on the phone. In sum, Zinman said he had obtained a photocopy of the *Oath* at the time of his visit to the gallery. He also explained that Hofmann was knowledgeable about early American printing and, in fact, had a facsimile printing of *The Whole Booke of Psalmes* with Zoltan Harazti's *Enigma of the Bay Psalm Book* in hand. Hofmann further showed his expertise at this early date by showing Zinman the unusual and obscure similarity of the ornaments that border the *Oath* to those in chapter four of the Bay Psalm Book. Apparently Hofmann hid this expertise from others when he spoke to them about the *Oath*.

All this seems like relatively basic information to me now. However, I clearly remember that when Zinman was telling me about the significance of the *Oath* and the fact that he believed it was a forgery, I was, if not totally baffled, somewhat confused about what he was saying. In retrospect, I think he made it as clear as one could over the telephone. By the time he explained the arrival of the Cambridge press to America, the significance of *New-Englands Jonas Cast Up at London*, the printing of the *Oath* and *The Whole Booke of Psalmes*—which he said was the same as the Bay Psalm Book—I felt inundated by what I then thought was trivial information, and I was sorry he had called. He had convinced me that there was something to the forgery idea; but considering what we had on our hands at the time, it seemed totally impractical to do anything about it then. But he did get my attention, and I conveyed the information to my associates.

I was particularly interested in the date when Zinman had seen the *Oath*. Zinman was not entirely certain of it, only that it was just before the Sotheby's auction in the spring. I had found a catalogue for a sale at Sotheby's scheduled for March 27, 1985, in Hofmann's evidence. It listed a copy of the *New-Englands Jonas Cast Up at London* as a book for sale. (See Appendix C). After additional phone calls, Zinman and I were able to place his meeting with Schiller and Hofmann on the twenty-fifth or twenty-sixth of March.

On November 13, I participated in an interview with Shannon Flynn, a friend and business partner of Hofmann's, who explained how Hofmann had tried to get Wilford Cardon and Duke Cowley, two Mormon businessmen from Mesa, Arizona, to invest in the *Oath of a Freeman*. He also related the astonishing news that Hofmann had gone back to Argosy and found a second copy of the *Oath*, which he had wanted Flynn to help him market through some connections Flynn had in Brazil. Flynn and his wife had seen the second *Oath* around the end of September 1985. Flynn did not know where the second *Oath* was at the time of the interview, nor did we. Flynn was told by Hofmann around August 20, 1985, that the sale of the first *Oath* had been completed for $1.5 million with a down-payment of $150,000.

About this time, I found two photocopies of documents in the Hofmann evidence dealing with the *Oath*. One was a photocopy of the *Oath* like the one Zinman had seen. It was different in that it lacked some distinctive markings on the recto. Zinman explained to me that there was writing on the verso of the *Oath* and the ink had bled through to the recto. Those marks were strangely lacking in this photocopy. Hofmann's own writing surrounded the text, noting specific words as well as a note on punctuation and the number of words contained in the *Oath*. The other was a photocopy of the text of the *Oath* that appeared in a book. (See Appendix D). At the time, these documents did not seem to be of any great value, except as proof that he had done some research about the *Oath*, which seemed logical given the fact that he had found it.

On November 25, I again spoke with Zinman by phone. He had become convinced that the *Oath* was a fraud, and he suggested we use the American Antiquarian Society to help with the investigation. Again, by necessity,

I told Zinman that it would have to wait until the foundation of the murder investigation had been completed. We were still dealing with a circumstantial case and basically had to prove that no one except Hofmann could have killed Christensen and Sheets. It was a large task, and the entire world seemed to be watching.

On December 14, I spoke with Duke Cowley on the phone. Hofmann had become acquainted with Cowley and Cardon through Shannon Flynn. Cardon had been Flynn's religious supervisor in Brazil some years before. Cowley explained that Hofmann had tried to get him and Cardon to invest in a second copy of the *Oath*, telling them that he had already sold one copy of it. On the sixteenth, I spoke with Cardon, who told me he had learned that Hofmann had never told him about the real status of the first *Oath*. I assume that because Cardon and Cowley had already invested in another venture with Schiller and Wapner, Cardon probably would have learned from them that Hofmann was not the sole owner of the *Oath*, and so had not been telling the truth.

Early in December, we found a canceled personal check for $2 in Hofmann's evidence. (See Appendix F.) Dated March 8, 1985, it had been written by Hofmann to a company named DeBouzek and had been found in Hofmann's home. Detective John Foster contacted the firm, which is an engraving company not far from the police department. The check had been endorsed by Jean DeBouzek, the store owner. No item in the store sold for $2, and no store record could be found that showed how the check was used. Furthermore, no one could identify the nature of the transaction. Although personnel at DeBouzek were aware of the case and Mark Hofmann, none of them could place him at the store at any time. For the time being, that was the end of the investigation of the canceled check.

About the third week of December, George Throckmorton and William Flynn, both forensic document examiners assigned to the case, advised us that the antiquarian manuscript documents that had passed through Hofmann's hands were probably forgeries. They said they had many questions to resolve and a lot of work to do before they could prove it in court. They had observed an unusual cracking of the ink on the documents from Hofmann that was not found on any of the hundreds of other genuine old documents they had examined.

By this time in the investigation, we knew of major prosecutable frauds perpetrated by Hofmann through formal and informal limited partnership schemes. These frauds totaled hundreds of thousands of dollars. Hofmann had lured investors into a variety of fraudulent schemes involving joint purchases of valuable historical documents (some of Mormon history, some of early Americana), document collections, book collections, loans using his children's book collection with forged inscriptions as collateral, and items he had on consignment from others. He had used the *Oath* on at least three occasions to attempt to or to successfully get his hands on someone else's money.

135

Hofmann acquired a signature loan of $185,000 from a Salt Lake bank with the sanction of a Mormon Church official, Elder Hugh Pinnock. On June 28, 1985, with the help of Steven Christensen. Hofmann stated in the application that the Library of Congress was going to purchase a document he owned for $1.5 million in the very near future and that he would be able to repay the loan. He said the document was the *Oath of a Freeman*. The stated purpose of the loan was to buy the McLellin Collection (a group of manuscripts supposedly of great importance for understanding the early history of the Mormon religion). However, we had already learned Hofmann had claimed to have purchased the McLellin Collection in New York with another businessman's money in April 1985. Hofmann told Christensen, Pinnock, and others that the collection contained many historical documents that were very negative about the personal life of Joseph Smith.

I knew at the time that the Library of Congress and Schiller and Wapner had ceased negotiations to arrange a sale of the *Oath* as early as June 6, 1985. The American Antiquarian Society had then entered into negotiations with Schiller and Wapner, but no agreement had yet been reached.

Hofmann had been lying to top church officials, bank officers, Christensen, Schiller, Wapner, et al. Most importantly, here he was with what was supposed to be the earliest document printed in English in America, and he was poisoning it with his fraudulent activities. Although the physical evidence was lacking, the *Oath* looked very phony to me at this stage. I hoped that in the future I would have the opportunity to carry its investigation to a successful conclusion.

Hofmann's next fraud using the *Oath* involved a local Salt Lake City businessman, Thomas Wilding, and his associates. On September 12, 1985, Hofmann told them that a man named Lyn Jacobs had a second *Oath* for sale in New York and that if Hofmann wanted to buy it he had to be on a plane that night. Hofmann already owed the Wilding group about $200,000 from previous deals. He told them he needed another $150,000 or so to acquire the *Oath* from Jacobs. The profit incentive offered by Hofmann was too much for them to pass up, so they cut him a check. More poison.

By the time of the bombings, Hofmann had promised payment of many personal debts from the proceeds of the sale of the *Oath*. Those promises far exceeded the amount of money he could expect to receive from the sale of the *Oath*. During an eighteen-month period preceding the bombings, Hofmann's frauds generated $2 million. Although the sum was large, Hofmann kept only a small portion of that amount for his personal use. Most of the money coming in from one investor was going out to another. He sometimes doubled an investor's principal in order to set him up for an even bigger deal in the future. As in all such scams, Hofmann eventually could not find enough money to cover the promise. He had specifically set October 15 as the day on which he would pay some of his debts. He told others that he would pay them the day the McLellin Collection was sold. He needed to come up with about $1 million that week. Unfortunately, he could only find about $330,000. At an impasse, he chose murder as a solution.

Most of the frauds were cases in which it could be argued in court that it was one man's word against another's or a misunderstanding about the details of the deals. But one fraud we uncovered involved a solid piece of physical evidence that we could prove Hofmann had used fraudulently. It was Ken Rendell's papyrus, which he had consigned to Hofmann on September 16, 1985. Rendell, a Massachusetts manuscript dealer, had contacted us right after the bombings to tell us about his relationship with Hofmann. Prior to that call we had found two pieces of papyrus. One had been in the trunk of Hofmann's car at the time of the bombing. There was only smoke damage on the plastic cover that protected it. The other piece had been found in Steven Christensen's safe-deposit box on October 17, 1985. Rendell identified the four-by-nine-inch piece in the safe-deposit box as part of the papyrus he sent to Hofmann on consignment, which had originally measured about twenty-four by nine inches.

Rendell and his assistant, Leslie Kress, were extremely cooperative and provided the information we needed to determine the provenance of the papyrus and to be able to prove it. I eventually found about twenty-five people who had seen the altered papyrus and had been told by Hofmann or Shannon Flynn that it was related to the history of the Mormon Church. Others had been told that it belonged to the elusive McLellin Collection. Hugh Pinnock, who had sanctioned the loan for the McLellin Collection, confirmed that Hofmann had told him and Steven Christensen that the papyrus in Christensen's safe-deposit box was part of the McLellin Collection. The Church official specified that it was something known as Facsimile Two in the Mormon Church's history. However, we knew that it came from a collection of Egyptian artifacts that at one time was owned by an Englishman named Solomon Pottesman and that Rendell had acquired the entire collection from Bernard Quaritch, Ltd., in London.

Rendell and Christensen knew each other because Rendell had authenticated the Martin Harris letter, also known as the Salamander Letter. Hofmann supposedly found it and then sold it to Christensen. With the papyrus, we had solid physical evidence that Hofmann was a fraud; and with the connection between Rendell and Christensen, there was a possible motive for Christensen's murder. Meanwhile, Hofmann had just passed his infamous polygraph test; and the defense attorneys and polygraph examiners were touting his innocence and telling us we had the wrong guy. Did we have a surprise in store for them.

I have digressed from the *Oath*, but I thought it was important to make the point that we knew with certainty what we had on our hands. Mark Hofmann was a total fraud. We also knew we had a long haul ahead when the county attorney's office nevertheless refused to file any charges.

About January 2, 1986, Zinman provided me with books on the history of the Cambridge Press and a facsimile of the Bay Psalm Book with Harazti's *Enigma of the Bay Psalm Book*. He told me that Charles Hamilton, a New York manuscript dealer, suggested how the *Oath* could have been forged using a photoengraved plate. Zinman also explained how simply ink is

137

made. Carbon for the ink could be obtained by burning wood from a period piece of furniture. He said that old paper is abundant. Combine these items and one would have the materials for a forgery. He suggested that if we could duplicate the broadside then we could prove it was a forgery. I suggested that with his expertise he should make it. He laughed and told me that if he made it he would sell it.

As the end of January arrived, we were promised that criminal charges would soon be filed against Hofmann. Throckmorton and Flynn had found out why the ink on the manuscripts had cracked and had put together a case they could take to court.

I contacted Keith Arbour of AAS, who told me that he had been a supporter of the *Oath* as a genuine document until recently. Based on scholarly research, he now had reversed his opinion and had come to the conclusion that it was a forgery. First, he believed that the use of the word "stablished" in the Schiller broadside was not proper. He explained to me the use of meter in the Bay Psalm Book and that the use of "stablished" in that format was proper, but not in the text of the *Oath*, which is not in meter. He also told me that the placement of the ornaments around the *Oath* is known in only one other place, the title of chapter four of the Bay Psalm Book, a fact that Hofmann had known. Arbour's conclusion about the *Oath* was that it was a modern-day forgery for two reasons. The forger had tried to tie the *Oath* to the Bay Psalm Book by using two unique characteristics found in it only four pages apart, and the forger had done so in ignorance of the use of the word "stablished" in meter form. (See Appendix D.)

Arbour explained to me his "ABC" theory. (See Appendix E.) The manuscript in the *Oath*, as adopted by the colony in 1634, contained a specific text. The next known text, which matches the manuscript version, is found in the printing of *New-Englands Jonas Cast Up at London*, printed in 1647. Arbour suggested a line of logic. By using the 1634 version as A and the 1647 version as C, then if Version B, having been written or printed between those dates, were discovered, the text should match the other two. Hofmann's version as B was not a match and therefore did not follow Arbour's model. Certainly, this would not be conclusive evidence but, combined with other factors, would weigh against the validity of B as the genuine document. Arbour sent me a letter explaining his theory in more detail. What was very important to me about this exchange was that someone with his degree of expertise was in our camp. We needed the recruits. It was also apparent that Arbour was going against the generally held feeling (at that time, at least) that the *Oath* was genuine, and I respected the forthrightness of his opinion. My notes indicated Arbour thought the purchase at Argosy Bookstore might have been a plant.

On February 4, 1986, charges were filed against Mark Hofmann and we took him into custody. He was charged with twenty-eight felonies, two of which carried the death penalty. Many more charges could have been filed, but enough was enough. He was released on bail four days later.

The investigation continued at full strength. On February 19, 1986, a breakthrough in the case took place. Papers found in Hofmann's home led to phone calls that revealed further evidence substantiating the investigators' theory that Hofmann was Mike Hansen.

The calls determined that a Mike Hansen had ordered photoengraved plates of Deseret currency in Denver, Colorado, in May and June 1984. Shortly after those orders were placed, Mark Hofmann sold sets of Deseret currency to several purchasers. The discovery of this information opened the door to the uncovering of many printed forgeries. Many of those printed forgeries had handwriting that also was forged. Michael Zinman's desire to prove the *Oath* was a forgery was starting to become more important to the case.

After finding a canceled check to Salt Lake Stamp, a local printing company, we searched its premises and found evidence that we would later tie to Hofmann's printed forgeries. One order was done in his own name. Another was in Mike Hansen's name. We also later found Hofmann's fingerprint on the Hansen work order. While at Salt Lake Stamp, we learned some good news. There were only two photoengraving stores in Salt Lake: Utah Printing and DeBouzek.

Up to this point, I had been reluctant to search all the printing companies in Salt Lake where I though Hofmann might have had plates made; and so I was very relieved to find out there were only two. Also, I hadn't believed Hofmann would use local sources since he traveled so often. After finding his use of Salt Lake Stamp, the idea of searching the stores' records was a little more appealing. But I still wasn't too enthusiastic about the idea, because we had already been to DeBouzek in December and had found nothing.

One of the prosecutors assigned to the case was David Biggs. I had been asked to bring Biggs along if I went to the printing business for investigative work. I called Biggs and told him I was going to DeBouzek to see if anyone could identify Hofmann's suspected printed forgeries. I thought that in the process of making a plate an engraver would become familiar with it. Since Hofmann's products were not part of run-of-the-mill wedding invitations or logos, an engraver might remember the work.

Biggs and I contacted Jack Smith, who had been a photoengraver for forty-one years with DeBouzek. After explaining our purpose, we showed Smith the photocopy of the *Oath* that Zinman had sent. Smith looked at it for fifteen or twenty seconds. He then looked at me with a quizzical expression and said confidently: "I made that." My hopes were building. Smith excused himself for a few minutes and returned with a negative of the *Oath*. The photocopy and the negative were identical except for the lack of marks made by the bleeding through from the writing on the verso of the *Oath*.

Printed at the top, and centered above the title, were the words "Hansen #4." The phrase was covered with red cellophane to keep it from showing up on a photosensitive plate. At the bottom, under the text of the *Oath*, was a typed inscription. It read: "This 'Quaker Catichism' (*sic*) was printed opposite the title-page in the 1653 edition of Cotton's book. Enlarged." (See Appendix F.) Smith excused himself again and returned with the combined work order and receipt, dated March 25, 1985. The customer was Mike Hansen. Smith also presented us with another *Oath of a Freeman* negative and the receipt. (See Appendix F.) This *Oath* had the same title; however, the text did not resemble the Schiller *Oath*, and was in verses that started out with "Give thanks all ye people." It looked like a poem.

The receipt was the most interesting part to me. Mike Harris was the customer this time. Here was a new Hofmann alias for us. There was a phone number on it. It was Mark Hofmann's home phone number, with which I was intimately familiar. The best part was that March 8, 1985, was the date five days before Mark Hofmann supposedly so innocently purchased the *Oath of a Freeman* at the Argosy Bookstore. Arbour was a prophet.

Gerry D'Elia and I returned to DeBouzek to complete the search of the files. We found two more orders by Mike Hansen for printing plates that we tied to two other documents that had gone through Mark Hofmann's hands. More negatives for printing plates were found in Salt Lake and in Kansas City, all ordered by Mike Hansen.

Since we had subpoenaed Hofmann's travel records from a local travel agency, I was able to consult them and found that Hofmann had purchased airline tickets to New York. One trip was from Salt Lake on March 11, 1985, with the return flight on March 13. The next was on March 26, 1985, at 6:30 a.m.

We now had a pretty good argument substantiating the following scenario: Hofmann ordered the "give thanks" *Oath* on March 8 at DeBouzek; made the document; flew to New York on the eleventh; planted it at Argosy; bought it on the thirteenth; flew to Salt Lake; made the artwork for the Schiller *Oath*; sent a photocopy to Schiller without the writing on the verso; ordered the plate from DeBouzek on the twenty-fifth; produced the document that night; traveled back to New York on the twenty-sixth; showed it to Schiller and Zinman; and then had dinner with them that evening. To help in discussions with other investigators, I took to calling the *Oath* in Schiller's possession simply "the *Oath*." The "Give thanks all ye people" version I called "*Oath* Jr."

Many tasks remained to resolve the forgery of the *Oath of a Freeman* beyond a reasonable doubt. None was more important than having our forensic document examiners, Throckmorton and Flynn, examine the *Oath* itself. I contacted Schiller's attorneys about arranging an examination, but no agreement could be reached. We were willing to see it anywhere, any time, any place; but apparently we had too many restrictions to satisfy them. The American Antiquarian Society, through Marcus McCorison, offered to arrange an examination on a formal basis, which was satisfactory to us. However, it was not to be. Eventually an examination was done, but not until after the preliminary hearing.

Late in March, additional charges were filed against Hofmann based on the evidence we had discovered about the printed forgeries. They were scheduled to be heard in court along with the previously filed charges. The *Oath* was not charged, although the Mike Hansen/Mike Harris evidence associated with the *Oath* would be used to build the circumstantial case against Hofmann.

I became concerned, due to the very defensive attitude and posture of the Schiller/Wapner camp, that we were in for a giant battle to overcome their position. I believed that Throckmorton and Flynn should take on another expert to beef up the odds of getting the *Oath* forgery resolved more quickly and with fewer difficulties. Throckmorton and Flynn were completely inundated with preparing for the upcoming preliminary hearing in which they were going to have to put their entire careers on the line, and I thought that it wouldn't hurt to give them an extra hand. I passed my thoughts on to Salt Lake County Attorney Ted Cannon, who was head of the office in charge of prosecuting Hofmann. Cannon was also a major asset to our investigative team once we got into the printed forgeries, because he had been a printer by trade for seventeen years prior to becoming a lawyer. He often made valuable observations to speed up our understanding of the printed forgeries. Cannon informed me that my idea was acceptable and that I should find the expert. I contacted the local head of the ATF office, Jerry Miller, and asked him if they had someone in their national lab who could do the job. He notified me that Marvin Rennert might be available.

One of the loose ends in the investigation of the *Oath* that I wanted to tie up was "*Oath* Jr." I had wondered what the text of "*Oath* Jr." was in reality, and if we could possibly find out where and when Hofmann had acquired it.

Arbour told me that Arthur Schrader of the Sonneck Society could probably help me with it. I contacted him by phone, and he told me the text was probably that of a post-Civil War hymn. He referred me to Dr. Wayne Shirley of the Library of Congress. I contacted Dr. Shirley, briefed him on the overall problem, and asked for his assistance. He told me that all of the music stored in the Library of Congress could be accessed by the first line of a song or hymn. I sent him a copy of the text. He responded by sending me a photocopy of "The President's Hymn" housed at the Library of Congress. (See Appendix G). It was the text of "*Oath* Jr." with a different title, and had been commissioned by Abraham Lincoln at the end of the Civil War.

An examination made clear that the copy at the Library of Congress was not Hofmann's source. Dr. Shirley informed me that most state historical societies had a copy of this particular hymn and that still other copies could be in private hands. I decided not to pursue this angle any further.

A constant problem in this case, as in most murder cases, was ordering priorities. It was usually a problem of crisis management. There were always hundreds of things to do at the same time in the Hofmann case. The order of priorities changed continually as new information or evidence came to light. I seldom got to take a part of the case to its logical conclusion, as I would have liked.

One of my priorities was to locate Hofmann's source for the photocopy of the text of the *Oath* found in his house. I had noticed earlier that at the top of the photocopy the phrase was "New-Englands Jonas Cast Up at London." I was quite certain what it was: the text of the *Oath* as found in this seventeenth-century book. I then needed to know which copy of the book Hofmann used to make the photocopy. If I knew where and when, it could be very important, especially if Hofmann had obtained it before he allegedly knew anything about the *Oath*.

I contacted the New York Public Library and had several helpful conversations with Miriam Mandelbaum of the Rare Book Section. Eventually, I asked her to send me a photocopy of the page containing the *Oath*'s text in the New York Library's copy of *New-Englands Jonas Cast Up at London*. Throckmorton compared the two for me and verified that they matched because of the similarities between the two versions' many flaws from wear, aging, etc. I was not able to identify the date when Hofmann obtained that photocopy.

Another question that Rennert and Zinman posed to me was whether or not Hofmann had taken a facsimile printing of the Bay Psalm Book and cut it up to make the *Oath*. Rennert and I decided to look at the possibility that Hofmann cut up whole words to construct the *Oath*. The most prominent word from my point of view, because of Arbour's observations, was 'stablished.' Hofmann was a frequent user of the New York Public Library, so I requested Mandelbaum to take a photograph of the page with the word 'stablished' from the New York Public Library's copy of the Bay Psalm Book. Rennert looked at it. His opinion was that if Hofmann had used whole words, this was not one of his sources. The juxtaposition of the letters was clearly different.

I had several conversations during the next few weeks with James Gilreath of the Library of Congress. I was curious about what he and his staff had concluded about their study of the *Oath* that made them believe the *Oath* was genuine. He was, of course, curious about what we had that made the *Oath* a forgery.

Gilreath told me that so far they had found nothing wrong with the type in the *Oath*. It matched the Bay Psalm Book, although if I recall correctly, they had not found exact matches to any letters in the book. He explained that one of the stronger reasons to believe that it was genuine was the bite of the type. First of all, it was the proper depth for the press that it was allegedly produced on; and secondly, and most importantly, there was a slight variation in the depth of the bite of the individual letters. He and his staff did not think that a forger could have been that exact.

We discussed chain lines in the paper of both the Bay Psalm Book and the *Oath*. He told me that they were not an exact match. This was not unexpected, he explained, because apparently the paper brought over to America for the Cambridge Press was acquired from several different sources and therefore differences would be natural. The paper was consistent with what one would expect to be used to print the *Oath*. I explained to Gilreath that in Hofmann's evidence we had found a book that taught papermaking, and that by reading about chain lines in it I had gained a rudimentary understanding about them. I also explained that Hofmann appeared to have been aware of bite depth since he actually had a type-depth gauge.

After speaking at length with Gilreath, I told him of the discovery of the negatives and of the Mike Hansen aliases, etc. I felt with him, as I had with some other people in the case, that disclosure of some evidence was much more important than simply asking them to trust my opinion. I shared a fair amount of information that was known only to the investigative team.

Gilreath provided the county attorney's office with a copy of the Library of Congress's report on the examination of the *Oath* and high-quality photocopies of the photographic documentation made during that examination. (See Appendix H.) This was beneficial for our understanding of their point of view about the apparently valid aspects of the forgery.

Zinman told me of a rumor that Hofmann had acquired the *Oath*, used it to make a negative, and then in his greed made a second *Oath*. This rumor alleged Hofmann had obtained the *Oath* from the Mormon Church in his dealings. He then made up a copy to be planted and obtained the receipt, because he could not disclose the true provenance.

On April 11, 1986, David Biggs told me to go to George Throckmorton's house at 9:00 p.m. with all of the evidence and the case file on the *Oath of a Freeman*. He told me that he had learned from Thomas Wilding that Wilding and Associates owned the second *Oath*. The second *Oath* would be at Throckmorton's house that night for examination, and Throckmorton needed the negative of the *Oath* from DeBouzek to do a comparison.

I did as requested and met Throckmorton, Wilding, and sergeants Mike George and Dick Forbes from the Salt Lake County Attorney's Office. George informed me that he had flown with Wilding to Idaho that day and picked up the second *Oath* from an associate of Wilding.

Wilding told me that Hofmann had given him the second *Oath* not long before the bombings as collateral against the money Hofmann owed him. It must have been after Shannon Flynn and his wife saw it at the end of September 1985, because Wilding had not relinquished control of it. Wilding said he had taken the second *Oath* and shown it to Schiller in New York not long after the bombings.

Throckmorton's conclusion that night after he made the examination was that the second *Oath* had been made from the negative. Throckmorton had explained to me a number of times after we began finding negatives that certain characteristics are transmitted from a negative to any product. Multiple products bear the same traits that descend from the negative, as well as some that appear during the printing process. He explained that the traits are microscopic and that they would not have been passed on in the photographic process. He called these traits trash marks.

The preliminary hearing got under way on April 14, 1986, the same day the US bombed Libya. The early focus of the hearing was the murders. Later, the documents and frauds were brought in. The preliminary hearing lasted until May 22, 1986, when Judge Paul Grant bound Hofmann over for trial. The investigation continued throughout the hearing.

On April 15, I called Gilreath about using an expert at the Library of Congress to look at the Wilding *Oath*. He invited us to come to Washington. We decided not to. We had hoped they would send someone to our location. The cost of the investigation was getting exorbitant and the trip was not a necessity.

We kept ourselves apprised of most of the activities having to do with the *Oath* that were outside our arena. On April 17, we received information that the Schiller-Wapner *Oath* was being tested using of the cyclotron at the University of California at Davis. I was also informed that Rennert would be joining the document examiners' team. He arrived on April 19 and looked at the evidence about the *Oath* at Throckmorton's house. Bill Flynn was there with Throckmorton. Rennert was given an introduction to the general document investigation by Flynn and Throckmorton, and Flynn had his first opportunity to see the negative of the *Oath*.

On the twentieth, Rennert called me and told me that he, too, had determined that the second *Oath* had been made from the negative. Rennert said that a flaw had been found in the emulsion of the negative, and that the flaw was transferred during the photographic process to the etched magnesium plate. Then, it had actually been transferred in the printing process to the *Oath*. Good-quality representations that I had seen of the Schiller copy displayed the flaw prominently. That fact would damn the *Oath* in New York with no other evidence needed.

Pending the formal examination of the Schiller copy, the forensic experts could state that the negative was the master from which both known copies of the *Oath* descended. The flaw was not a characteristic that could be transferred from one *Oath* to the negative and then to the second *Oath*. This ruled out the possibility that Hofmann might have found a genuine copy of the broadside, had a negative made, and then produced a bogus second copy. The flaw was inherent in the materials of the negative, which generated the characteristic in the finished products. Both copies were children of the negative.

Finally, negotiations had progressed enough that an examination of the Schiller *Oath* was scheduled for June 25, 1986. Throckmorton and Rennert met at the United States Postal Laboratory in New York City, where they examined the *Oath* for an hour, concluding that it was a forgery. Their determination was made from observing the trash marks and the flaw from the negative, as well as the cracked ink on the verso caused by Hofmann's having artificially aged the iron gall ink.

The sale of the *Oath* by Argosy Bookstore was investigated twice: once earlier in the year by ATF Special Agent David Cummings, stationed in New York, and a second time in July by sergeants Mike George and Dick Forbes of the Salt Lake County Attorney's Office. It was determined that Vera Marvin made the sale and filled out the handwritten receipt. Marvin remembered the sale because Hofmann had asked for the receipt, and handwritten receipts are provided only upon request. Marvin had made out fewer than two dozen handwritten receipts in seven years at Argosy.

Hofmann had specifically requested the receipt. Marvin was shown the *Oath* and "*Oath* Jr." by George and Forbes. When shown the *Oath*, she said that she didn't recognize it; but when shown the "*Oath* Jr." she said the item she sold was about its length. However, she did not identify it with certainty. She also did not identify Hofmann as the purchaser but said the buyer did physically resemble him.

Hofmann had had problems of provenance on a few of his other documents. It appeared that he tried to take care of this problem in the case of the *Oath* by trying to provide an actual provenance. In retrospect, his special request for a receipt at Argosy cast suspicion on his innocence. Hofmann was not known for keeping good financial records, and so his deliberate effort to document the sale of the *Oath* immediately raised doubts about the authenticity of the broadside.

We had seen a Silver Reed typewriter during the searches of Hofmann's home. Having observed the typed words on several of Hofmann's negatives, including the statement at the bottom of the *Oath* negative, we wondered whether these typewritten notes could be matched to a sample of type from the typewriter we'd seen in the house. In the fall, I arranged through Hofmann's attorneys to obtain the typewriter and have it examined by Throckmorton. Throckmorton concluded that the type on the negatives was consistent with samples taken from Hofmann's typewriter. He explained that the type on the negatives matched the brand of typewriter and type ball Hofmann owned. Due to the good quality of the modern typewriter balls and their lack of flaws, he could not say that Hofmann's typewriter was the exact source.

Although enough evidence had been developed to put the case against the *Oath* to rest in our minds, other work was brought to light after this examination. Roderick J. McNeil, a man who seemed to be a master of many things, entered into our investigation. McNeil, who lives in Montana, had developed a technique for determining the approximate length of time that iron gall ink has been on paper. This subject was a critical matter in the Hofmann forgeries, since nearly all of his forgeries involved the use of iron gall ink. If McNeil could use his tests on Hofmann's forgeries and his results were as we expected them to be, we would have bolstered the case tremendously with additional scientific evidence.

McNeil's examination used a scanning auger electron microscope to measure the migration of ions from the written line of iron gall ink. He examined Hofmann documents and obtained the results we expected. The ink was applied to the paper substantially later than the alleged dates. This set of tests did not include the Schiller *Oath*, but it did include the Wilding *Oath*.

McNeil first saw the Schiller *Oath* in November 1986. He performed no tests on it at that time but did test in it early 1987. The printing ink had enough iron in it to enable it to be tested as easily as the iron gall ink on the verso. Both tests indicated that the *Oath* was not genuine.

During the rest of 1986 we continued to smooth out the case for the expected trial, set for the following March. In the fall of 1987, the New York District Attorney's Office became involved in the case at our request. We thought that the additional pressure that would be brought to bear on the

Hofmann defense team if multiple jurisdictions had charges filed against Hofmann would work to our advantage. Also, New York was probably the appropriate arena for the prosecution of the forgery of the first *Oath*. Most of the witnesses lived in that area, and a major part of the crime actually took place there. Our attorneys therefore contacted the district attorney's office in New York, and its staff began collecting the information needed to prosecute the case. Grand jury subpoenas were sent out to some of us as witnesses, but we never appeared in New York because of what transpired in Salt Lake City.

Just before Christmas of 1986, we were informed that a plea agreement was being negotiated, which eventually came to fruition in January 1987. Hofmann pled guilty to the murders and to two counts of fraud. In exchange for his plea, the death penalty was dropped, and he promised to disclose everything about the crimes with which he had been charged and matters related to those crimes.

The plea agreement, negotiated by lead prosecutor Robert Stott, did not allow anyone except the attorneys to interview Hofmann. My questions would be asked by proxy. The interviews began in February 1987 and ended months later when Hofmann refused to answer more questions. Just after the interviews began, I received a phone call from Nicolas Barker of The British Library. He was working in the Los Angeles area and wanted to tell me about his examination of the *Oath of a Freeman*. He also wanted to know what we had discovered.

The plea agreement had stepped up public pressure. Everyone was trying to find out what Hofmann was saying before it would be formally made public. Because of that constraint, I asked Barker if he could wait until the confessions had progressed significantly. We agreed to meet in the spring before he returned to England.

We did so early in June. Barker and I spent the entire day together going over the case. He shared his evidence with Jim Bell, George Throckmorton, and me, explaining his background and expertise in early printed documents. He had seen and examined the Schiller *Oath* in July 1986, and he had determined that it was a forgery for several reasons that he had told Schiller. He outlined those reasons to me and provided a report that explained his findings in depth.*

The results of the Hofmann interviews were published at the end of July 1987. Hofmann was questioned about the *Oath* during those interviews, confessing to forging it. He gave his account of his research: the making of both *Oath*s and "*Oath* Jr.," including the composition of the ink, the source of the paper, the printing of the document, the making of the original artwork, and more. He also provided his version of the marketing of the *Oath*. In summary, the investigation of the *Oath* proved the document to be a forgery in several ways, including scholarly examination, printing errors, fo-

* *Editor's Note:* Nicolas Barker would not allow the report he gave Farnsworth to be reproduced in this volume.

rensic evidence, fraudulent marketing, and the confession of the forger.

An overall look at Mark Hofmann's career is also helpful in seeing how the *Oath* fits into the big picture. Hofmann's operation with the forged *Oath* was about the same as the one he used in other forgeries. He usually dangled the bait before his victims. Unreasonably large profits were available to the victim if he chose to invest or get involved in a document deal. In the case of the *Oath*, Justin Schiller and Raymond Wapner ended up doing all the work in marketing and authenticating the *Oath* while Hofmann sat back and waited for his share of the money.

The major documents forged by Hofmann, which he claimed to have found, divided into three categories. The first occurred when Hofmann identified a set of circumstances in history, usually Mormon history, that could possibly have occurred and then created a document to fit the situation. A good example was the Martin Harris 1830 letter, known as the Salamander Letter, Hofmann's most significant Mormon find, which alters the known history of Joseph Smith's first vision. The second category was his use of a document that was known to have once existed, but whose whereabouts and text were unknown. He then made up a transcript to fit the known facts and created the document. An example was the Joseph Smith III blessing, a document that authorized the succession of the leadership of the Mormon Church. The third category, which included the *Oath*, was when Hofmann identified an unlocated document that had a known text, and he then made an appropriate artifact. In this case, he made more than one.

Hofmann was credited with finding many valuable historical documents. The *Oath* was his most important find. He did buy some valuable items and he sold some, occasionally after he altered them by adding pages and inscriptions. In reality, he found no valuable historical documents.

Hofmann was a complete fraud in representing himself to be a good Mormon. In all of his dealings, he deceived his family, his best friends, and all of his associates. He tried to rearrange the known history of the Mormon Church. He has dampened the market for Mormon documents and has had a negative impact on the Americana market.

Hofmann has affected the lives of an inestimable number of people by his criminal activity. Religious convictions have been disturbed. Reputations have been tainted and ruined. Jobs have been lost. Businesses have been financially depleted. Families have been destroyed, and lives have been lost. For these losses Mark Hofmann is spending the rest of his natural life in prison.

Proper credit cannot be given, nor can I personally express enough gratitude, for the work done by so many people who contributed to the resolution of this case. I worked with an amazingly talented group of investigators and lawyers and then had the good fortune and pleasure to deal with many others outside of the criminal justice system who helped put all the pieces of the puzzle together. I hope I have acknowledged their efforts sufficiently in this chronicle.

147

APPENDIX A

Evidence from Mark Hofmann's Van
(Photocopy of 1602 Document Reduced)

OLD AND RARE BOOKS

ARGOSY BOOK STORE, INC.
116 EAST 59th STREET • NEW YORK, N.Y. 10022 • (212) PLAZA 3-4455

Sold to:

3/13/F1
INVOICE

For Mayor	5 —
For Representatives	5 —
Oath of 2 Free Men	25 —
George Washington – port	7 50
Martha Washington – port.	5 00
a	47 50
the –	3 92
↑	51 42

Pd.

Mense Aprilis Anno R: R: nae Elizabeth: xxxvij.

James Digges one of the messengers of her
Maiestes Chamber ordinary allowance for being
sent &c with letters for the messadge to the
Comaundement of the right hoble the Lorde
Tresorer of England from the Court at
Whitehall to & beyond London, to the
right worll mr Nicholas Gorges at
his house neere Morney where he
delivered the same, And so retorned
with Answere, as appeareth he said &c.
James Digges for it to be allowed
for his travaile therein paines taken
rated by mr William Killigrew
and paid by one of the Tellers of
her Maiesties receipte as aforesaid.

T. Buckhurst

mr Taylor I pray you pay three poundes
on disbursementes &c

Wm: Killigrew

Jhon m [illegible] xxviij
Novr 1612

J. Buckhurst Lord Treasurer Queen Elizabeth
Sackvile Lord Buckhurst afterwardes Earl of Dorset

APPENDIX B

Michael Zinman's Letter to Keith Arbour

Zinman's Photocopy of the 'Oath' with His Notations

CONFIDENTIAL — NO DISTRIBUTION *for your files*
mike Zinman

November 25th 1985

Dear Keith,

You asked that I put down on paper what transpired when first I
saw the Oath, and I will try and do so, as I believe it may prove
useful in the future.

Without attempting to pinpoint the date from memory, I can tell
you that one Monday or Tuesday evening earlier this year Justin
Schiller called me and told me that he thought a customer of
his had found the Freeman's Oath.

He said it in an understated but excited way, and asked if I
would or could come down and see it that night.

[You can fix the date because the next day *Augsme* he went to the NYPL
and had Frank Matson withdraw the Bay Psalm Book from an exhibition
case - this was on Tuesday or Wednesday, I remember, and Matson
can probably more accurately find the exact date]

Schiller's call came in the late afternoon, about 4 or 4:30,
and there was no reason for him to believe I could or would come
down. To this day I can't explain why in fact I did go, but go
I did. I got to the Gallery about 5 or 5:30, and was introduced
to Mark Hoffmann by Justin. I don't recall who else was there,
but I don't think Ray was.

Shiller had the document out on his desk to the right of the
entranceway, and Hoffmann showed it to me. My instant reaction
was that it was no good, and I said so. My first question was
where did it come from, and I got this story ~~that~~ *about* Hoffmann, who
Schiller said was a coin dealer from Utah, and a customer of
Justin's for rare childrens books.

I think Justin related the story about how Hoffman presumably
purchased the Oath and found out what it was. Hoffman was present
at all times during this conversation. What was said was that
Hoffmann had come to New York to look over some lots at Sothebys,
or even possibly to do some coin business, and had stopped at
Argosy Bookstore to browse around. He said that he purchased
a few items, one of them being a broadside which he said had
been in a file of 18th century English Broadsides. As I recall
he said he had purchased only broadsides, and showed me a bill
while I was at the Gallery with the item listed as "Oath of a
Freeman" for $25. It was, as I remember the 3rd or 4th line
down of items bought, but I can't remember if there was a name
on the bill.

In fact, I did not see the invoice itself, but rather a xerox
copy of the invoice with the Oath below it. Freemann gave me
later that evening that particular copy of the Oath, tearing off
the top part which had the invoice from Argosy. I still have
the xerox of the Oath, I mean the one he gave me.

Back to the story.

Hoffmann or Justin related to me that after Hoffmann's trip to
New York, he was reading the Sotheby Catalog on the flight home,
and saw the New England's Jonas cataloged. He said he remembered
it jogging a familiar thread, and I seem to recall thathe said
that he had recently purchased a document very much like that, and
that when he got to Utah, he looked at what he had previously
bought and it was basically what was written up in the Sotheby
Catalog.

[One point. I am sure Hoffmann said he did not have the oath
with him when he flew back to Utah with the Catalog. Now, we can
most probably find out when he flew back, and we can find out
when the catalog became available. It would be interesting to
check out the date of the Argosy invoice and see if it falls
into a believeable time frame, that is sufficiently before the
Sotheby Catalog, and of a time that Hoffman can prove he was in
New York.]

Anyway, Hoffmann told me that he did some checking in Utah, and
was more and more excited, and as he did not know anything about
this sort of stuff, contacted Justin, who contacted me.

Well, among the first questions I asked him was why was the paper ↗ That is, what was the physical condition he found the oath in
so white, and how did he find it. He told me that it was glued
to a lousy cheap type of cardboard (my words, but my impression
of what he described is correct) and that when he soaked it off
in Salt Lake City, the chemical reaction of the paper and the
water must have naturally bleached the paper, inferring that it
was yellower or darker before he washed it. He specifically answered when
~~stressed when~~ I asked him whether he had bleached it, and he denied
it emphatically, saying the color of the paper came out in the
wash. I asked him if he had the cardboard, but he said he didnt
know at the time of the value of the Oath, and so had thrown it
out.

I then commented on the fact that whatever form the Oath might
have appeared, it would not be as I saw it then, at least in my
mind, and I questioned specifically the ornamental border and the
right hand justification. Hoffmann then showed me how a similar
type border appeared on the title page of the Psalm Book, and
then showed me where it appeared in an exact duplicate, in book
four, I recall. The point was that he had the Harazti book at
the Gallery and pointed out the border and I believe the type
face.

Justin pointed out that he was very excited about it because he
felt he knew 17th century handschrift, and that the ms inscription
on the verso of the document was just that.

We went round and round,and I kept handling the Oath (I never
did swear to it, though), and I recall that either or both
Justin or Mark pointed out the similarity of the type of the
Oath and the Psalm Book.

Most importantly, I was made aware of Hoffmann's ignorance
in not only early American imprints, but books as well, and that
he only dabbled in documents from time to time, having his main
business as a coin dealer.

Anyway, after a while we went out to dinner and a discussion
took place about the value of the document. It again was my
impression that Hoffmann and Schiller were looking to compare
its value in some way to the Psalm Book, and did I have an idea
of what the Psalm Book was worth. I told them I thought it
was worth about 1 to 1.2 million dollars, and that the Oath was
of equal or somewhat greater value. When asked, I said I would
rather have the Psalm Book, but others might not. It was my
feeling thatthey had tentatively set a price for the Oath in the
500 thousand range, but raised it after my discussion.

Another impression. I think when Justin called me no one else
had seen or heard of the Oath. He said the next day that he had
spoken with the Library of Congress and I believe they were
coming up to see it immediately. Again, it might be useful to
see if the dates jibe.

I think that's all I can recall, at least at this late hour.
My impression of Hoffmann is a puzzling one, when I think of it
at this moment. He was a very quiet person, and did not volunteer
much, letting Justin do most of the talking. I don't want to
consider if I was set up, which I amy have been, because I don't
think I have the antennae to sense that sort of stuff, and my
guess would have no real foundation in fact.

What followed is known to others, and the peculiar history of
the Oath and its travels can be documented elsewhere.

The best news is that I learned yesterday that as is usually
the case, when something of such a momentous nature occurs, it
brings other examples to light. Well, I was told another copy
of the Oath was known. Seems Mr. Hoffmann found two of them,
and had sold a share in the second one to a Salt Lake Individual.

How marvellous. I think that the AAS should consider a proper
medal of recognition be presented to Mr Hoffmann (with a
duplicate struck in anticipation for his next discovery)

THE OATH OF A FREEMAN.

I. A.B. being (by Gods providence) an Inhabitant, and Freeman, within the iurisdiction of this Common-wealth, doe freely acknowledge my selfe to bee subiect to the govenement thereof, and therefore doe heere sweare, by the great & dreadfull name of the Everliving-God, that I will be true & faithfull to the same, & will accordingly yield assistance & support thereunto, with my person & estate, as in equity I am bound: and will also truely indeavour to maintaine and preserve all the libertyes & privilidges thereof, (submitting my selfe to the wholesome lawes, & ordres made & stablished by the same, and surther, that I will not plot, nor practise any evill against it, nor consent to any that shall soe do, butt will timely discover, & reveall the same to lawefull authoritee nowe here stablished, for the speedic preventing thereof. Moreover, I doe solemnly binde my selfe, in the sight of God, that when I shalbe called, to give my voyce touching any such matter of this state, (in which freemen are to deale) I will give my vote & suffrage as I shall iudge in myne owne conscience may best conduce & tend to the publick weale of the body, without respect of persoanes, or favour of any man. Soe help mee God in the Lord Iesus Christ.

Handwritten annotations:

This is The first copy
of the freemans oath I gave to me
private 14½ mm I gave to me
of Justin Schiller's -
The top part applied if had
Bill showing of
The A7897 Bill showing of
to have been purchased first

The bottom was cut of by the photostat

APPENDIX C

Sotheby's Catalogue

SOTHEBY'S

FOUNDED 1744

Fine Printed And Manuscript Americana from the Collection of Mrs. Philip D. Sang

NEW YORK
WEDNESDAY, MARCH 27, 1985

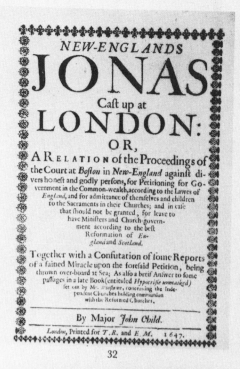

32

□ 33 [CLEMENS, SAMUEL L.] The English Version of the Polyglot Bible, containing the Old and New Testaments. *London, n.d.*

8vo. Several stamps throughout reading "The Mark Twain Library. Redding, Conn.," 1 leaf loose. Contemporary blind-stamped morocco; worn, front joint cracking

ASSOCIATION COPY, from the library of Mark Twain, with 3 marginal annotations in the handwriting of his wife, Olivia Langdon Clemens: at Exodus 20, "Susie began to learn the com. March 18th 1877 — finished July 1877"; at Psalms 23, "Susie finished learning Jan 1878"; at Matthew 5, "Susie finished learning the beatitudes March 11th 1877." Clemens and his family owned or referred to more than 25 copies of the Bible

Gribben, *Mark Twain's Library*, p. 69

$300/500

□ 34 CLEVELAND, GROVER, *Twenty-second and Twenty-fourth President*. The Public Papers . . . March 4, 1885 to March 4, 1889. *Washington, 1889*

Tall 8vo. Some marginal spotting. Original blind-panelled cloth; rubbed

First edition. PRESENTATION COPY, inscribed and signed by Cleveland on front flyleaf: "Robert Bennett Esq from Grover Cleveland June 4, 1890"

$300/400

□ 35 COOLIDGE, CALVIN, *Thirtieth President*. The Price of Freedom: Speeches and Addresses. *New York, 1924*

8vo. Frontispiece. Blue cloth

First edition. PRESENTATION COPY, inscribed and signed by Coolidge on front free endpaper: "To Albert D Matthai with regards Calvin Coolidge"

$150/250

□ 36 CRANE, STEPHEN. The Red Badge of Courage: An Episode of the American Civil War. *New York, 1895*

8vo. Title-page in red and black; some marginal spotting and creased corners, 1 very short marginal tear, 2 very short closed marginal tears, marginal paper flaw to first leaf of ads, a few leaves roughly opened at fore-edges. Original decorative buckram; slightly spotted, restored worn dust jacket. Red cloth box with maroon morocco label

First edition, first issue

BAL 4071; Grolier *American* 98; Johnson, *High Spots*, p. 25; Williams and Starrett 3; Wright 1257

$700/800

□ 32 CHILD, JOHN. New-Englands Jonas Cast Up at London. *London: for T.R. and E.M., 1647*

Small 4to. Title within an ornamental border; B2 with neat marginal repair into text, final leaf closely trimmed affecting last line of text and "finis." Modern calf; a little rubbed

First edition. A refutation of Winslow's *Hypocrisie Unmasked* (1646) that illustrates the conflict over civil and religious rights between the Puritan authorities and settlers not of the Congregational fold. This book also provides the earliest reprint of "The Freeman's Oath," the first issue of Stephen Daye's Cambridge press, of which no copy of the original printing survives

Church 478; JCB III, p. 353; Sabin 12705; Wing C3851

$1,500/2,000

APPENDIX D

Evidence from Mark Hofmann's Home
(Photocopies of the 'Oath' and the 'Jonas' Page Enlarged)

THE OATH OF A FREEMAN.

I·A·B·being (by Gods providence) an Inhabitant, and Freeman, within the jurisdictio of this Common-wealth, doe freely acknowledge my selfe to bee subiect to the governement thereof; and therefore doe heere sweare, by the great & dreadfull name of the Everliving-God, that I will be true & faithfull to the same, & will accordingly yield assistance & support therunto, with my person & estate, as in equity I am bound: and will also truely indeavour to maintaine and preserve all the libertyes & privilidges thereof, submitting my selfe to the wholesome lawes, & ordres made & stablished by the same; and further, that I will not plot, nor practice any evill against it, nor consent to any that shall soe do, butt will timely discover, & reveall the same to lawefull authoritee nowe here stablished, for the speedie preventing thereof. Moreover, I doe solemnly binde my selfe in the sight of God, that when I shalbe called, to give my voyce touching any such matter of this state, (in wh. ich freemen are to deale) I will give my vote & suffrage as I shall judge in myne owne conscience may best conduce & tend to the publick weale of the body, without respect of personnes, or favour of any man. Soe help mee God in the Lord Iesus Christ.

Jurisdiction
do
self   be   G
do here swear
        and dreadfull
and   and
    thereunto
        and
ndeavour   truly maintain
liberties and priviledges
    self
and established
                or
    or so
        but and reveall
iour . tblished lawefull athorit,
speedy
    bind self
shal be

        deal
and   mine own
    and publike
        weal
persons So me
    J

Words: 48/225   punctuation:

14. IF any man rise up by false witnesse, wittingly, and of purpose to take away any mans life, he shall be put to death. *Deut.* 19-16, 18, 19.

15. IF any man shall conspire or attempt any invasion, insurrection, or publike rebellion against our Common-wealth, or shall endeavour to surprise any Town or Towns, Fort or Forts therein; or shall treacherously or perfidiously attempt the alteration and subversion of our frame of Polity or Government fundamentally, he shall be put to death. *Num.* 16; 2 *Sam.* 3. & 18. & 20. *Per exemplar.* Incre. Nowel, *Secret.*

THE OATH OF A FREE-MAN.

I (*A.B.*) being by Gods providence, an Inhabitant, and Freeman, within the Jurisdiction of this Common-wealth; do freely acknowledge my self to be subject to the Government thereof: And therefore do here swear by the great and dreadful Name of the Ever-living God, that *I* will be true and faithfull to the same, and will accordingly yield assistance & support thereunto, with my person and estate, as in equity *I* am bound; and will also truly endeavour to maintain and preserve all the liberties and priviledges thereof, submitting my self to the wholesome Lawes & Orders made and established by the same. And further, that *I* will not plot or practice any evill against it, or consent to any that shall so do; but will timely discover and reveal the same to lawfull Authority now here established, for the speedy preventing thereof. Moreover, *I* doe solemnly bind my self in the sight of God, that when *I* shal be called to give my voyce touching any such matter of this State, in which Freemen are to deal, *I* will give my vote and suffrage as I judge in mine own conscience may best conduce and tend to the publike weal of the body, without respect of persons, or favour of any man. So help me God in the Lord Jesus Christ.

C 2

APPENDIX E

Keith Arbour's Evidence

FOUNDED 1812

 American Antiquarian Society

185 SALISBURY STREET
WORCESTER, MASSACHUSETTS, 01609, U. S. A.

April 3, 1986

Kenneth Farnsworth
Detective Division
Salt Lake City Police Department
450 South, 300 East
Salt Lake City, Utah 84111

Dear Ken:

The A-B-C idea in its simplest form: Let A stand for the 14 March 1634
manuscript version of the oath. Let C stand for the 1647 Child printing
of the oath (the earliest extant printing of known date). And let B stand
for the 1639 Cambridge printing, of which the Hofmann-Schiller broadside
may or may not be the sole extant exemplar. ("Exemplar", OED sense 5,
avoids the troublesome ambiguity previously caused by "copy".)

It is certain that C was printed from a descendant of A. For various
reasons we can consider it probable that that descendant was B. The line
of descent, then, is A-B-C. Because B represents an intermediate stage of
descent (or of change, since texts change as they descend) we can expect
that B will resemble both A and C more closely than A and C resemble each
other. This expectation is fulfilled in the relationship between A, the
Hofmann-Schiller broadside, and C. For instance: (1) A is a one-paragraph
version of the oath, as is Hofmann-Schiller, whereas C is in two paragraphs;
(2) where A reads "wherein" C reads "in which" and Hofmann-Schiller agrees
with the latter. In both of these places A and C disagree; and B resembles
first one, then the other. For this reason, the Hofmann-Schiller oath ought
to be examined as if it were printed before, not after, C(Child, 1647).

What one does not expect to find in a clear A-B-C line of descent is an important
reading that is common to A and C with which B disagrees. I think that the word
established is such a reading. All known authentic versions of the oath include
the word (or spelling) established twice. The Hofmann-Schiller broadside
disagrees and instead twice prints stablished. If this reading originated by
chance in B, why did it not descend to C? If it did not originate in B, from
whence did it originate? Why was stablished preferred to the otherwise standard
reading, established? If preferred, why did stablished not descend to C?

"Stablished" appears twice in The Whole Booke of Psalmes (Cambridge, 1640), as
"stablisht" (two syllables) in line 3 of psalm 93 and as "stablished" (three
syllables) in line 5 of the same psalm. In this verse translation of psalm 93,
lines of 4 metrical feet (eight syllables) are coupled with 3-foot lines (six
syllables). The psalm comprises 6 such regular couplets: no line is a single
syllable too short, or a single syllable too long. "Established" (and
"establisht") has too many syllables for this verse form. "Stablished" is
used because the verse form demands it.

JOHN JEPPSON, 2ND
PRESIDENT

MARCUS A. McCORISON
DIRECTOR AND LIBRARIAN

JOHN B. HENCH
ASSOCIATE DIRECTOR

BRUCE G. DANIELS
TREASURER

It is possible that "stablished" appears twice in the Hofmann-Schiller broadside
because the printer of this broadside wanted to "tie" his or her work to The
Whole Booke of Psalmes. The printer of this broadside may have thought that the
substitution of "stablished" (from psalm 93) for the otherwise invariable oath
reading "established" was a subtle way to tie the two pieces together, but failed
to consider why "stablished" appears in psalm 93. The oath is a prose piece in
which meter is of no concern. I think that this substitution of word-forms is
an unambiguous sign of modern forgery. "Stablished" as it appears in the Hofmann-
Schiller broadside originated in The Whole Booke of Psalmes. It does not descend
to C because it found its way into B long after C was printed.

This is a rather quick and superficial consideration of a more involved line of
thought. It is subject to considerable qualification and elaboration. It is my
opinion only, not that of the American Antiquarian Society. It is worth further
consideration only if it rings true to established textual scholars as a good
working hypothesis.

Sincerely yours,

Keith Arbour
Head of Readers' Services

KA/mtb

cc: Robert Mathiesen

TO: Nicolas Barker
FROM: M. A. McCorison
DATE: 23 December 1986
SUBJECT: Textual analysis of Oath of a Freeman, prepared by Keith
    Arbour of the AAS staff. NOTE: users of this material must
    give proper credit to Mr. Arbour and the AAS staff.

'The Oath of a Freeman': Summary of Conclusions

We have compared the text (herein referred to as E) of the Schiller-Wapner
Galleries broadside printing of the 'Oath' with four authoritative texts,
viz. (A) the version of the freeman's oath adopted by the Governor and Company of Massachusetts on 14 May 1634 and entered on the page numbered 114
in the first volume of the company's records; (B) the contemporary copy of
A entered on the page numbered 5 in the first volume of the company's
records; (C) the oath printed in Child, New England's Jonas, London, 1647;
and (D) the version of the oath printed in The book of the general lawes
and libertyes, Cambridge, 1648.

A and B differ in many accidental, but only two substantive readings: where
A reads "wholesome lawes & orders made", B reads "wholesome laws, made";
and where A reads "as I shall iudge in myne owne conscience may best
conduce", B reads "as I shall in myne owne conscience iudge best to
conduce". C reproduces the substantives of the A versions of these phrases;
D reproduces the substantives of the B versions. From this evidence we
have positted two lines of descent: A-B-D and A-C. Because E includes the
phrases "as I shall judge in myne owne conscience may best conduce" and
"wholesome lawes, & ordres made" we must examine the status of E in relation to the A-C line of descent.

A and C differ in many accidental and four substantive or quasi-substantive
readings, viz.

1.	Version A:	common weale]	commonwealth	Version C	
2.	A:	nor ... nor]	or ... or	C	
3.	A:	text in one paragraph]	text in two paragraphs	C	
4.	A:	wherein]	in which	C	

From the circumstances of the publication of New England's Jonas and from
an explicit statement in its text we know that Evans 1 was an intermediary
in the A- C line.[*] For this reason we expect the text of Evans 1 to

---

[*] External evidence (the body of historical information regarding the
drafting, printing, re-printing, and revising of the freeman's oath from
1634-1648) led us to conclude: (1) that beyond any reasonable doubt, no intermediate version in the A-C line was printed after C (1647); and (2) that
it is probable that only one printing (i.e. Evans 1) of one intermediate
version in the A-C line was executed between 1634 and 1647.

1

resemble both A and C more closely than A and C resemble each other. Be
cause this expectation is realized in E, which agrees with A in readings 2
and 3, and with C in readings 1 and 4, we have scrutinized E as a candidate
for intermediary status in the A-C line.

Collation of E with A and C disclosed many variants peculiar to E. Three
variants (two pairs of parentheses and the hyphenization of "Everliving-
God") are problematic but have not lent themselves to conclusive investigation. We have concluded that two others, both occurances of the spelling
"stablished" in place of "established" (as in A, B, C, D, and all other
authoritative texts), fall outside the limits of accidental variation that
could be attributable to 17th-century compositorial interference. We have
compared these variants with the authoritative appearances in the printed
and MS sources of the otherwise invariable "established." In addition, we
have made a limited examination of the use of both forms in contemporary
literature. We have concluded that "stablished" is an interpolation from a
line of verse located on leaf Y3r of The whole booke of psalmes, Cambridge,
1640.

The "Bay Psalm Book" translation of Psalm 93 on Y3r-v comprises verse in
alternating lines of four and three metrical feet. Forms of "stablish" occur in two of the four-foot lines:

    line 3: himselfe: the world so stablisht is,
    line 5: Thy throne is stablished of old:

We strongly suspect that a person, failing to comprehend the significance
of the demands of verse on the translator, concluded that these lines contained compositorial spelling variants for "established." Therefore, we
conclude that "stablished" was lifted from Psalm 93, line 5, and was mis-
takenly used in an attempt to present version E (the Schiller-Wapner Galleries broadside) as an authentic specimen of the earliest work from the
press in Cambridge, Massachusetts.

APPENDIX F

Evidence from DeBouzek Engraving
& Colorplate Co.

DATE REC'D	Mar 8 - 85	Nikki Harris		OUR ORDER NO.	540

DATE SENT	1 8 85

WANTED

ORDERED BY / MOUNT / OTHER — DEL TO: 788-5444

COPIES	PLATES	LINE	HALFTONE
1	1		

NO.	SIZE	KIND	DESCRIPTION	PRICE	COST
1	3¾ x 3¾		The oath of a freeman		45.00
				tax	2.58
					47.58

TIME CHARGES — DESIGN O. — HOURS — SQ.I. — COST

EXP. NO. H. L. S-P

R M F

MAT.

DESIGN

TOTAL

THE OATH OF A FREEMAN.

1. Give thanks, all ye people, give thanks to the Lord,
   Alleluiahs of freedom, with joyful accord:
   Let the East and the West, North and South roll along,
   Sea, mountain and prairie, one thanksgiving song.

   Chorus after each verse.
   Give thanks, all ye people, give thanks to the Lord,
   Alleluiahs of freedom, with joyful accord.

2. For the sunshine and rainfall, enriching again
   Our acres in myriads, with treasures of grain;
   For the earth still unloading her manifold wealth,
   For the skies beaming vigor, the winds breathing health:
   Give thanks—

3. For the Nation's wide table, o'erflowingly spread,
   Where the many have feasted, and all have been fed,
   With no bondage, their God-given rights to enthrall,
   But Liberty guarded by Justice for all:
   Give thanks—

4. In the realms of the Anvil, the Loom, and the Plow,
   Whose the mines and the fields, to Him gratefully bow
   His the flocks and the herds, sing ye hill-sides and vales
   On His ocean domains chant His name with the gales.
   Give thanks—

5. Of commerce and traffic, ye princes, behold
   Your riches from Him whose the silver and gold.
   Happier children of Labor, true lords of the soil,
   Bless the Great Master-Workman, who blesseth your toil.
   Give thanks—

6. Brave men of our forces, life-guard of our coasts,
   To your Leader be loyal, Jehovah of Hosts:
   Glow the Stripes and the Stars aye with victory bright,
   Reflecting His glory—He crowneth the Right.
   Give thanks—

7. Nor shall ye through our borders, ye stricken of heart,
   Only wailing your dead, in the joy have no part:
   God's solace be yours, and for you there shall flow
   All that honor and sympathy's gifts can bestow.
   Give thanks—

8. In the domes of Messiah, ye worshiping throngs,
   Solemn litanies mingle with jubilant songs;
   The Ruler of Nations beseeching to spare,
   And our empire still keep the elect of His care.
   Give thanks—

9. Our guilt and transgressions remember no more;
   Peace, Lord! righteous Peace, of Thy gift we implore;
   And the Banner of Union, restored by Thy hand,
   Be the Banner of Freedom o'er All in the Land.
   And the Banner of Union, etc.
   Give thanks—

THE OATH OF A FREEMAN.

I·AB· being (by Gods providence) an Inhabitant, and Freeman, within the iurifdictiõ of this Common-wealth, doe freely acknowledge my felfe to bee fubject to the governement thereof; and therefore doe heere fweare, by the great & dreadfull name of the Everliving-God, that I will be true & faithfull to the fame, & will accordingly yield affiftance & fupport therunto, with my perfon & eftate, as in equity I am bound: and will alfo truely indeavour to maintaine and preferve all the libertyes & privilidges thereof, fubmitting my felfe to the wholefome lawes, & ordres made & ftablifhed by the fame; and further, that I will not plot, nor practice any evill againft it, nor confent to any that fhall foe do, butt will timely difcover, & reveall the fame to lawefull authoritee nowe here ftablifhed, for the fpeedie preventing thereof. Moreover, I doe folemnly binde my felfe, in the fight of God, that when I fhalbe called, to give my voyce touching any fuch matter of this ftate, (in wh. ich freemen are to deale) I will give my vote & fuffrage as I fhall judge in myne owne confcience may beft conduce & tend to the publick weale of the body, without refpect of perfonnes, or favour of any man. Soe help mee God in the Lord Iefus Chrift.

This "Quaker Catichism" was printed opposite the title-page in the 1653 edition of Cotton's book. Enlarged.

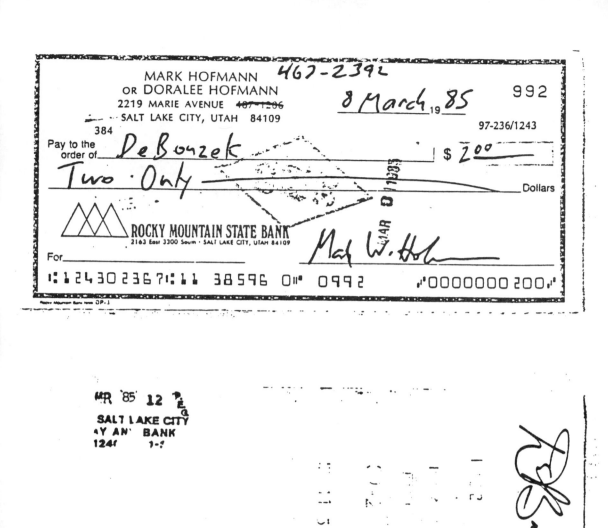

MARK HOFMANN
OR DORALEE HOFMANN
2219 MARIE AVENUE 487-1206
SALT LAKE CITY, UTAH 84109

467-2392

8 March 19 85

992

97-236/1243

384

Pay to the
order of *DeBouzek*

$ 2⁰⁰

Two · Only

Dollars

ROCKY MOUNTAIN STATE BANK
2163 East 3300 South · SALT LAKE CITY, UTAH 84109

MAR 0 1985

Mark W. Hof

For

⑈1243023671⑈11 38596 0⑈ 0992 ⑈0000000200⑈

MR '85 12
SALT LAKE CITY
NY ANY BANK
124

MR '85 08
ANY BANK 21 6
ERSTATE BK OF UT.
LAKE CITY, UTAH

31-2

0255267 A 4020 5650

24 042 030835 4046

⑈5140 1404

⑈5468 0810

APPENDIX G

'The President's Hymn'

Duplicate

733

The President's Hymn:

GIVE THANKS, ALL YE PEOPLE,

IN RESPONSE TO THE PROCLAMATION

OF THE

PRESIDENT OF THE UNITED STATES,

RECOMMENDING A GENERAL THANKSGIVING,

ON NOVEMBER 26th, 1863.

————————— ◆ —————————

PUBLISHED BY

A. D. F. RANDOLPH, 683 BROADWAY, NEW-YORK.

Library of Congress
MUSIC DIV

CLASS. M

ACC. NO. 107003

1640
B

Received by Mail.
5-5-86
Bee
F33

JB
486

Received by Mail 5-8-28 Bull 753

Give Thanks, all ye People.

With spirit.

1. Give thanks, all ye peo - ple, give thanks to the LORD,

Al - le - lu - ias of free - dom, with joy - ful ac - cord;

Let the East and the West, North and South roll a - long,

Sea, moun - tain and prai - rie, One thanks - giv - ing Song.

CHORUS.

Give thanks, all ye peo - ple, give thanks to the LORD,

Al - le - lu - ias of free - dom, with joy - ful ac - cord.

JB - 486

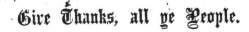

Give Thanks, all ye People.

1. Give thanks, all ye people, give thanks to the Lord,
Alleluias of freedom, with joyful accord:
Let the East and the West, North and South roll along,
Sea, mountain and prairie, One thanksgiving song.

Chorus after each verse.

Give thanks, all ye people, give thanks to the LORD,
Alleluias of freedom, with joyful accord.

2. For the sunshine and rainfall, enriching again
Our acres in myriads, with treasures of grain;
For the Earth still unloading her manifold wealth,
For the Skies beaming vigor, the Winds breathing health:
Give thanks—

3. For the Nation's wide table, o'erflowingly spread,
Where the many have feasted, and all have been fed,
With no bondage, their God-given rights to enthral,
But Liberty guarded by Justice for all:
Give thanks—

4. In the realms of the Anvil, the Loom, and the Plow,
Whose the mines and the fields, to Him gratefully bow:
His the flocks and the herds, sing ye hill-sides and vales;
On His Ocean domains chant His Name with the gales.
Give thanks—

5. Of commerce and traffic, ye princes, behold
Your riches from Him Whose the silver and gold.
Happier children of Labor, true lords of the soil,
Bless the Great Master-Workman, who blesseth your toil.
Give thanks—

6. Brave men of our forces, Life-guard of our coasts,
To your Leader be loyal, Jehovah of Hosts:
Glow the Stripes and the Stars aye with victory bright,
Reflecting His glory,—He crowneth the Right.
Give thanks—

7. Nor shall ye through our borders, ye stricken of heart,
Only wailing your dead, in the joy have no part:
God's solace be yours, and for you there shall flow
All that honor and sympathy's gifts can bestow.
Give thanks—

8. In the Domes of Messiah, ye worshipping throngs,
Solemn litanies mingle with jubilant songs;
The Ruler of Nations beseeching to spare,
And our Empire still keep the Elect of His care.
Give thanks—

9. Our guilt and transgressions remember no more;
Peace, Lord! righteous Peace, of Thy gift we implore;
And the Banner of Union, restored by Thy Hand,
Be the Banner of Freedom o'er All in the Land.
And the Banner of Union, &c.
Give thanks—

					EXR NO.	H.	L.	S-P

Date: Mon 25-85 Mike Hansen

OUR ORDER NO. 621
YOUR ORDER NO.

BILL TO

ORDERED BY

MONN]

OTHER

TIME CHARGES
DESIGN O.
HOURS

COPIES	PLATES	LINE	HALFTONE	KIND

NO.	SIZE	DESCRIPTION	PRICE	COST	SQ.I.
1	9 X 7	2½ act of w Greenwich		37.00	
		Tax		2.13	
				39.13	

Bill Custr 25-85
Invoice

	R	M	B	F

MAT.

DESIGN

TOTAL

APPENDIX H

Library of Congress Photocopies

OGC

THE LIBRARY OF CONGRESS

WASHINGTON. D. C. 20540

OFFICIAL BUSINESS
PENALTY FOR PRIVATE USE. $300

199

FIRST CLASS MAIL

RECEIVED
APR 2 3 1986

COUNTY ATTORNEY

Ted Cannon, County Attorney
Office of the Salt Lake County Attorney
231 East 4th Street
Salt Lake City, Utah   84111

CONFIDENTIAL

CONFIDENTIAL

Salt Lake County Attorney

2 of 3

The Oath of a Freeman
Photographic print of Beta Radiograph

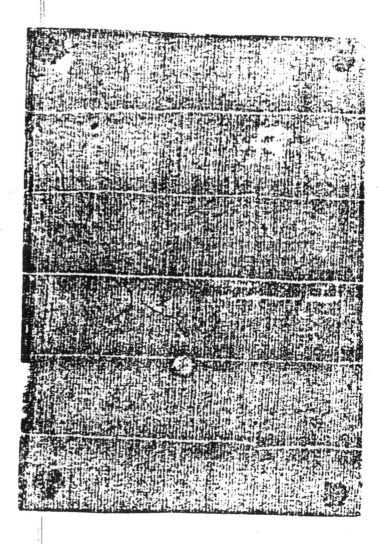

THE OATH OF A FREEMAN.

I. A B. being (by Gods providence) an Inhabitant, and Freeman, within the iurisdictiõ of this Common-wealth, doe freely acknowledge my selfe to bee subject to the governement thereof; and therefore doe heere sweare, by the great & dreadfull name of the Everliving-God, that I will be true & faithfull to the same, & will accordingly yield assistance & support therunto, with my person & estate, as in equity I am bound: and will also truely indeavour to maintaine and preserve all the libertyes & privilidges thereof; submitting my selfe to the wholesome lawes, & ordres made & stablished by the same; and further, that I will not plot, nor practice any evill against it, nor consent to any that shall soe do, butt will timely discover, & reveall the same to lawefull authoritee nowe here stablished, for the speedie preventing thereof. Moreover, I doe solemnly binde my selfe, in the sight of God, that when I shalbe called, to give my voyce touching any such matter of this state, (in which freemen are to deale) I will give my vote & suffrage as I shall judge in myne owne conscience may best conduce & tend tò the publick weale of the body, without respect of personnes, or favour of any man. Soe help mee God in the Lord Iesus Christ.

THE OATH OF A FREEMAN.

AB·being (by Gods providence) an Inhabitant, and Freeman, within the iurifdiction of this common-wealth, doe freely acknowledge my felfe to bee fubject to the government thereof: and therefore doe heere fweare, by the great & dreadfull name of the Everliving-God, that I will be true & faithfull to the fame, & will accordingly yield affiftance & fupport thereunto, with my perfon & eftate, as in equity I am bound: and will alfo truely indeavour to maintaine and preferve all the liberty es & privilidges thereof, fubmitting my felfe to the wholefome lawes & orders made & ftablifhed by the fame; and further, that I will not plot, nor practice any evill against it, nor confent to any that fhall foe do; but will timely difcover, & reveall the fame to lawfull authoritee nowe here ftablifhed, for the fpeedie preventing thereof. Moreover, I doe folemnly binde my felfe, in the fight of God, that when I fhalbe called, to give my voyce touching any fuch matter of this ftate, (in which Freemen are to deale) I will give my vote & fuffrage as I fhall judge in myne owne confcience may beft conduce & tend to the publick weale of the body, without refpect of perfons, or favour of any man. Soe help mee God in the Lord Iefus Chrift.

THE OATH OF A FREEMAN.

I·A·B· being (by Gods providence) an Inhabitant, and Freeman, within the jurisdictio of this Common-wealth, doe freely acknowledge my felfe to bee fubject to the government thereof; and therefore doe heere fweare, by the great & dreadfull name of the Everliving-God, that I will be true & faithfull to the fame, & will accordingly yield affiftance & fupport therunto, with my perfon & eftate, as in equity I am bound: and will alfo truely indeavour to maintaine and preferve all the libertyes & privilidges thereof, fubmitting my felfe to the wholefome lawes, & ordres made & ftablifhed by the fame; and further, that I will not plot nor practice any evill against it, nor confent to any that fhall bee done, butt will timely difcover, & reveall the fame to lawefull authorites nowe here ftablifhed, for the fpeedie prevēting thereof. Moreover, I doe folemnly binde my felfe, in the fight of God, that when I fhalbe called, to give my voyce touching any fuch matter of this ftate, (in which freemen are to deale) I will give my vote & fuffrage as I fhall judge in myne owne confcience may beft conduce & tend to the publick weale of the body, without refpect of perfonnes, or favour of any man. Soe help mee God in the Lord Iefus Chrift.

THE OATH OF A FREEMAN.

I AB. being (by Gods providence) an Inhabitant, and Freeman, within the iurisdictio of this Common-wealth, doe freely acknowledge my selfe to bee subject to the governement thereof; and therefore doe heere sweare, by the great & dreadfull name of the Everliving God, that I will be true & faithfull to the same, & will accordingly yield assistance & support thereunto, with my person & estate, as in equity I am bound: and will also truely indeavour to maintaine and preserve all the libertyes & privilidges thereof, submitting my selfe to the wholesome lawes, & ordres made & stablished by the same; and further, that I will not plot, nor practice any evill against it, nor consent to any that shall soe do, butt will timely discover, & reveall the same to lawefull authoritee nowe here stablished, for the speedie preventing thereof. Moreover, I doe solemnly binde my selfe, in the sight of God, that when I shalbe called, to give my voyce touching any such matter of this state, (in which freemen are to deale) I will give my vote & suffrage as I shall judge in myne owne conscience may best conduce & tend to the publick weale of the body, without respect of persones, or favour of any man. Soe help mee God in the Lord Iesus Christ.

THE OATH OF A FREEMAN.

I AB. being (by Gods providence) an inhabitant, and Freeman, within the iurisdictio of this Common-wealth, doe freely acknowledge my selfe to bee subject to the governement thereof; and therefore doe heere sweare, by the great & dreadfull name of the Everliving-God, that I will be true & faithfull to the same, & will accordingly yield assistance & support therunto, with my person & estate, as in equity I am bound: and will also truely indeavour to maintaine and preserve all the libertyes & privilidges thereof, submitting my selfe to the wholesome lawes, & ordres made & stablished by the same; and further, that I will not plot, nor practice any evill against it, nor consent to any that shall soe do, butt will timely discover, & reveall the same to lawefull authoritee nowe here stablished, for the speedie preventing thereof. Moreover, I doe solemnly binde my selfe, in the sight of God, that when I shalbe called, to give my voyce touching any such matter of this state, (in which freemen are to deale) I will give my vote & suffrage as I shall judge in myne owne conscience may best conduce & tend to the publick weale of the body, without respect of personnes, or favour of any man. Soe help mee God in the Lord Iesus Christ.

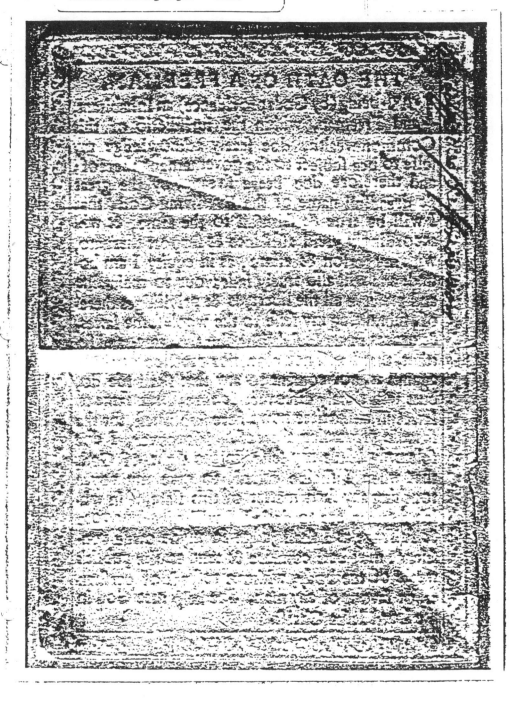

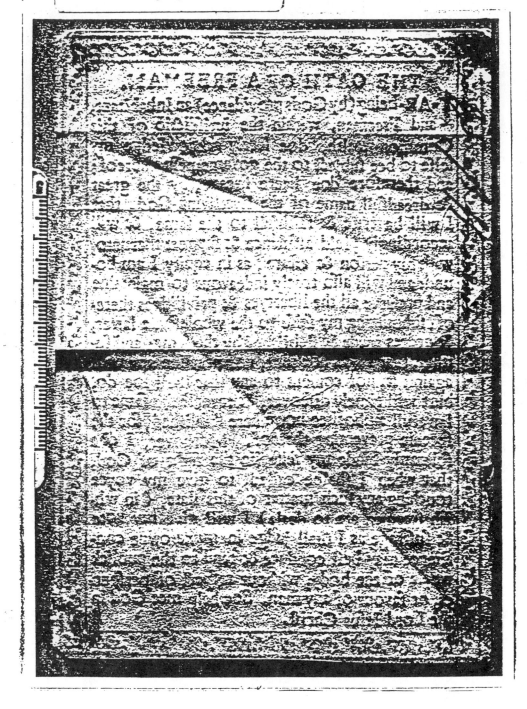

*Excerpts about the 'Oath' from the
'Mark Hofmann Interviews,' with the
Office of the Salt Lake County Attorney*

Office of Salt Lake County Attorney

DAVID E. YOCOM
COUNTY ATTORNEY

MARK HOFMANN INTERVIEWS

INTERVIEWS CONDUCTED AT
UTAH STATE PRISON BETWEEN
FEBRUARY 11 AND MAY 27, 1987

TRANSCRIPTS, SUPPLEMENTS AND EXHIBITS

000022

Volume 1

Editorial Note:

David Biggs	—	Deputy Salt Lake County Attorney
Robert Stott	—	Deputy Salt Lake County Attorney
Ron Yengich	—	Attorney representing Mark Hofmann
Brad Rich	—	Attorney representing Mark Hofmann
Mike George	—	Salt Lake County Police Department sergeant
Lyn Jacobs	—	A collector of Mormon books who was unwittingly used by Hofmann in several of his schemes.

All answers are given by Mark Hofmann during these interviews.

Excerpt of Interview Conducted on
March 12, 1987

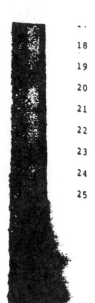

18   MR. BIGGS: Back on the record. Let's begin

19   speaking, and certainly I don't think we'll get done in a

20   half hour with the Oath but let me give you what I've got on

21   that and see how far we can go. I'm showing you a, what

22   looks to me to be a plate on a piece of wood.

23   A   That's what it looks like to me too.

24   Q   And I'm also showing you a negative and a Velox

25   and a receipt of another document titled the Oath of a

230

1   Freeman. And a kind of oldish looking printed document.

2   The Oath of a Freeman, let me start with the

3   Oath, if I can describe it as that. Do you have any

4   familiarity with that?

5   A   Yes, I had that made and printed.

6   Q   Okay, I'll show you the receipt under the name

7   Mike Hansen, 448-4584

8   Q   Did you use the name Mark Harris or Mike

9   Hansen?

10   A   I would get the word Hansen was used, but

11   Harris was written down but it's hard to me to say.

12   Q   Is that your telephone number?

13   A   I believe that used to be one of my telephone

14   numbers, yes.

15   Q   I'll tell you right now it is. Also there is a

16   $2 check written on your checking account around that same

17   time. Do you happen to know what the $2 was for? To

18   DeBouzek Printing, I'm speaking of.

19   A   The only thing I can imagine would be I only

20   had $45 with me and it looks like the cost of this was $47

21   so I would have, or when I had $45 with me, I mean in cash,

22   so I would have written a check to make up the balance.

23   Q   Where did you-- The problem is, of course, that

24   DeBouzek doesn't know for sure. They don't have anything

25   for sure for $2 so they said obviously he didn't have enough

231

cash. The Oath of a Freeman that starts out the first line,
"Give thanks, all yee people give thanks to the Lord". Why
did you have that done?

A   My intention was to use this, a printing from
this at Argosy Bookstore in order to, well, my intention was
to smuggle or take into Argosy Bookstore a printing of this
priced at $25, which I recall I wrote on the back. And
purchase it for $25, getting a receipt from them with the
title Oath of a Freeman on it and use that receipt in order
to establish a provinence for the document, which actually
was not used. I decided I did not like the appearance of
this document so I made some new artwork and copied with a
photocopy machine, on to a piece of old paper, my version of
the Oath of a Freeman, and I used that for the purpose that
I originally intended to use this one for.

Q   Similar technique to the one that Lynn Jacobs
described?

A   Yes. He taught me that technique. Now, I
don't know if you want this on the record or not but Lynn
Jacobs, as far as the technique he used was not to defraud,
you know, so I hate to associate him with any forgery
techniques since he was not a part of any of this.

Q   So that is the plate that you had prepared on
March 8th. You didn't actually use the printed material
from that plate to salt, if I may use that term, Argosy

1   Book?

2   A   That's a good term. No, I did not. I used the

3   same idea but not this identical printing.

4   Q   Why $25?

5   A   Having looked at items on the second floor of

6   Argosy Book in their Broadside or print, or engravings

7   department, that seemed to me to be a reasonable price for

8   what appeared to be a 19th Century document of this type.

9   Q   Why is the Oath of a Freeman title so much

10   larger than the body?

11   A   That is the title.

12   Q   Any intent on your part?

13   A   Yes. It is common to have a title larger

14   than the text and I believe that on the document that I

15   salted Argosy Bookstore with, which like I say, is not

16   identical with this, also had a larger title than the text.

17   Q   What are the differences between the one on the

18   Velox and the one you actually ended up Xeroxing and

19   salting into Argosy Book?

20   A   It's smaller than this one and I got the text

21   from another source. It wasn't this poem.

22   Q   What is the source of that poem, by the way?

23   A   Again, I had another cheap 19th Century print

24   which I believe I cut up or either that or I Xeroxed it off

25   and cut it up from what appears to be a poem or song.

233

1   Q   And that is what you actually did salt in

2   Argosy Book?

3   A   Yes.

4   Q   Okay. I don't have--

5   A   Now when you say that's what I actually salted,

6   not this but the other thing I used, yes.

7   Q   Right. I should be more specific when I say

8   those things. Now, March 25th, 1985 there's receipt, M.

9   Hansen for Oath of a Freeman. No, I don't have it, the

10   receipt or the negative and I don't know where it is but

11   it's around. Is that you as well?

12   A   Yes. The receipt would have been for a plate

13   similar to this, yes.

14   Q   It had a little disclaimer on the bottom. Did

15   you type that on there?

16   A   I typed it on a piece of paper and put it on

17   the artwork, that's correct.

18   Q   Did you take it off of that plate before you

19   printed up the Oath?

20   A   Before I printed this one I did, yes. I am not

21   sure what the margins are around the other one. That is in

22   New York City still, I presume.

23   Q   You presume correctly. They're still holding

24   on to that. After you got the plate of the Oath of a

25   Freeman that you used to print the Oath of a Freeman--

234

1   A   I know what you mean.

2   Q   What did you do with the plate on March 25th,

3   1985?

4   A   I am not sure if it was on that day but soon

5   thereafter I used it to print.

6   Q   If this will refresh your recollection, I can

7   tell you that approximately between 6:00 and 7:00 a.m.   the

8   next day you were on a plane to New York.

9   A   Yes.   I probably would have stayed up all night

10 printing, which actually would only take a few minutes but

11 then aging the document, manufacturing ink probably at the

12 same time, both the printing and the writing ink.

13   Q   How did you prepare the printers ink for the

14 Oath?

15   A   I knew that this document would be scrutinized

16 so I took pains to assure that the ink would not differ from

17 the 17th Century printing ink.   I manufactured the ink.

18 I'll go in to the process I used but I don't know if you

19 want it on the record.

20   Q   Heck, why not?

21   A   Off the record a minute.

22   DISCUSSION HELD OFF THE RECORD

23   Q   You were describing for us the ink manufacture.

24   A   Yes.   I got some, I obtained some paper from

25 the same time period,   approximately.

235

1   Q   Where?

2   A   This paper would have probably come, would have

3 definitely come from Brigham Young University Library. The

4 paper did not have printing on it, which I guess they'll be

5 happy to hear that. That paper I burnt in an apparatus to

6 make carbon black. The reason I went through this trouble

7 is because I thought that there was a possibility that a

8 carbon 14 test would be performed on the ink.

9   Q   Do you know what book this paper came out of

10 that you used to produce the carbon black?

11   A   If you want to take me in shakles to the

12 library I could point it out to you but I don't know that I

13 can describe the exact location.

14   Q   Are there 17th Century books just sitting on

15 the shelves?

16   A   Yes, there are. Mostly they would have been of

17 a religous nature. Early religous books aren't particularly

18 valuable. But yes, it is possible to just get them off the

19 shelf.

20   Q   Go ahead.

21   A   The apparatus that I used had a glass tube

22 chimney which caught the carbon and that's how I accumulated

23 it. It was mixed with a linseed oil.

24   Q   Any special linseed oil?

25   A   It would have been chemically, it was

1 chemically pure linseed oil which I treated to some extent.

2   Q   How did you treat the linseed oil?

3   A   Well, I'm going into all of this. You are just

4 dying to hear this; aren't you. The linseed oil was heavily

5 boiled, which thickens it and then it was burned.

6   Q   Why?

7   A   I was basically following a recipe from 17th

8 Century ink making recipe.

9   Q   Where did you get that?

10   A   From a book. I know you will ask me where I

11 saw the book, which I again, I can probably find for you but

12 I can't describe. I believe it is on, it's a microfilm book

13 from that time period in the University of Utah Library but

14 I can't remember the title of it.

15   Q   Okay, go ahead.

16   A   I also added some tannic acid or at least a

17 solution of tannic acid which had dried. It was made from a

18 leather binding from that same time period which had been

19 boiled in distilled water until it turned a nice brown

20 color. There's also some bees wax added, just ordinary bees

21 wax, nothing special to it, and I believe that's all.

22   Q   And that made the printers ink?

23   A   That was the printers ink.

24   Q   After you made the printers ink, you have the

25 plate, picked it up on the 25th, you're at your house where

237

1   you lived?

2   A   Right, I was downstairs in my office and

3   printed it. I would have rolled the ink on to the plate. I

4   would have put the paper, that I haven't yet described where

5   I got that, on the plate. A piece of felt behind it,

6   another thick metal copper plate on top of it all and

7   pressed with a C-clamp.

8   Q   A C-clamp?

9   A   A C-clamp.

10   Q   One clamp?

11   A   A single C-clamp, as I remember. Again, it may

12 have been moved around.

13   Q   Did you have only one piece of paper at that

14 time to print on?

15   A   Yes, I did.

16   Q   Were you a little concerned that maybe you

17 wouldn't get it right the first time?

18   A   I don't think so. For one thing this was the

19 first attempt by the Day Print Shop to make an impression

20 and if it was crude or didn't look quite right I didn't

21 think it would be too great of a concern.

22   Q   Did you alter the plate in any way? Grind down

23 any of the letters?

24   A   Yes, I did.

25   Q   Why was that done?

238

1   A   For a couple reasons. One being so that it
2   could not be identified as being printed from a zink plate
3   which I guess is the best reason of all why I did it.
4   Q   How did you do it?
5   A   First of all, the whole plate would have been
6   treated in some process with iron wool to round out the
7   corners of the lettering. Some of the letters would have
8   been ground even finer with a small drill containing a fine
9   grinding tip stone. In fact, I believe that was done first
10   and then afterwards the whole thing was iron wooled.
11   Q   Any rhyme or reason to which letters were
12   ground down by you?
13   A   None that I remember, although-- In other
14   words, it doesn't seem it was too random but I can't think
15   of how I--
16   MR. RICH: Did you test out your final product
17   on a piece of modern paper to see how it looked on the
18   paper?
19   A   Yes, I'm sure I did.
20   MR. RICH: He's a lot bolder than I am. A lot
21   of things he just did it, knew worked and went ahead and
22   printed it.   I would take a ream of paper and go through it
23   to be sure it worked.
24   A   You tell me what I did do.
25   MR. BIGGS: I wish we could remember it

239

specifically. I remember reading in the Library of Congress
analysis that went on for umteen hundred pages, they say it
obviously came from printing letters because they were
different. They pressed on the paper in different amounts
and so that it was down further in to the paper and so
forth.

     A   Part of that would have been the uneveness of
the pressure applied by the C-clamp which again is typical,
I believe of the crude printing that would have been done.
And the other is I believe that too, some letters I
purposefully ground down. I can't remember though how or
what method I used or how I decided. It may have been
random but I can't remember how I did that.

     Q   The paper that you used, 17th Century piece of
paper for the Oath?

     A   Right.

     Q   Where did you get it?

     A   I had previously looked at a copy of the Hymn
book, a genuine copy. I also studied a microfilm of it
which showed the laid lines in the paper and my effort was
to duplicate those laid lines which in going through
numerous volumes I succeeded in doing. The paper I believe
was in, within five years of the date. It's very close to
the date of the alleged or it least the, not the paper, I
shouldn't say but the printing that was put on the paper is

240

1   very close to the date that the Oath of a Freeman would have

2   been printed.

3   WHEREUPON, the interview was adjourned at the

4   hour of 5:00 p.m.

5   --------------------------------

6

7

8

9

10

11

12

13

14

15

16

17

18

19

20

21

22

23

24

25

Excerpt of Interview Conducted on
March 17, 1987

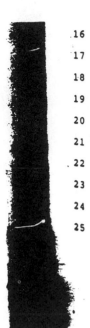

16   Q   When we ended last time we were discussing the

17   Oath of a Freeman and I brought some things today that I

18   didn't have last time. I finally got my investigator out of

19   bed and he was able to find them for me. You will see on

20   this sheet is the negative of what is entitled the Oath of a

21   Freeman.   It's about 4 by 7 and on the other side is a

22   receipt. Least start with that receipt. Do you recognize

23   it?

24   A   No, I don't recognize it but I presume that is

25   the receipt that was written out at my direction.

244

1	Q	And it's in the name of Mike Hansen?
2	A	That's correct.
3	Q	Did you use that name?
4	A	Yes.
5	Q	The date is March 25th 1985. Is that date

6 recognizable to you?

7   A   I'm pretty bad with dates but that is

8 undoubtedly the date that I ordered this negative or a plate

9 made from this negative.

10   Q   One other thing that we made reference to last

11 time but I didn't have with me. Back on March 8th when you

12 had the DeBouzek Printing Company print up a Oath of a

13 Freeman, which was actually the Presidential Oath--

14   A   Yes, that's right.

15   Q   They received this as partial payment.

16   A   Yes, a $2 check from me from Rocky Mountain

17 State Bank.

18   Q   And that was in discussions having to do with

19 the fact that you probably only had $45 and the bill was

20 $47?

21   A   That's what I said.

22   Q   But you don't have any recollection of it?

23   A   I have independent recollection of using a

24 check when I ordered some plates from Kansas City for that

25 purpose. Meaning that I had insufficient cash. But I

1   really don't remember the exact purpose for this check

2   although I can't think of any other possibility.

3   Q   That would have been the, Kansas City would

4   have been the Immigrants Guide, would it not?

5   A   That's right.

6   Q   Now, let's turn over and look at this. Do you

7   recognize that?

8   A   I don't believe that I ever saw the negative

9   before but I certainly recognize the photograph.

10   Q   What is it?

11   A   It is the Oath of a Freeman, meaning the one

12 with the border around it that purports to be from the 17th

13 Century.

14   Q   Who created the artwork from which that

15 negative was produced?

16   A   I did.

17   Q   Now the receipt for the preparation of the

18 plate says March 25th. How long did it take you to develop

19 the artwork that you took in on the 25th for DeBouzek to

20 make the plate from?

21   A   Several days. Probably more than a week.

22   Q   How long had you been developing-- Maybe the

23 best word to use would be how long was the conceptual stage

24 for the Oath of a Freeman?

25   A   Probably more than a month before I actually

1   began working on it. Meaning in that time I was doing

2   research on it.

3   Q   Where primarily was the research done?

4   A   I started out in the University of Utah

5   Library. They have a printed facsimile edition of the Bay

6   Psalm Book. Also have a copy, I believe, of two different

7   volumes of that book on microfilm. I studied all three of

8   those sources. In fact, that is the source of the type that

9   was used in preparing the artwork. I also used it to

10   research such things as the spelling of words, the

11   characteristics of the printings.

12   Q   Let me show you something that was taken from

13   your materials. Are you familiar with that?

14   A   Yes, this would have been, I believe a Xerox of

15   a Xerox of the Oath.

16   Q   Now is that your Oath? That is to say, after

17   you had the artwork done and the plate made up, did you

18   somehow enlarge a Xerox of that or does this come from

19   another source?

20   A   Yes. This would have been, I believe, a Xerox

21   of the Oath which is possessed by Justin Schiller which I

22   enlarged after making the forgery in order to show parallels

23   between the Psalm Book and the copy of the Oath.

24   Q   There's been quite a lot of--

25   A   Let me read this for a second.

247

1   Q   Sure. There's handwriting on the left side.
2   Is that your handwriting?

3   A   Yes, it is. Yes, I believe this would have
4   been composed by me after the forgery had been completed.

5   Q   Okay, now Mark, there's been a lot of
6   contention about actually where you got, how should I put
7   it, the body of the text.

8   A   Yes, that's also some of the research I did at
9   the University of Utah Library. I found two or three
10 different sources for the Oath, all of which varied slightly
11 in words and so forth.

12   Q   Can you recall those sources?

13   A   What I thought was the best source, the
14 earliest source was a journal of, I believe one of the
15 governors in the Massachusetts Bay Colony. If I heard his
16 name I could probably tell you if that was correct or not.

17   Q   I can't remember. I can remember reading about
18 a couple of governors. Was it an actual reprint of his
19 journal?

20   A   Yes. It was a type script, copy of the
21 journal.

22   Q   At the University of Utah Library?

23   A   The University of Utah Library. It's on the
24 4th floor, north wall. If you took me there I could walk
25 you right to it. I keep saying that to get out of the

248

1   prison. If you want to take me for a field trip, I could

2   walk you to it.

3   Q   We very well might do that because we have not

4   been particularly successful, from the Bible at the USU

5   Library in finding the sources you've described to us.

6   How did you come to that source? In the card

7   catalog or how?

8   A   Yes. My first search would have undoubtedly

9   been in the card catalog, although I'm not sure if you look

10 under Oath of a Freeman it would be listed there. What I

11 did was research the early days of the Massachusetts Bay

12 Colony and in going through early journals and other

13 references, not only to get an idea of the early printing

14 done but also the, what I believe to be the composure of a

15 legal document such as this. In going through as much

16 material as I could find I came across an early version

17 which was probably taken from the original, first edition of

18 the Oath in the journal.

19   Q   And you don't remember the name of the book,

20 the journal?

21   A   Let's see, I remember there was a journal was

22 one of my sources, which I believed to have been taken

23 directly from the original Oath, printed Oath. I also

24 remember a copy of the actual laws which were passed in this

25 period. There was a copy of the Oath which was ordered to

1   be printed and the words that were, what the Oath consisted

2   of, the actual wording. That was another one of my sources.

3   I think I described before in how I composed the characters

4   in the Anthon Transcript. I have, I think some knowledge of

5   how a document is, the sections examined and it is put in a

6   chronological sequence with the other versions or sources of

7   the Oath. My purpose, of course, was to make this the first

8   printed version. It differs from any of the other single

9   sources that I used and that was my intention.

10   Q   Okay.

11   A   So in other words, you would not find the exact

12   wording in any source that you see here in the composure

13   which I made.

14   Q   So your composition intent is similar to your

15   composition intent in the Anthon Transcript?

16   A   To make it look like it was the first printed

17   source, that's correct.

18   Q   Now the border?

19   A   I tried to make it look like it was after the

20   text approved by the either legislature there, but before

21   any other printed source. In other words, to make it look

22   in between that so that it fit chronologically in between

23   those.

24   Q   Did you do that with the spelling of the words

25   to some extent?

250

1   A ·   To some extent. The spelling I believe

2   reflects the spelling of the composer who composed the Bay

3   Psalm Book.

4   Q   How about the border?

5   A   The border also came from the Bay Psalm Book.

6   Q   I have somewhere in this book of mine here a

7   page from Book 4 of the Bay Psalm Book and it has, or

8   appears to have--

9   A   Yes, this is the page of the 90th Psalm and it

10   has the same type face as what I used in creating the

11   border. Particularly look at the right, the furthest right

12   character on that page. It is identical to the characters

13   which I composed in the border of the Oath.

14   Q   How is it physically done?

15   A   Pardon me?

16   Q   How is it physically done? Tell me the process

17   by which the very last character of the 4th Book, Psalm 90

18   Book, the border--

19   A   These designs also appear in other pages in the

20   book. It was a simple matter of Xeroxing from the facsimile

21   of the Psalm Book several Xeroxes of the pages which I

22   wanted to copy the flourishes or designs. I then used a

23   razor blade, actually an Xacto knife to cut out the letters

24   and the designs that I wanted. I glued them on a piece of

25   paper and that was on, and then after they were glued on a

251

1   piece of paper I Xeroxed my composure and that was the

2   artwork which I took into DeBouzek. I didn't mention that I

3   used glue. I cut them out, I put a little dot of glue on

4   the back and stuck them on the piece of paper using lines on

5   the paper on which I was composing, to line up the letters.

6   Q   I think you told me this but tell me again

7   because I've obviously forgotten. The type face for the

8   body of the Oath of a Freeman, where that came from?

9   A   Came from the Psalm Book also. The Bay Psalm

10   Book.

11   Q   Any particular place or just where you could

12   find the appropriate letters?

13   A   Where I could find the appropriate letters that

14   were distinct. Back in those days when they set type it was

15   done differently than we do it now. One of the techniques

16   they used after they set it was to drive it into a piece of

17   wood using a wooden mallot, which obviously deformed a lot

18   of the letters. My intention was to choose letters which

19   could not be identified as being the exact letters used in

20   the Psalm Book. I guess, first of all I should say that

21   it's fairly common in valuable books to have several.

22   Several centuries ago, they can identify, the experts I

23   should say, can identified the person who made the font.

24   Also, if the same exact letter type was used more than once

25   in setting up the book and in other books printed by the

252

1   same printer. In fact, they can even tell if it was a

2   printer that went out of business, who he sold his type to

3   by another contemporary printer who used the identical type.

4   All these features were taken into

5   consideration. And after cutting out the letters, pasting

6   them on a sheet, then making a Xerox of that artwork, I used

7   a technical pen. I think I described that before. To

8   actually deform some of the letters the way I wanted, which

9   are different, the deformations, than what exist in the Bay

10 Psalm Book. In other words, knowing that an item of this

11 importance and value would be very closely scrutinized, I

12 took all precautions I could think of to mislead the experts

13 who would examine it.

14   Q   On the negative which, of course, you had not

15 seen, but the plate came from that negative, there's a

16 little disclaimer down at the bottom.

17   A   Yes.

18   Q   And did that come out on the plate that you

19 picked up from DeBouzek?

20   A   That was on the plate, yes it was.

21   Q   And when you printed your Oath of a Freeman,

22 which you took back to New York, how did you get rid of that

23 statement at the bottom?

24   A   I believe that when I took it to New York I was

25 in such a hurry to print it up to take it the next day, I

                            253

1   don't believe that I removed that disclaimer, as you call

2   it, on the bottom. I believe that I trimmed the Oath down,

3   which Schiller owns or has possession of. Strike the word

4   owns, will you? I believe that I trimmed it. Trimmed the

5   bottom off it to such an extent that it would not appear,

6   although it was probably printed on the piece of paper. On

7   this Oath which you got from Wilding it was obviously

8   removed. I can't remember exactly when I did that but I

9   must have. I probably ground it off or I may have cut it

10   off with a hacksaw.

11   Q   I may be getting ahead of myself but how many--

12   A   In fact, I did cut it off with a hacksaw, as I

13   remember.

14   Q   How many original forged Oaths of a Freeman did

15   you do in March of '85?

16   A   Just the one, which is possessed by Justin

17   Schiller.

18   Q   So the one you gave to Wilding, Jensen, et al.,

19   that was done after at a different time?

20   A   Yes.

21   Q   Than the Justin Schiller?

22   A   Yes. That would have been done probably the

23   day before Wilding received it, much later. I had no

24   intentions at the time that I produced the Oath, which is

25   now in New York, of ever producing another one. However, I

                              254

1   still had the plate and I was at that time under

2   considerable pressure to satisfy Wilding, et al. And that

3   is when I produced the other copy of the Oath. My intention

4   was never to let it be marketed.

5   Q   What was your intention?

6   A   Thinking that that would be too great a

7   coincidence to have two copies of the Oath. My intention was

8   when the Oath, owned by me, which was in the possession of

9   Justin Schiller, when they sold it use that money and claim

10   that that was this particular Oath and pay off my debtors,

11   namely Wilding and company and never to have the second Oath

12   known on the market.

13   Q   And they would have given you back the second

14   Oath?

15   A   Well, yes. The original idea was that I would

16   maintain possession of it anyway and so my belief was there

17   would be no way of them nothing when one Oath sold that it

18   was a different Oath than the one which they believed they

19   had an ownership interest in/

20   MR. BIGGS: After you had the Oath printed,

21   after you printed the Oath, now we discussed how you did it

22   with a C-clamp?

23   A   That's right.

24   Q   And making your own ink but you don't recall,

25   and I'm sure you told me, the process by which you went

255

1   through to locate the piece of paper that you actually used

2   to print the Oath on, that Schiller and Wapner has in their

3   possession in New York. Can you tell me again about that?

4   A   Yes, I think I mentioned in looking at both the

5   microfilmed copies and the original copy of the Bay Psalm

6   Book owned by the New York Public Library that I determined

7   how wide the laid line should be.

8   Q   Is that another word for chain marks? I've

9   heard experts say chain marks?

10   A   Yes.

11   MR. GEORGE: I'm sorry Mark, what did you call

12 it?

13   A   Laid, L-a-i-d. The chain marks in this copy

14 run vertically. The laid lines run horizontally. There's

15 greater distance between the laid lines than the chain

16 lines.

17   MR. BIGGS: Explain to me what a laid line is.

18   A   The paper was hand made back in those days on a

19 metal screen, on a copper screen at this period. The screen

20 gave certain indentations on the paper and that is what

21 those lines are. That's also how water marks were formed is

22 by taking one of the wires and bending it to a certain

23 initial or number or shape or whatever and having that on

24 the screen.

25   Q   Now, are you saying that the paper in the Bay

1 Psalm Book has lines that go both ways, vertically and

2 horizontally?

3   A   Yes. If you look at it you will see that that

4 is true of all laid paper. Any paper before around 1795 has

5 that and around 1795 is when they started using a wove-type

6 screen.

7   Q   The vertical lines are very close together on

8 that paper and the horizontal are further apart.

9   A   That's correct. Anyway, in studying the paper

10 I determined the spacing which should exist on the laid

11 lines, the horizontal lines, that run furthest distance

12 apart. And with that knowledge I looked through several

13 books from around the same period of time, 1620s, in an

14 effort to locate a piece of paper which would match the

15 dimensions which the Bay Psalm Book has as far as the paper.

16 The dimensions meaning the spacing of the lines, which took

17 considerable effort. I started out at the University of

18 Utah Library going through material. I then spent time at a

19 couple other places, I don't know if I want to be on the

20 record, but I succeeded in finding the paper at the BYU

21 Library.

22   Q   Which library is that?

23   A   I believe it's called the Harold Bee Library.

24   Q   Where at in that particular library?

25   A   I believe it was on the 4th floor in the

257

1 southeast corner, or area. East of their microfilm section,

2 which I believe is on the same floor as the microfilm. And

3 I can walk right to it.

4   Q   Can you remember the book it came out of?

5   A   I can't remember the book but let me see, I

6 believe it was a Latin book. Let's see, is that true?

7 Interestingly, the book I am thinking of also has the same

8 border flourishes that I used, the same font was used but it

9 was from the same time period. It was printed, I believe in

10 England. I can't remember for sure but it might have been

11 in Latin.

12   MR. GEORGE: Latin did you say?

13   A   Latin, yes and has the same flourishes but I am

14 not sure if it was Latin or not, but I do remember it had

15 the same flourishes which I thought was interesting.

16   MR. RICH: How did you extract these pages from

17 these books?

18   A   Buy tearing them out.

19   Q   What did you do to finish the edge after you

20 had it out?

21   A   To finish the what?

22   Q   The torn edge?

23   A   The idea was, and with practice I succeeded

24 quite well in tearing so it was rather difficult to see

25 where the page was removed. Very close to the spine.

258

1   Q   What about the page that was-- This doesn't
2   show evidence of being torn out of a book, does it?
3   A   No, it would have been trimmed. This is a very
4   poor job compared to, at least in my opinion, compared to
5   the copy that is in New York.
6   MR. BIGGS: For the record, what he is talking
7   about is the second Oath printed by himself that was given
8   to Wilding, et al. for collateral, correct?
9   A   That's correct/
10   Q   The Oath that you printed up in the evening
11   hours of March 25th and 26th-- By the way, where was that
12   printing done again?
13   A   It would have been done in my downstairs office
14   in my house.
15   Q   There is a little something written on the
16   back, on the verso.
17   A   This is is the one in New York.
18   Q   Correct.
19   A   Yes, it's Elizabethan handwriting which says,
20   as I remember, Oath of a Freeman, or something, Oath of the
21   Freeman or Oath of Freeman, something like that.
22   Q   Did you do that?
23   A   Yes, I did.
24   Q   When?
25   A   Well, since I only had one night to prepare

259

```
 1    that Oath it would have been done at that time.  In between
 2    the time I picked up the plate and when I left the next
 3    morning to go to New York.
 4              Q    Why did you do that?
 5              A    The main reason would have been to give
 6    validity to the Oath.  It would allow the document to be
 7    tested, not only for printing ink as far as the composition
 8    but also the handwriting ink on the back, on the verso.
 9              Q    What type of ink did you use?
10              A    Ink of my own composure.  Tannic acid, ferric
11    sulfate, probably gum arabic and logwood, as I remember.
12              Q    What did you use to write it with?
13              A    Quill pen.
14              Q    Well, is this the first time you used a quill
15    pen?
16              A    No.
17              Q    You know, all of the others once we've
18    discussed, we've talked about, you said  steel nibb pen.
19              A    Yes, I believe a quill pen was also used in the
20    1825 letter to Josiah Stoal and various other documents.
21              Q    Did you create the quill that you wrote with?
22              A    Yes, I did.
23              Q    Out of what?
24              A    A feather and a razor blade.
25              Q    Any particular type of feather?
```

```
1         A    I believe it was a turkey feather.

2         Q    Where does one get a turkey feather?

3         A    I wish I could give a better answer for that

4    but I believe it was a feather which we just had in the

5    house. I can't tell you why we had it. Let's see, I

6    believe, no, this one-- I've used feathers before which are

7    dyed, like the kind that little kids use to pretend like

8    they're Indians or something. They seem to be the most

9    common type for me to find. But this particular one, as I

10   remember, it was a turkey feather. It wasn't dyed. In a

11   drawer where I had, in fact, I can tell you the exact drawer

12   since you have been through the house. In the hallway

13   there's a cupboard in the upstairs hallway with two drawers.

14   In the bottom drawer I have various nicknacks and odds and

15   ends.

16        Q    We found some batteries there.

17        A    Yes. In fact, you left some batteries there

18   also which I was surprised at. Some C batteries.

19        Q    Where at?

20        A    Even after your third search or whatever. It

21   was in that same drawer.

22        Q    Was the quill still there that you used?

23        A    No. I would have, after putting a nibb on it,

24   carving a tip and using it I would have, I believe,

25   destroyed it. Let's see, I  think I mentioned before that I
```

261

1   burned some material in my fireplace but I don't believe
2   that I said that that was the common way for me to get rid
3   of material. Just about whenever we had a fire in that
4   fireplace I would put some scrap papers or other materials
5   in a brown paper bag downstairs and bring them upstairs.
6   Bring that bag upstairs and throw the whole bag in the fire.
7   Q   After you wrote on the back-- By the way, did
8   you print it before you wrote on the back or vice versa?
9   A   I would have written on it after it was printed
10   which can be distinguished, incidentally.
11   Q   How so?
12   A   By the oils in the ink keep, the oils in the
13   printing ink keep the handwritten ink from the diffusing
14   evenly. In other words, where the writing went over a
15   letter, if you look with an ultraviolet light using a
16   microscope you can see that that ink hasn't diffused as much
17   as where it goes over a piece of paper which has no writing
18   underneath it, no printing underneath it.
19   Q   How did you know that?
20   A   By the time I forged the Oath I considered
21   myself a pretty good forger. I thought I had a pretty good
22   knowledge of different techniques that would be used in
23   analyzing it.
24   Q   Had you ever done that, looked through a
25   microscope under ultraviolet light at printed and written

1   material?

2   A   Yes, I have. I've studied that. You will be
3   interested to know that I also, even before the preliminary
4   hearing, spoke to Ron about my fears as far as the cracking
5   was concerned.

6   Q   Oh, really? You had seen that cracking before
7   yourself?

8   A   Yes, although I didn't know the cause of it
9   until the preliminary hearing as far as the gum arabic and
10   undoubtedly when somebody reads this transcript they'll keep
11   gum arabic out of the formula.

12   Q   We are doing an invaluable service here I
13   guess. Did you attempt to age the document after it was
14   printed and the verso was placed on it?

15   A   Yes. That's when I would have aged it. As far
16   as the oxidizing of the writing on the back, the
17   handwriting, I believe that would have been done with
18   ammonia. It might have also been done with suction. I
19   believe I described that technique before.

20   Q   But it was usually hydrogen peroxide that you
21   used?

22   A   Well, the idea was to draw the ink through the
23   paper as it was being oxidized. Incidentally, the chemical
24   reaction in oxidizing ink is very complex but I know from
25   experience using-- Let's put this off the record or you are

1 not even interested in it probably.

2   Q   Off the record a minute.

3   DISCUSSION HELD OFF THE RECORD

4   MR. BIGGS: After your process was completed

5 and you got on the plane at 4:00 o'clock in the morning on

6 the 26th of March, where did you go and what was your

7 intent?

8   A   My major intent was undoubtedly to show a copy

9 that I had produced of the Oath to Justin Schiller to

10 excite him, as much as I could in New York concerning its

11 discovery and make whatever efforts I could to sell it.

12   Q   Did you have any inclination at the time that

13 you got to New York how much you were going to sell it for

14 or how much you thought it would be be worth on the open

15 market?

16   A   I felt it would be damn valuable. Yes, I had a

17 good idea of what the Bay Psalm Book was selling for and I

18 thought this would be at least as available as that because

19 for one thing, it's an earlier, in fact, the earliest

20 printing in the new world, or at least in English. There

21 were a few Spanish items printed earlier. The actual

22 content of the Oath concerning the rights of free men in

23 America, I believe would make it equally as valuable. In

24 fact, my belief was that it would be more valuable than the

25 Bay Psalm Book.

1   Q   Well, there was some talk at one time of
2 placing it in a display case right next to the Declaration
3 of Independence and the Constitution. Did you have any
4 inclination it was going to be that big?
5   A   For the reasons I just gave, it wouldn't be
6 surprising. It is obviously a valuable historical document.
7 I wasn't too concerned with having it displayed with the
8 Declaration of Independence. My major concern was making as
9 much off of it as I could.
10   Q   Why did you use Schiller and Wapner? Why not
11 just do it yourself?
12   A   I had a good relationship with them and I
13 thought that they were, they had better contacts than I in
14 making whatever negotiations.
15   Q   What was your initial negotiation with them
16 concerning what they would be paid for acting as your agent
17 in the sale of this Oath originally?
18   A   Originally it was that if it sold for one
19 million dollars or more, we would split 50/50 the proceeds.
20 If it sold for less than a million dollars, I had a right to
21 decline, in which case they were to receive nothing.
22   Q   Was this a written agreement?
23   A   Or in other words, I would keep it myself.
24   Q   Was this in writing?
25   A   No. It wasn't in writing, strange as it may

1   seem.

2   MR. GEORGE: So less than a million you had

3   right of refusal?

4   A   That's correct

5   MR. BIGGS: Any talk about who to sell it to

6   or attempt to sell it to?

7   A   Are you talking about originally or with the

8   passing of time?

9   Q   When you had these initial discussions with

10   Schiller and Wapner?

11   A   Yes. The original idea was on their part was

12   that it was an item which belonged or should be sold to the

13   Library of Congress.

14   Q   Now, I'm going to show you a series of letters

15   starting with, looks like May, well, April 8th. Library of

16   Congress letter received from M. Raymond Wapner, Justin

17   Schiller to be an authentic printing of the Oath of a

18   Freeman, 1638, telling what it is they were going to do.

19   A   Yes.

20   Q   Did you see that letter?

21   A   Yes, I believe I did. I believe that they sent

22   me a copy of this. That Schiller/Wapner sent me a copy of

23   this correspondence.

24   Q   Now, when you found out what the Library of

25   Congress was going to do to your counterfeit Oath, did it

                              266

1   cause you any concern?

2   A   No. In fact, I was wondering why they weren't

3   doing more extensive testing on it than this but then I was

4   told this was just the initial work that was going to be

5   done on it.

6   Q   Now, I'll show you a letter, May 5, 1985, where

7   the Library of Congress, John C. Broderick, is asking them

8   to make an offer. I mean, that is to say, asking Schiller

9   and Wapner to say how much they want for it and so forth.

10   Were you familiar with that letter?

11   A   Yes, I probably had a copy of this sent to me

12   also but at least I would have been told about it over the

13   telephone through Schiller and Wapner.

14   Q   Now, this is after you had gotten $150,000 from

15   Rust for the McClennin Collection in April of '85?

16   A   Right, that would have been correct.

17   Q   Now this is a letter of May 14, 1985 from

18   Schiller and Wapner to Mr. Sullivan of the Library of

19   Congress detailing what they wanted as far as price, as far

20   as confidentiality and so forth. Did you help compose that

21   letter or know the contents of what they were doing?

22   A   No, I didn't know the contents of it except in

23   a general vocal way with Schiller/Wapner. I pretty much

24   gave them free ride to do what they could to sell it. I

25   remember receiving a copy of this letter, however, or at

1   least seeing a copy of it while I was in New York.

2   Q   May 23rd. The Library of Congress writes back

3   to Schiller and Wapner telling them what has to be changed.

4   "The price, 1.5 million seems to be excessive. However, we

5   prefer to withhold further comment on the price quotation of

6   1.5 million until we have certain things", and one of the

7   things they wanted was a little more on the provenance or

8   some provenance at this particular time.

9   A   Yes.

10   Q   Were you aware of this letter?

11   A   Yes, I was. I believe it's all a normal part

12   of negotiations.

13   Q   How did you feel about that letter?

14   Did you feel that the Library of Congress was going to

15   purchase it eventually or what?

16   A   Yes. Schiller and Wapner indicated that they

17   believed it would be sold to them.

18   Q   For how much? Were you still thinking of 1.5

19   million?

20   A   In that ballpark.

21   Q   On May 30, 1985 we have a letter from Schiller

22   and Wapner back to the Library of Congress stating what they

23   accepted and what they didn't accept, sticking with the 1.5

24   million dollars as the price and on the provenance, upon

25   agreement to purchase the document a complete and full

1   provenance as is known to us and our client, will be done

2   provided to the Library.

3   Had you given Schiller and Wapner the story

4   that we discussed last time concerning the purchase of the

5   Oath in Argosy Bookstore?

6   A   Yes, they knew that when they first saw the

7   Oath, that's where I purported to have received it or

8   purchased it. They also had, I believe a copy of the

9   receipt from Argosy Bookstore.

10   Q   At this time, May 30th of '85, had they given

11   that information to the Library of Congress, as far as you

12   know?

13   A   I don't believe so, although they may have done

14   so privately, confidentially.

15   Q   Were you trying at that time to develop any

16   further provenance? Did it concern you they might not

17   accept that as satisfactory?

18   A   No. I had afterwards gone to Argosy Bookstore

19   with a Xerox of the Oath and the receipt and talked to the

20   lady who had allegedly sold it to me. Interestingly, she

21   claimed to have recognized the Oath and I felt like that

22   source was, or that provenance was secure as far as that's

23   where I obtained it. She informed me that there would be no

24   way for Argosy Bookstore to discover where they had received

25   it since they purchased large collections and thousands of

269

1   items at a time and so I felt no one would know the source

2   other than Argosy Bookstore. But I felt like Argosy

3   Bookstore would acknowledge that this was the source where I

4   had purchased it.

5   Q   Do you remember the name of this lady at Argosy

6   Book?

7   A   No, but if you take me to New York I can point

8   her out to you. There are two ladies that worked up on the

9   second floor on the Broadside print map area. She is the

10   older of the two. Schiller knows her name.

11   MR. BIGGS: You actually showed her a Xerox of

12   your forgery?

13   A   Yes. Well, in fact, it was even before I took

14   it to Schiller/Wapner when I arrived in New York. I had the

15   receipt with me from a couple two or three weeks earlier and

16   I did not show them the, show her the original but I did

17   show her a Xerox and the receipt and she said something to

18   the effect that, of that is a pretty important discovery.

19   But I don't believe she realized at the time how important

20   it would become.

21   MR. GEORGE: Let me see if I can understand

22   it. Prior to bringing the Oath to Schiller and Wapner, you

23   went back to Argosy about three weeks later, showed her a

24   Xerox copy of what you had produced to sort of entrench in

25   her own mind that this is, in fact, what she had sold?

1   A   Yes.

2   Q   And then went to Schiller and Wapner with it?

3   A   That's correct

4   MR. BIGGS: If she looked at it and said boy,

5   I would have known if I sold him this and I never sold it to

6   you and it was never in our collection, what would you have

7   done?

8   A   Probably have thought of a new source for the

9   Oath. I wasn't fearful, however, because it really doesn't

10   look anything outstanding like she would handle numerous

11   items everyday.

12   MR. RICH: And you knew they didn't log stuff

13   in originally?

14   A   Right, I knew that and I wasn't fearful of any

15   of this when I showed her the receipt. In fact, I believe

16   it was all on the same copy. I believe I had a Xerox of

17   this and receipt underneath it and I asked her-- My

18   intention was I asked her, I told her I was interested in

19   this Oath and I would be willing to buy further copies of it

20   and she said that she would look. And she went through some

21   material for a while with me or pulled out some material for

22   me to go through and then afterwards I told her that I

23   thought it was a valuable item and explained to her that the

24   first item printed in America was the Oath of a Freeman and

25   this might be the first one. And she said, that's nice, or

271

1   something like that, but it never entered her mind, I'm

2   sure, although I tried to impress on her that it was

3   extremely valuable. She made some comment about that other

4   people had found some pretty valuable things there before.

5   Q   Okay, now we go to a letter, June 5, 1984,

6   Library of Congress writing to Mr. Schiller saying the

7   price, the Library of Congress is not prepared to purchase

8   this document at the quoted price of 1.5 million and

9   provenance. You did not respond to this essentially

10   important requirement. Before L. C. could agree to

11   purchase this document we would have to receive evidence

12   that your title to this document is clear and there are no

13   conflicting claims. Your warranty referred to in item eight

14   above would have to apply to both the authenticity of the

15   document and the chain of title.

16   Did you get a copy of that letter?

17   A   If I didn't receive a copy I was at least read

18   that paragraph because I remember it.

19   Q   Any problems?

20   A   It didn't cause any problems with

21   Schiller/Wapner so it didn't with me. They knew that we had

22   no knowledge of its prior history before Argosy and the

23   major concern wasn't so much with provenance but the

24   possibility that Argosy, when they discovered how valuable

25   it was they could somehow make some claim on it. Which

1   Schiller/Wapner attorneys said they could not make.   In

2   other words, that was lawfully mine.

3   Q   What about the paragraph on the--

4   A   It didn't-- This paragraph did not cause any

5   excitement on Schiller/Whapner's part and therefore, I

6   thought that it was not that important.   That we could tell

7   them it was attained from Argosy, that they have told us

8   that they cannot tell us or give us, provide any information

9   where they received it from so that's as good as it gets.

10   Q   What about the paragraph on the purchase price,

11   where they say, ain't going to buy it for 1.5 million?

12   A   Schiller/Wapner were still quite certain that

13   they would make the purchase of the document, I believe, at

14   this point.

15   Q   For the same amount?

16   A   In that ballpark.

17   Q   Now, we go to June 6th, '85 and Schiller/Wapner

18   writing back to Library of Congress and saying the document,

19   we want 1.5.   Consequently this is to confirm the

20   arrangements for picking up the Oath.   If you guys don't

21   want it for 1.5 we'll pick it up and sell it.

22   A   Right.

23   Q   Did you know this was going to be happening?

24   A   Yes, I did.

25   Q   What was the strategy behind that?

273

1   A   Again, what I was informed was they were still

2   very interested in it but rather than dragging out

3   negotiations any longer than possible, this was considered

4   the best strategy to actually pick up the document. There

5   were a couple other institutions which had, who also had

6   expressed interest in the document and when the option

7   expired for the Library of Congress, I believe, let's see, I

8   can't remember the Society for some strange reason, who had

9   the option--

10   MR. GEORGE: American Antiquarian?

11   A   Right, American Antiquarian Society had an

12   option on it.

13   MR. BIGGS: American Antiquarian Society, June

14   6, 1985, is a letter to Mr. Schiller from them stating the

15   conditions of possible sale, by Marcus McGarrison.

16   A   Yes.

17   Q   And then, of course, we have a return of the

18   document on June 14th, 1985 from the Library of Congress and

19   then the American Antiquarian Society writes on June 17th

20   1985. This is what we need, full proof of ownership,

21   proofs independently developed by the agent on behalf of the

22   owner of its authenticity?

23   A   Yes.

24   Q   Then there is some document on August 5th

25   concerning, therefore and so forth. Okay, on August 12th,

1   '85, the American Antiquarian Society writes Justin Schiller

2   and makes some observations concerning the Oath, right?

3   A   Yes.

4   Q   And wants it sent to New Mexico for a

5   cyclotron test?

6   A   Yes.

7   Q   Did you know anything about cyclotron testing

8   at the time you prepared the document?

9   A   Yes.

10   Q   Did it concern you that it may be tested by

11   cyclotron method?

12   A   No.

13   Q   Why not?

14   A   Because I felt that the document would pass.

15   Incidentally, I never heard. Did it or didn't it?

16   MR. BIGGS: Well, it depends on who you talk

17   to. If you talk to Schiller and Wapner, it passed. But if

18   you talk to the people who actually did the tests, they were

19   not that positive about it.

20   MR. RICH: I'm sure when you called them they

21   were backing up as far as they could.

22   A   Yes, I'm sure if it wasn't for the other

23   suspicion, i.e. the bombings, etc., I believe it would have

24   passed very well.

25   MR. BIGGS: Now, we have a letter from

```
1   American Antiquarian Society, August 27, 1985. There it
2   says, Dear Raymond, we are interested in buying it, but
3   these are the two requirements that we need. The price is
4   lowered drastically to a level that reflects its true
5   importance and value, and they were offering $250,000 and if
6   the counsel for the Society approves its purchase at their
7   meeting on October 15, 1985, assuming that the proofs are in
8   by that date. Were you aware of that August of '85?
9        A    I don't believe I saw that copy of this
10  correspondence but I was told of it.
11       Q    This was, of course, also after you got
12  $150,000 from Rust, after you got $185,000 from First
13  Interstate Bank and just before you had gotten another
14  $160,000 from the Wilding group. Did you still think you
15  were going to get more than $250,000 for the Oath?
16       A    Yes. Again, Schiller/Wapner indicated that in
17  private negotiations with these people and others that it
18  would receive or be purchased for much more than that and I
19  was confident of that at this point. Although I had reached
20  the point where I became desperate enough for liquid money,
21  for cash, that I offered and they a agreed to purchase my
22  share in the document for $150,000. You know about all
23  that, I presume.
24       Q    Schiller and Wapner?
25       A    Yes.
```

276

1   Q   No, they never told us that. Did they give you
2 the $150,000?
3   A   No. They had arranged-- They were not going to
4 make the purchase. They had another party who was going to
5 make the purchase who they had arranged for.
6   Q   Was this after this date, August 27, 1985?
7   A   Yes. In fact, it surprises me you don't know
8 this information because when Steve Christensen and myself
9 met with Harvey Tanner at First Interstate Bank, Harvey
10 Tanner called Schiller/Wapner to verify that I was to
11 receive, without question, in other words, without
12 possibility of the deal falling through or anything, the
13 $150,000 on a certain day, which was sometime in September
14 of '85. I can't remember the exact day. But Harvey Tanner,
15 you've talked to him I presume.
16   Q   Yes.
17   A   You probably just don't remember all of this as
18 far as I'm sure your investigators have all of this
19 information.
20   Q   I remember but Harvey Tanner remembered a
21 little differently. He indicated that he called Schiller
22 and Wapner and asked them specifically if the deal was going
23 to go through for the sale of the Oath and that Mr. Wapner
24 assured him the sale was going to go through to the Library
25 of Congress. Now, of course, this is long after the Library

277

1   of Congress had given back the Oath

2   A   I believe that he's confused   the

3   one that said Library of Congress   I was

4   in the office when Tanner talked with Sch   The

5   only concern was on the part of Mr. Tanner   the

6   $150,000 would become available to me and

7   Schiller/Wapner would agree to wire the mon   First

8   Interstate Bank.

9   Q   Did they ever do that?

10   A   No. Soon after the bombings the person, the

11 purchaser backed out of the deal. But I remember I was, I

12 am the one that told Harvey Tanner that it was to the

13 Library of Congress and not Schiller/Wapner. The only thing

14 Schiller/Wapner agreed upon was that $150,000 would become

15 available to me on a certain day and that with my approval,

16 which I then gave, that money would be wired to First

17 Interstate Bank

18   MR. BIGGS: Let me ask you, on August 27,

19 1985 were you told or did you see this letter that would

20 indicate that the American Antiquarian Society was going to

21 vote on the purchase of the Oath on October 15, 1985?

22   A   I believe I was. I was also, I believe told at

23 this point that, from Schiller/Wapner, that the document

24 would still not sell for under a million dollars. In fact,

25 I had told them that I would not sell the document for

1 under a million dollars and they agreed that they wouldn't

2 want me to and if I didn't, at this point they were going to

3 receive no money for all of their effort. But they still

4 felt confident enough when I talked to them before, that it

5 would sell. They told me not to worry about that

6 possibility that it wouldn't. In other words, they would be

7 out all of their time and effort.

8   Q   Was there any connection in your mind between

9 the vote by the American Antiquarian Society on October 15,

10 1985 and the bombs going off on October 15, 1985?

11   A   Was there any connection?

12   Q   Yes.

13   A   Yes. The connection was the money factor. I

14 was obviously very desperate for money at this point and so

15 that is the connection. I might also mention that

16 Schiller/Wapner, besides carrying on this written

17 correspondence, they were also verbally negotiating with the

18 American Antiquarian Society, the Library of Congress and

19 others and they told me that all though the $250,000 figure

20 was in writing, they agreed that the document was worth more

21 than that and so not to take that seriously.

22   Q   And one last question before we stop for a

23 minute so Mr. Rich can go get a guard. Hypothetically if

24 the American Antiquarian Society had been able to and did

25 vote to purchase your Oath on October 15, 1985 for about a

279

```
1    million dollars, what would that have done to the financial

2    hole that you dug yourself into by that time?

3         A    It would have relieved me from it.  Hence, I

4    guess you want me to say the bombings would not have taken

5    place.

6         Q    I don't want you to say that unless it is true.

7         A    I'll say it since it's true.

8              BREAK FROM 10:45 to 11:00 A.M.

9              MR. BIGGS:   After the first printing in March

10   of '85 what was done with the plate?

11        A    I kept it until I would guess a week before the

12   bombings.

13        Q    What was done with it at that time?

14        A    It would have been kept in a paper sack with

15   various other plates in my, in the closet in my downstairs

16   office.

17        Q    How was it destroyed?

18        A    I believe in fire.

19        Q    Where did you get the paper for the second

20   Oath, the one that was given to the Wilding group for

21   collateral?

22        A    The book, the first paper for the first Oath

23   came out of was a series of volumes so I had already

24   identified where the paper could be had so it didn't take me

25   long to drive down to Provo and pilfer a copy from the BYU
```

280

1   Library from their old library.

2   Q   What about the ink for the second Oath?

3   A   It is not as sophisticated as it was for the

4   first Oath. In other words, I don't believe it would pass

5   the cyclotron, for example.

6   Q   You didn't use the technique of getting a piece

7   of paper from the period and burning it for the carbon?

8   A   No.

9   Q   Did you print any other Oaths other than the

10   two we know of, one in the hands Schiller and Wapner and one

11   that you see before you today?

12   A   I'm sure I made trial proofs probably just on

13   regular bond 20th Century paper which all would have been

14   destroyed. In other words, that I have made no other copy,

15   no. I would be surprised if you found a copy someplace.

16   Q   If it came through Brazil?

17   A   Oh, yes.

18   Q   There was that information that you had given

19   Shanon Flynn and talked to Carden concerning. Was there an

20   actual printed second Oath when you were talking to him?

21   A   No, my idea was to not. If it would have

22   happened, which was all speculation, and I was more or less

23   testing the waters anyway. I was never convinced that this

24   would take place but if it did it would have been not with

25   the Oath since like I say, the ink is wrong. But this copy

1 would have been, meaning the Wilding copy, would have been

2 destroyed and another one printed and shipped down to

3 Brazil, however that was supposed to work. But like I say,

4 that was never a serious consideration on my part, although

5 I know Shanon was thinking it would be an easy way to make

6 some money.

7   Q   Okay. Just before the first search of your

8 home, your mother went in and got a box of stuff and left

9 the home.

10   A   Who did?

11   Q   Your mother. Can you recall that? Did you ask

12 her to do that and did you know what was in the box?

13   A   No. This is the first I've heard of this. If

14 she went out of the home with a box of stuff it probably

15 would have been diapers for the kids or--, it was nothing

16 related. She took nothing besides clothes or food or

17 whatever, I'm sure. In other words, nothing related.

18   MR. RICH: I was part of the discussion where

19 she was going to go do that. I discussed in the hospital

20 with Dorie and your mother about needing something for the

21 kids or whatever.

22   A   I don't remember that at all. I had never

23 heard of that before.

24   MR. BIGGS: Okay. Mike, do you have any other

25 questions on the Oath?

282

```
 1              MR.  GEORGE:  Huh uh (indicating in the
 2   negative.).
 3              MR. BIGGS:   Brad?
 4              MR. RICH:    No.
 5              MR. BIGGS:   Mark, anything else that should be
 6   said concerning the Oath of the Freeman?
 7         A    I never went in to the other aging techniques
 8   other than the oxidizing the ink on the back.  Did you want
 9   me to go into anything else?
10         Q    Certainly.
11         A    I created foxing markings on it.  I folded it
12   repeatedly.  I browned the edges of the document.  I browned
13   the entire document.  I believe that I waterstained it.
14              MR. RICH:    That document doesn't look anything
15   like this one does.
16         A    No.  This is a lot nicer copy.
17              MR. RICH:    How did you create the foxing?
18         A    With a fungus, a red fungus.
19              MR. BIGGS:   How did you learn how to do that?
20         A    Just asking myself what causes this on a
21   genuine old document and trying to imitate it.  Foxing is
22   caused by fungus.
23         Q    Had you done that before?
24         A    Yes.  I don't believe that any new technique
25   was used that hadn't been used except for the printing ink
```

1   manufacture that hadn't about used before.

2   Q   In our discussions with Mr. Stott and the

3   forged documents you've never talked about fungus before.

4   A   Let's see, that's because we have only so far

5   talked about--

6   MR. RICH: 19th Century documents?

7   A   We've only talked about the Anthon Transcript

8   and just starting on Joseph Smith the 3rd.

9   MR. RICH: The date is later. We've only

10   talked about those two documents.

11   A   I don't believe I've even talked about what I

12   did to age the Joseph Smith, 3rd document. Only the Anthon

13   Transcript.

14   MR. BIGGS: All right. Anything else?

15   A   Yes, but you want this off the record.

16   MR. BIGGS: Off the record.

17   DISCUSSION HELD OFF THE RECORD

18   MR. RICH: We've just had an off the record

19   discussion about the detailed techniques of forgery that

20   probably would serve no public benefit and would allow

21   potential forgers significant resources toward their trade.

22   A   And if I write a book you will learn a lot

23   more.

24   MR. GEORGE: I have two questions on the Oath

25   that came up in some of our investigation. We talked with

an expert down at Huntington Library on printing and he
looked at that and I guess part of it was he knew everything
was under suspicion at that time but he looked at that
document for a half hour, or hour or so and said to him he
thought it was a forgery and the reason why is that it
appeared to him that the words had been placed, the artwork
had been placed on a piece of paper because they were going
up and down rather than a flowing motion that printing
should have on it. Is that in fact, true?

A   I don't believe so. In fact, if it goes up and
down it's because I copied that characteristic from the Bay
Psalm Book and I believe in the Library of Congress report
that in fact, is looked upon as favorable.

I was going to say you asked me before on these
documents what I consider the giveaways to be. There is,
I believe, a couple giveaways, I believe on the printing
which I haven't heard mentioned by the experts as far as
characteristics which would establish it to be fraudulent.
One of them is on the 5th and 6th lines of the document
there is the word, subject, with the J in subject and
underneath it, the word do. The J extends below the top of
the letter D which could not happen in genuine type. I
discovered that the day I first showed the document to
Justin Schiller before I could do anything about it. And
was in fact, on the airplane coming back. So it would have

1   been like that night or the next day or something.

2   There are, I believe a couple others, or at

3   least one other place where that same sort of thing happens

4   where the typed letters seem to be going through each other,

5   which is impossible in normal type. I see another one, in

6   the first, in the parenthesis where it says in which free

7   men are to deal. In the first parenthesis on the top part

8   that parenthesis is higher than the bottom of the why in

9   the word my.

10   In looking at old type and if someone else

11 looked at old type they would be able to look at that

12 characteristic and right there be able to say that it was

13 made photographically rather than with a genuine type.

14   MR. GEORGE: Give that to me again.

15   A   The top of the parenthesis, in the letter Y in

16 my/

17   Q   People have talked about the border on that,

18 that the border is a little bit reversed and not quite what

19 they have ever seen in the Bay Psalm Book, not exactly

20 duplicated, and they thought you may have been reversing

21 some of the figures.

22   A   No, if you look at the Bay Psalm Book-- Now,

23 incidentally, this is not the same as the title page type.

24 This is, if you measure it, a larger figure than what

25 appears.

286

1   MR. RICH: That other page we were looking at
2   was the same, was it not?
3   A   Yes.   See, this is not the same but this is.
4   MR. RICH: You said it is like the last figure
5   and it is like the last figure reversed, right?
6   MR. BIGGS: It would be, if you Xeroxed it,
7   wouldn't it?
8   A   Each of these halves are different types which
9   are put together different ways. See, that is put together
10 different there. This one here is the one that is the same
11 as this one here where it starts out here.
12   MR. RICH: Referring to the second figure on
13 that 4th book title?
14   A   Yes. But actually there are two different--
15 Like if you had this half right there and turned it around
16 you will see that it is opposite of that one right there.
17 In other words, you cannot make that figure with that
18 figure. And it is also the same as you see in here, there
19 are two different figures that were used. You know, what I
20 mean?
21   MR. GEORGE: Some of the experts too have
22 talked about breakage in lines.
23   A   Yes.
24   Q   Were they intentional or mistakes?
25   A   No, that is how it is in the original or other

287

1   lines. You see the break in the lines?

2   MR. BIGGS: No, I don't think so.

3   MR. RICH: Doesn't that have it here at the

4   corner?

5   A   Oh, yes. The corners, yes. That was, it is

6   common. The lines were made with strips of metal and I

7   don't think that is uncommon to find them like even bent or

8   something right there. In fact, that would be if they were

9   just purely straight lines, that would be suspicious in my

10 mind, compared to looking at 17th Century printing.

11   MR. BIGGS: What was the artwork for the

12 lines? How was that done by you?

13   A   I believe from some old lines that I took from

14 an old book.

15   MR. GEORGE: Did you just burn your artwork

16 after you had it produced?

17   A   Yes, I probably would have just-- There was a

18 time when I would have just put it in the garbage but I

19 think at this time in my life I would have been more

20 cautious and would have been just, have just burned it. Put

21 it in a brown paper sack and thrown in the fire.

Office of Salt Lake County Attorney

DAVID E. YOCOM
COUNTY ATTORNEY

MARK HOFMANN INTERVIEWS

INTERVIEWS CONDUCTED AT
UTAH STATE PRISON BETWEEN
FEBRUARY 11 AND MAY 27, 1987

TRANSCRIPTS, SUPPLEMENTS AND EXHIBITS

000023 **Volume 2**

Excerpt of Interview Conducted on
April 1, 1987

20   MR. BIGGS: Just a couple questions before

21 your mind gets onto other tracks. We were talking about the

22 Oath last time. I went up to the University of Utah library

23 and I found two things in the area that you described to us.

24 One is a book called the Puritan Republic and on page 36

25 and 37 it has the text, the Oath of a Freeman. On the

302

```
1   second page of that copy I gave you is the records of the
2   Colony of Massachusetts Bay in New England wherein it has,
3   at least in the Oath of a Freeman as of 1634.  It changed,
4   apparently somewhat from 1631 to 1634.  Do either one of
5   those two reference materials look similar or can you recall
6   either one of those being used by you in the preparation of
7   the text of the Oath of a Freeman?
8           A       The records of the Colony of the Massachusetts
9   Bay Colony was certainly used.  I am not certain about the
10  Puritan Republic but it was probably taken from a source
11  which I would have used.
12              MR. BIGGS:   And one last question on the Oath.
13  Are there any other forging techniques or counterfeiting
14  techniques, I supposed is more appropriate, used on the
15  first Oath that we haven't already gone over?
16          A       Yes, there are.
17          Q       What would they be?
18          A       There was, I made a laquer which was included
19  in the ink which I don't believe I mentioned in the
20  ingredients.
21          Q       What was the ingredient of the laquer?
22          A       It's a boiled turpentine and linseed oil
23  combination.
24          Q       What was it used for?
25          A       To correspondence to early printing ink
```

303

1   recipes.

2   Q   Was it used on the second Oath?

3   A   No.

4   Q   Where did you get those recipes?

5   A   That's a question you asked before which I real

6   can't-- If you turned me loose in the University of Utah

7   library I could probably come up with it/

8   MR. BIGGS: We've been talking about a field

9   trip here. Are you saying the recipe came from the

10   University of Utah library?

11   A   I believe it was from the University of Utah

12   library. And I would even say that it probably came from

13   the first floor, but I hate to be even that specific since I

14   don't even know for certain that it came from the University

15   of Utah library.

16   Q   I should tell you that the research material

17   was in the same location that you described last time.

18   A   On the 4th floor?

19   Q   Yes, northeast corner. I did have a little

20   difficulty finding the Governor's Journal, Winthrop's

21   journal. I found the journal but was unable to find the

22   text of the Oath in that journal. There are three or four

23   volumes.

24   A   Must not have been his journal. Must have been

25   another governor's journal.

304

```
1          Q       All I did was go to the governor that was
2    governor from 1630 and 1640/ Any others techniques used?
3          A       Yes, there was other techniques in aging of the
4    paper.  I believe that there is a, what appears to be a book
5    worm's hole through the document.  When it is folded it goes
6    through two pages.
7          Q       How did you accomplish that?
8          A       That's a strange story.  We had some bags of
9    wheat down in our basement which were in a type of paper
10   bags which we found little bugs had eaten through and I
11   took, I thought that was interested so I took what looked
12   like a little fly and put it in a notebook and came by a
13   couple days later and it ate through a few pages.  So I
14   thought it was rather convincing, so I believe that that
15   document has bookworm holes in it.
16         Q       How did you do that?
17               MR. YENGICH:     That's a new one on me.
18         A       I believe I took a bug and stuck it in a book.
19   Put the Oath-- I've just changed my story.  I don't believe
20   that that was used on this particular document.  The reason
21   being--
22               MR. BIGGS:     It was an interesting story.
23               MR. YENGICH:     Is that true?  You did do that?
24   It's not a story in the Grimms Fairytails I take it?
25         A       What document did I do that on?
```

1   MR. YENGICH: Answer my question.   It is not a
2   story in the Grimms Fairytails? You actually did do that
3   with a document; is that right?
4   A   Yes. I'm thinking I wouldn't have done it on
5   that document since the next day I took it to New York and I
6   wouldn't 'have been able to leave the bug on it for a couple
7   days
8   MR. BIGGS: What document has bookworm holes
9   in it?
10   A   Tell me if you ever find a document with
11   bookworm holes in it. I'll be interested to see. It's
12   probably a printed document, as I remember. I believe it
13   would have been a printed document.
14   Q   Anything else about the first Oath, the
15   Schiller & Wapner oath, we could say?
16   A   I have to see it to say for certain, you know,
17   I may recognition a certain stain on it or something if I
18   had the original.
19   Q   If we had it we would show it to you.
20   A   It's similar to when you were asking me
21   techniques used on the Emma Smith Hymnal, you know, it was
22   more speculation than anything since I, as far as what
23   stains were added or how I did it, since I haven't seen or I
24   wasn't describing the book or looking at the book when I was
25   making those descriptions.

306

```
1        Q      One last question. You told us about Ozone to
2    age the ink and paper, make it brittle and you told us about
3    how you created the Ozone with a spark?
4        A      Right, it was a carbon spark.
5        Q      Wouldn't the Ozone dissipate rather rapidly?
6        A      Yes, it does.  But while it is being produced
7    it is in close proximity to the document and, therefore,
8    when it comes in contact with another molecule which would
9    change it to an O2, that other molecule has a good chance of
10   being on the document if it is in close proximity.
11       Q      Can you actually perceive a difference in the
12   paper and ink after that procedure is accomplished?
13       A      Yes, more so in the ink than in the paper.
14       Q      What does it do to the ink?
15       A      The greatest characteristic would be a browning
16   effect on the back of the page and browning around the edges
17   of the ink., a hazing effect.
18       Q      When we searched your car we found  an
19   envelope, the Argosy set but included in that was also
20   another document that looked very 17th Centuryish,
21   Elizabethan handwriting type document.
22       A      Yes, I know the document.
23       Q      Was that used as a model for the back of the
24   Oath or did you actually produce that document as well?
25       A      Neither.  It's a genuine Elizabethan document
```

307

Excerpt of Interview Conducted on
April 7, 1987

INTERVIEW, MARK HOFMANN

2 APRIL 7, 1987, 2:25 P.M.

3 PRESENT: Robert Stott, Esq., David Biggs, Esq.

4 Ronald Yengich, Esq.

5 MR. BIGGS: I have one further question on

6 the Oath that came up from a discussion I had with Marv

7 Leonard. He's an expert in the Treasurey Department, and he

8 had been going through your Oath and he called me and he

9 said well, would you ask Mr. Hofmann where he got the

10 lettering, and I didn't tell him that we had already

11 discussed it, and he went on and said there are many of

12 these letters that I cannot find in my perusal of the Bay

13 Psalms Book, and in particular the large I at the front

14 doesn't appear anywhere in the book, to his knowledge. But

15 he said a lot of them are similar to the Bay Psalms Book and

16 he wondered if somehow you had touched the Xerox up with

17 some type of pen so they didn't look exactly identical to

18 those in the book.

19 A Yes, I believe I said before I did that on

20 purpose in order to cause that confusion. In other words,

21 the lettering he identified as coming from the same type as

22 the Bay Psalms Book, although the individual letters, many

23 of them are altered to the extent that they cannot be found

24 in the Psalms Book.

25 Q What about the large I at the beginning?

313

1 I'm showing you now a page from the New England Kastep in

2 London. They look similar but--

3   A   Yes. Well, as you can see, this is, okay, from

4 Jonah's Kastep in London. For example, if this, this

5 capital I was one of the capital Ies in the Bay Psalms Book,

6 I would have touched up the top of it where you can see

7 there is a little indentation. And made it all that similar

8 yet different from what appears in the Bay Psalms Book.

9   Q   One last thing. We got this out of your home

10 and it looked like you had been doing diction and spelling

11 analysis on your Oath?

12   A   Yes.

13   Q   What were you comparing it to?

14   MR. STOTT: Would you describe that for the

15 record?

16   MR. BIGGS: I'm showing him a blown up

17 version of his Oath and on the side or margin is writing

18 that looks like it's in Mr. Hofmann's handwriting?

19   A   I'm certainly comparing it to something you but

20 I can't say for certain what without seeing different copies

21 of the Oath and making comparisons. Do you have anything

22 you want to show me to have me compare?

23   Q   No

24   MR. STOTT: Do you remember doing that?

25   A   Obviously this was done after. Yes, I believe

314

1   this would be done on a Xerox of the Oath after I printed

2   it. So I don't believe this predates the Oath as far as its

3   manufacture. I did several comparisons I remember, some of

4   them with just Schiller and in an attempt to, for one, show

5   my naivety, and in interest in determining how my Oath would

6   compare to other copies.

7   MR. BIGGS: So to the best of your knowledge

8   the large I--

9   A   If I had a Xerox copy of the Bay Psalms Book I

10 could possibly show you which I, I altered to make that but

11 it certainly came from the Bay Psalms Book as did all of the

12 lettering.

13   MR. BIGGS: Thank you.

14

Excerpt of Interview Conducted on
April 22, 1987

1

2   PRESENT: Mr. Brad Rich, Mr. David Biggs, Mr. Mark Hofmann

3   MR. BIGGS: We were talking about the use of

4   03 or Ozone to age ink in paper.

5   A   Yes, you keep bringing that up. That must be

6   mysterious.

7   Q   I'm sorry because I'm not understanding how it

8   is done. What is actually used to create that?

9   A   The reason why you don't understand it is I

10 understood from our last meetings comment, was that Ozone

11 cannot be stored, or in other words, you don't put it in a

12 bottle and keep it. I used it while it was being

13 manufactured.

14   Q   How did you manufacture it?

15   A   With an electric spark.

16   Q   Was it in some type of container?

17   A   Yes, it was. It was enclosed in glass. It

18 was, the Ozone was manufactured by an electric spark with

19 actually a spoon. This was a simple apparatus, I used a

20 spoon to protect the paper from the sparks and it went

21 around in the container.

22   A   Try it and I'll show you. Shall I draw you a

23 diagram?

24   Q   Yes, and Mr. Rich can keep it since they've

25 been keeping everything else.

363

1   A   This rectangular shaped vessle is an aquarium,
2   probably about a five gallon aquarium which I can produce,
3   if you are interested in seeing it. On top of it I'm
4   drawing a line which represents a piece of glass which is
5   covering the top of it. Draped along the side and the
6   bottom is another curved line which represents a piece of
7   paper. This is out of scale, incidentally, because it was a
8   lot more compact or crowded within the aquarium than I'm
9   drawing it. Now I'll draw the electric system. Here is a
10 plug that goes into a 110 volt outlet. One of the pieces of
11 wire is going into the aquarium underneath the glass lid.
12 The other one is going into a jar which was a simple bottle
13 such as is used to preserve jam, or whatever. Another wire
14 is coming out of that and under the glass and in to the
15 aquarium. The jar is filled with water and salt, which I'm
16 labeling H20 plus NACL. The wires come together to form a
17 spark junction and, I can't think of anything else so that's
18 it.

19   Q   Now you've drawn it, now tell me how it works.
20   A   The water and salt solution keep the circuit
21 breaker or fuse from being blown if the wires touch. I
22 forgot to draw my spoon. The spoon is protecting, it is
23 bent and in a position to, it's a curved line between the
24 spark junction in the diagram. It protects the paper from
25 any stray sparks or whatever, which I don't think would have

364

been a problem but after going through the trouble of
manufacturing a document I was usually pretty careful to
keep it from getting burned up. The spark in the oxygen
atmosphere forms 03 which is Ozone and the Ozone comes in
contact with the paper.

Q   How did you manipulate the spoon and the spark
about the glass over the tank?

A   Without any particular care. All I did was I
formed a spark junction and then stuck the spoon in to
protect the paper from that junction. I am not sure I know
what you mean. It wasn't tricky to do.

Q   Did you manipulate the spoon or?

A   No, I formed the junction so it could be left
without being-- What happens is the electricity eventually
wears the junction out and you have to replace the wires.

Q   Could you actually see the visible change in
the document while this process was being performed?

A   Yes, you could see in the printing ink. I
believe the comment was made earlier about the change in the
ink and the paper which actually isn't the case. I didn't
make that comment but in your re-examination you said
something about the change in the paper. I saw no change in
the paper but I did in the ink and that was a browning or
hazing effect.

Q   Did the paper become more brittle?

365

1   A   Probably, but not that I noticed or, I didn't
2 do any experiments to determine how that was affected.
3   Q   Do you want to sign that and give it to Mr.
4 Rich? Just for the record, we would indicate that Mr.
5 Hofmann has given the document to his attorney. One
6 question, did you ever get $150,000 from Schiller and
7 Wapner?
8   A   No.
9   Q   We talked about the fact they purchased your
10 option. Did they ever give it to you?
11   A   No. The bombing interferred with that
12 transaction.
13   Q   Did you use different ink or can you remember
14 using different compositions of inks on the handwritten
15 White Notes?
16   A   Yes, I believe I did. I think I mentioned that
17 last time.
18   Q   This process of Ozoning your documents and you
19 can answer this yes or no. Was that performed on more than
20 the first Oath?
21   A   It was not performed on the second Oath.
22   Q   Was it performed on any another documents?
23   A   Not that I am charged with.
24   Q   That was my next question. So the answer is
25 yes, it was performed on other documents but the next

366

1   question is no, not on any other documents we've charged?

2   A   I am not saying it was or was not performed on

3   another documents. Write that as a note and we'll get to

4   that.

5   MR. RICH: If the question is of the other

6   documents that were charged were there any of those that

7   were, on which Ozone was used?

8   A   No, there are not.

9   MR. RICH: Okay, let's leave it at that.

10   Let's let Yengich deal with that in his infinite wisdom.

11   MR. BIGGS: Thank you. I don't have anything

12   further.

13   A   Let's see. I had one another comment to make.

14   As I first initially gave you the composition of the ink. I

15   left out originally that there was a shellac, meaning a

16   pinegum-turpentine shellac added in the ink for the first

17   Oath.

18   Q   That's interesting because I had notes and

19   there's two different indications on that as far as ink.

20   A   What I was going to say was that the ink for

21   the second Oath did not include that and it was not as

22   sophisticated of an ink as far as using old carbon, for

23   example, for the carbon black or whatever. And I don't

24   believe that the second Oath contained that burned shellac

25   mixture combination.

367

Notes on Contributors

THOMAS CAHILL is professor of physics at the University of California at Davis and since 1980 director of the Crocker Nuclear Laboratory. In 1977, Dr. Cahill and Dr. Richard Schwab cofounded the Crocker Historical and Archaeological Projects at Davis, an integrated team of humanists and scientists involved in nondestructive analysis of documents and other objects of art and archaeology. The authors are also contributors to Gregory Moller, Dennis Dutshke, Dan Wick, and Alan Pooley, "The Vinland Map, Revisited: New Compositional Evidence on Its Inks and Parchment," volume 59 of *Analytical Chemistry* (1987).

KENNETH C. FARNSWORTH, JR., has been a police officer for the Salt Lake City Police Department for almost two decades. At the time of the investigation of murders linked to the forgery of the *Oath of a Freeman,* he had been a homicide squad detective for a year and a half and also had served as a hostage negotiator for the Salt Lake City Police Department. Mr. Farnsworth was born and raised in Utah.

JAMES GILREATH is an American history specialist in the Rare Book and Special Collections Division at the Library of Congress. He is responsible for interpreting the Division's Americana holdings to the general and scholarly public and for making acquisitions for the collections. He is the author of many books, articles, and facsimiles about American history and the history of American books, including *Federal Copyright Records* (1987), *Thomas Jefferson's Library* (1989), and "American Book Distribution" in *Needs and Opportunities in the History of the Book: America, 1639-1876* (1987).

MARK HOFMANN, on January 23, 1987, pleaded guilty to two counts of second-degree murder for killing Steven Christensen and Kathleen Sheets, one count of second-degree felony for theft by deception for the forging of the "Salamander Letter," and one count of second-degree felony for fraud for obtaining money from Alvin Rust, a Salt Lake City coin dealer, in order to purchase an imaginary collection. He was sentenced to life imprisonment and entered the Utah State Prison at Draper, Utah. On January 29, 1988, his parole was denied, and a majority of the parole board recommended that he spend the rest of his life in prison.

MARCUS A. McCORISON has been the librarian of the American Antiquarian Society since 1960 and the director and librarian since 1967. The American Antiquarian Society is an independent research library in Worcester, Massachusetts, that specializes in books printed in America before 1877. Mr. McCorison is the author of *Vermont Imprints, 1778-1820* (1963) and the editor of a new edition of Isaiah Thomas's classic *The History of Printing in America* (1970).

WALTER C. MCCRONE is an internationally known expert in chemical microscopy. He founded the McCrone Research Institute in 1956, an independent teaching institute for the study of microscopy and crystallography. He received his undergraduate and postgraduate education at Cornell University. Dr. McCrone's best-known work is the six-volume *The Particle Atlas* (1973-79).

RODERICK J. MCNEIL is president of McNeil Technologies in Polson, Montana, which was founded in 1986. His firm performs consulting work for a variety of clients on numerous scientific subjects, including water purification and biochemical separation. Microscopy is a sideline passion of Mr. McNeil's. He received a master's degree in chemistry from South Dakota State and has been involved in document examination for about nine years.

ROBERT MATHIESEN studies medieval manuscripts and early printed books in a variety of languages and alphabets and is deeply involved with the possible applications of high technology to that field of study. He is a professor at Brown University in the Department of Slavic Languages and on its Committee for Medieval Studies. Among his publications are *The Great Polyglot Bibles: The Impact of Printing on Religion in the Sixteenth and Seventeenth Centuries* (1985) and "The Making of the Ostrih Bible," in volume 29 (1981) of the *Harvard Library Bulletin*.

MARVIN G. RENNERT is currently the chief of the Atlanta Forensic Science Laboratory of the Bureau of Alcohol, Tobacco, and Firearms in the Department of the Treasury. At the time of the investigation of the *Oath*, he was a forensic document examiner for the Washington, D.C., office of the Bureau, for which he had worked since 1975. He has a master of arts in forensic science from Antioch University School of Law in Washington, D.C.

JUSTIN G. SCHILLER has been reading, collecting, and researching rare children's books since the age of nine in 1952. In 1959 he began to issue rare book catalogues to help finance his college education. He was elected a member of the Antiquarian Booksellers Association of America in 1967. Among the world's leading specialists in rare children's literature, he is a member of the American Antiquarian Society, the Grolier Club, and the Association Internationale de Bibliophile. He and partner Raymond Wapner operate Justin G. Schiller, Ltd., in New York City.